QUR'AN

IN CONVERSATION

QUR'AN

IN CONVERSATION

Michael Birkel

BAYLOR UNIVERSITY PRESS

Cover Design by *the*BookDesigners
Cover Images: © Shutterstock/emran, faberfoto-it
Book Design by Diane Smith

Library of Congress Cataloging-in-Publication Data

Birkel, Michael Lawrence.
 Qur'an in conversation / Michael Birkel.
 292 pages cm
 Includes bibliographical references and index.
 ISBN 978-1-4813-0097-1 (hardback : alk. paper)
1. Qur'an—Criticism, interpretation, etc.—History. I. Title.
 BP130.45.B57 2014
 297.1'226—dc23

                          2014002730

Printed in the United States of America on acid-free paper with a minimum of 30% post-consumer waste recycled content.

For Gwen

In tranquility, love, and compassion
—Qur'an 30:21

CONTENTS

ACKNOWLEDGMENTS

My greatest debt of gratitude is to the Muslim scholars and religious leaders who led me on this journey into the Qur'an and whose voices are heard in the pages to come. Thank you for the hospitality that allowed me to be a guest in your spiritual community.

Before initiating any of the conversations that are the core of this book, I traveled to the headquarters of the Islamic Society of North America to explain my proposed project to Safaa Zarzour, Secretary General of ISNA. He immediately offered his full endorsement of this project, for which I am grateful.

I gladly acknowledge my debt to my mentors in interreligious engagement, particularly to Shanta Premawardhana, Jay Rock, Peter Makari, and Saoud El-Mawla. My first teachers concerning Islam and Muslim culture were Musa Khalidi and Kelley Lawson-Khalidi, whose friendship launched me on this journey. Imam Umar al-Khattab was kindly supportive of this project from the beginning, and I am grateful. Thanks also to Robin Anderson for her helpful conversation and insight.

I have learned much from my Muslim students over the years, and I want to thank all of them, particularly Sara Ababneh, Sara Adem, Ra'ed Abu Ghazaleh, Asaad Alkhouli, Shanoz Aqnazarbekova, Rossa Darni, Hassan Halta, Shuruq Harb, Lailul Ikram, Su'ad Jarbawi, Kübra Zehra Kaşıkçı, Tamer Mahmoud, and Iyad Manassra.

Support from the Professional Development Fund of Earlham College and from the Trueblood Chair allowed me to carry out this work. Thanks also to my departmental colleagues Mary Garman, James Logan, and Lyn Miller, and to our departmental administrative assistant Sarah Emmer and student assistant Laura Miller.

I am thankful to Kecia Ali for suggesting to me that I consider Baylor University Press, and grateful to the staff of that press, especially to its director, Carey Newman, for his enthusiastic response to my proposal and for his editorial guidance, and also to his colleagues Jordan Rowan Fannin, Karla Garrett, Jenny Hunt, and Diane Smith.

INTRODUCTION

A little Scripture can be a dangerous thing. "If someone has a stubborn and rebellious son who will not obey his father and mother . . . all the men of the town shall stone him to death" (Deut 21:18, 21).[1] "Slaves, obey your earthly masters" (Eph 6:5). A religion with these verses as its fundamental guiding principles could be a threat to human well-being. Children would not be safe; human equality would be only a dream, and not even a religiously sanctioned dream. Yet no Christian theologian argues that these quotations from the Bible are at the core of Christianity. At the same time, no one can contend that these words are not in the Bible.

The Bible, as an anthology, presents its religious community with two tasks. One is to *discern* what the core message of its Scripture is. If asked to identify the central verses of the Bible, different Christian groups would choose different texts, but it is unlikely that most would choose these. When asked a similar question in his day (Matt 22:34-40), Jesus chose Deuteronomy 6:5 and Leviticus 19:18, which speak of love of God and love of neighbor. Not all Christians would agree with Jesus' choices,[2] but the story from the Gospel of Matthew does illuminate the task.

The second task is to *interpret* Scripture. Since Scriptures are complicated, a community needs to articulate how it will read its own authoritative texts. It must find a way to explain passages that can, at first sight, seem to be in tension with that core message.[3] Otherwise the risk is a free-for-all, and people can defend killing their own disobedient children and enslaving other people.

1

Islam and its holy book are much misunderstood in our day. Many of the reasons for this predate the tragedies of September 11, 2001, but they are nonetheless exacerbated by recent acts of Muslim extremists. Intentional misrepresentations of Islam abound,[4] yet there are many non-Muslims who want to understand but find an initial effort to read from the Qur'an to be perplexing.

Like the Bible, the Qur'an is a complex book. Its arrangement is not particularly thematic, nor is it chronological. The language is powerful, but the style can strike newcomers as elliptical. Some of its fruit is low hanging, but much remains out of reach for the uninitiated.

This book is written for readers of goodwill who are curious to learn more, who are rightly suspicious of rancorous distortions of Islam, and who would like to hear thoughtful Muslims themselves talk about their Scripture in ways that outsiders can comprehend. This volume is not another introduction to the content of the Qur'an; such books already exist.[5] Instead, it focuses on the two tasks mentioned above. Based on conversations with more than twenty Muslim scholars and religious leaders, it explores how the Qur'an is interpreted among North American Muslims.[6]

The prevailing image of Muslims in the media tends to be one of exotic but backward people from far away. Islam is portrayed as oppressive of women, intolerant of other faiths, zealous to impose a tyrannical theocracy, and incapable of freedom of thought. The voices gathered here show Islam as it is believed, understood, and lived out in North America. They discuss gender equality, religious pluralism, and social justice, and demonstrate a breadth and depth of intellectual vitality. They also do not all agree with one another.[7] Nor is such agreement required in Islam, where the tradition values diversity of thought.

Their words show a diversity of approaches to reading Scripture. Some are centered in traditional modes of interpretation. Others challenge some traditional readings, though from a perspective that is committed to what they see as the core message of the Qur'an. Just as some of the Qur'an echoes the Bible, some of their methods of interpretation will look familiar to Christian or Jewish readers. These Muslim thinkers also show a range of interactions with the Western intellectual tradition, past and present.

As religious scholars and leaders, the Muslims gathered here are important; many are relatively young and will play a significant role in shaping the future of Islam in North America. Their interpretations of the Qur'an are informative, and they are also beautiful. They bear witness to how their

Scripture comes to life even as it gives life to believers. Their spiritual hospitality offers readers the opportunity to consider what it might be like to be guests in the house of another faith, not necessarily as potential converts but as respectful visitors who can stand firmly rooted in their own convictions and yet meet others at the boundaries between them that both separate communities and still somehow join them.

KNOWLEDGE HIDDEN
AND MANIFEST

Say: "My Sovereign, increase my knowledge."
—Qur'an 20:114

I was a treasure that was unknown, so I desired to be known. So I created a creation, and I made myself known to them.
—Hadith Qudsi[1]

To read Scripture is to acquire knowledge, but what kind of knowledge is available? Some languages, such as German and Spanish, use different verbs to distinguish between knowing information (*wissen, saber*) and knowing a person (*kennen, conocer*). The latter is suggestive of a deeper acquaintance than "how to do something." As humans, we ourselves have a desire to be known. Islamic monotheism seeks so stridently to preserve God's uniqueness that it rejects anthropomorphisms, such as speaking of God as a person, yet in Islamic tradition God too desires to be known, and this is the motivating impulse to create the universe. In Islam, knowledge of God is central to the religious life. Islam is not alone in this regard. In the Christian tradition, for example, the sixteenth-century reformer John Calvin agreed and began his magisterial *Institutes of the Christian Religion* with the same topic.[2] The Eastern Orthodox John of Damascus began his *Exposition of the Orthodox Faith*[3] with the same theme, as did the great Catholic theologian Thomas Aquinas[4] and the medieval Jewish theologian-philosopher Maimonides.[5]

A thoughtful faith must consider what human beings can know about God. This leads to reflection on the concept of revelation as a divine communication. A theology of revelation ponders the human capacity to know, on the one hand, and God's freedom to engage in self-disclosure and yet to remain to a considerable extent unknowable, on the other. Some degree of knowledge about God becomes manifest, but much is still hidden.

Knowledge of God and of reality—one of the ninety-nine names of God is al-Haqq, the Real—is at the heart of Islam.[6] The Qur'an provides moral guidance and offers counsel, comfort, and mercy, but it also reveals the character of God. This chapter brings together a variety of voices and insights into the theme of hidden and manifest knowledge. It begins with reflections on the opening words of the Qur'an as a revelation of what kind of God is speaking and offering knowledge. Because such knowledge entails a moral response, the relationship of humans as created to God as the Creator emerges as a theme. God is first of all a source of compassion, and then communicates God's will, which offers direction for believers.

The Mother of the Book
OVAMIR ANJUM

The very first chapter or sura of the Qur'an is called al-Fatiha, the Opening. It is considered one of the early revelations of the Qur'an, sent down to Muhammad through the angel Gabriel in the first years of Muhammad's prophetic career. The Opening occupies a central role in Muslim devotion. In the round of required daily ritual prayer, Muslims recite this sura at least seventeen times each day.

Ovamir Anjum holds the Imam Khattab Chair of Islamic Studies in the department of philosophy at the University of Toledo. His scholarly work combines interests in theology, ethics, politics, and law in classical Islam. He has great interest in al-Ghazali, Ibn Taymiyya, and Ibn Qayyim[7]—intellectual giants from the classical period of Muslim tradition. His book *Politics, Law, and Community in Islamic Thought: The Taymiyyan Moment* was recently published by Cambridge University Press. A major current project is a translation and analysis of Ibn Qayyim's massive spiritual classic *Madarij al-Salikin*, which is a fourteen-hundred-page commentary inspired by a single verse of al-Fatiha. As he expounded upon the first sura, the themes of divine knowledge and divine self-disclosure loomed large in the background, which helps to explain why he turns so frequently to the great mystics of Islam as conversation partners in his quest to understand how to know and how to speak about God.

— ﷲ —

Al-Fatiha is the Mother of the Book. It is said that all of what people say about Islam is a commentary on the *sunna*, the teachings of the Prophet. And all of the sunna is nothing but a commentary on the Qur'an. And all of the Qur'an is nothing but a commentary on the beautiful names of God. The Qur'an and all of Islamic tradition are essentially a commentary on what it means to live in a world created by God, to live in a world in which perhaps even "creation" as a metaphor falls short. People have used the metaphor of a constant emanation from God, not something simply created and then disconnected. Creation is a metaphor that we use for ourselves. God has used it because that's the closest thing.

And so how do you figure out what it means to live in this extremely wondrous world that at the same time is an extremely tragic, sad, and depressing place, with what humans have made of it? These are really strong passions that one brings to the reading of the text. And of course one also reads in a situated way. My own place is to live in a world which on the one hand is disconnected from God, rebellious against God, yet also finds time to fight in the name of God constantly. That's how I look at my own reading of the Qur'an, especially of al-Fatiha.

In the name of Allah who is most merciful and ever merciful[8]

When one reads and recites al-Fatiha as a conversation with God, what one thinks of is not limited to what it says, because what al-Fatiha says is just the beginning of all things. In a philosophical moment, I think of it as contextualization of creation. It is as though you've found a first ray of life and consciousness. You look around at being and existence. You would ask questions, and if you were living in a world where this existence was good, you would hear, *Bismillah ir-Rahman ir-Rahim*, "In the name of Allah who is most merciful and ever merciful." So the first thing you hear about the being that you are in is that it is good. You hear that we are going to begin to know in the name of Someone, about whom you know nothing except that He is most merciful and always merciful. So there is some goodness, something compassionate about the world, which is a very optimistic thing. I contrast this with a Greek concept of God, where God or the gods may be jealous of human knowledge and therefore punitive or competitive with humans. The God that you hear in the Qur'an is always, always merciful and compassionate. That's the first thing you hear when you're beginning to know anything about anything.

Praise is due to Allah, the master of the worlds

Alhamdullilah. Praise is due to Allah, who is now the Rabb, which means both owner or master and also the caretaker and caregiver. Muslims often use the word *tarbiyah*, which means to raise children or to educate children. The word for "education" in Arabic is often *tarbiyah*. Before the child proceeds to the state of advanced knowledge, what a mother does to a child is *tarbiyah*. Then the teacher comes and begins the process of giving knowledge. So even prior to knowledge is raising the child, preparing the child. That is the original sense of the word *rabb*. Rabb is far more motherly than fatherly, far more intimate care than simply education. The word also means ownership, but intimate care, even of things that are not related to cognition, and prior to cognition. Rabb is lord, caregiver of the worlds.

The most merciful and ever merciful

Arrahman Arrahim. Once again the same attribute of *rahman*, which is the name of my daughter. I love that attribute so much. My first daughter is named Rahma. Mercy is something that we all wish for and want and hope for each other. When you begin the Fatiha, the sense that you get is that of the beginning of all beginnings. Someone is introducing Himself or Herself—"Him" and "Her" is not an attribute appropriate to God, but I'm going to use the English convention. In two brief sentences, God has four times said that He is compassionate. And the difference between Rahman and Rahim is something ultimately irrelevant to the first, if you will, mystical reading of the text. By mystical

reading I do not mean esoteric but rather to think that everything is connected and somehow speaking to you, as opposed to
it saying to you anything objective or noetic. Rather, it is saying
something is communicating. When you read the Qur'anic text,
the sense that you get is of God being eager to communicate,
eager to make you feel good to begin with. God is telling you
that it is a good world because the one who created and takes
care of all this is merciful, as opposed to someone who is mean
and who would not reward goodness, or somebody who would
be jealous of what you have. And therefore mercy and compassion are the appropriate attitudes for this existence, as opposed
to competition or overcoming of nature or reducing the endow-
ment to your service.

Master of the day of recompense

Malik means "master," and a variant reading means "king." Both
are metaphors. That's what language can do, provide metaphors.
It's there for humans to communicate with each other about
their mundane existence. C. S. Lewis,[9] who is one my favorite authors, says that language is much better at communicating
emotions than other things for which it is used, such as descriptions of people or places. Communicating emotion is one thing
that only language can do, as opposed to a map of a place, which
you can draw much better. So what the Qur'anic language is
doing is saying that God has come down, if you will, to human
level. Without, of course, the idea of the story or myth of incarnation, but God has come down to us to speak in a rational language that we can understand. That itself is to me no less of
a step or gesture of compassion or mercy or sacrifice than the
Christian understanding, metaphorical or literal, of the sending
down of the Son for the incarnation. God, who is completely
infinite, absolute, and transcendent, has come down to speak to
us in our language. The Qur'an is therefore the Word of God
for Muslims as Jesus is the Word of God for Christians, and the
Qur'an itself speaks of Jesus as the Word of God, as *kalimah*,
a word from God. The comparison to be made is not so much
between the Qur'an and Bible as between the Qur'an and Jesus.

I was recently reading a Christian theologian, Hans Küng,[10] who writes insightfully about this.

Master of the Day of Judgment or *din*. *Din* is often translated as "religion" or as a "way or system of life." In Arabic, the root of it goes back to the idea of a transaction, barter, or loan. *Din* is used both for a religious way of life and also for how God then will deal with you and barter with you for what you have done with your life on that day. That's why it's called the day of recompense. Justice is an essential meaning of *din*. Note that justice is mentioned only after mercy is mentioned four times.

You alone we worship and you alone we ask for succor

This is the verse that Ibn Qayyim's fourteen-hundred-page commentary is on. Scholars of spirituality say that all of the Qur'an is summed up in al-Fatiha, and all of al-Fatiha is summed up in this verse. We start to know at the very beginning that God is mercy. Then that God is also just. Then a new phase of al-Fatiha begins with this verse, in the center of the sura. This is the first point at which we as conscious beings enter into the sura. It deals with the question "Who are we?" Our relationship is that we are the ones that worship God and that seek God's help. So it's a two-way relationship. Worship is the reverence or the ultimate love that we give to God. Ibn Taymiyya says that the best way to understand worship is not to think only of what one does on Fridays. Think of a person who loves someone so much that he says, "I worship you." It is ultimate love, for Ibn Qayyim, but it is also ultimate obedience, disciplined and reverent love that one gives to God and God alone. In return, one asks for help. One asks for help, first and foremost, with worship itself. You cannot worship God except by God's grace and mercy. It's something that you recognize. You get there only if you have God's grace. So what you are asking for is an increase of love itself. "I give my ultimate devotion, but help me do that."

Guide us on the straight path

Now the prayer begins, after establishing the world that we live in and the relationship that we have to this ultimate reality, to God. Guide us to the straight path. There is a sense in which this

straight path needs no further specification because the path is
to God, and the mercy of God, and the justice of God, and the
relationship with God. The direction of this path is fairly clear.
The point is to ask for guidance. Guidance to that path is what
we're asking.

Then the path is further specified, in a historical, human,
social kind of way. Rather than the only true way, it speaks of
the path of those who have already earned blessings and gifts for
you, the path of those before us. It's a tradition-endorsing prayer.
We are not the innovators. We're not the first ones to try to figure out how to worship You, God. People before us have done
so. Make us like them. It's also a very humble prayer: we are not
asking to be better than all those before us. Rather, guide us to
their path. For the first time in this prayer, there is the sense
that there is the possibility of turning away from God, despite
the mercy and justice of God, and the relationship—and all the
goodness that has been evoked so far.

*Not the path of those who have incurred wrath, not the path of
those who have gone astray*

Traditional commentators have seen this as referring to two
different kinds of response. Some people have incurred wrath
because they knew and knowingly disobeyed. Others have gone
astray unwittingly, because they did not know, but that is a layer
of meaning that is hinted at but not explicit in the Qur'an. Yet the
two kinds of error do incur the wrath of God. This is a Qur'anic
etiquette throughout the Qur'an. Evil is not attributed to God.
Muslims, those who submit, those who take up this path, are
to be aware that you have the possibility of knowledge now that
you've asked for guidance. God has given the Qur'an as guidance, and to abandon that knowledge would be to incur God's
wrath. Not to take the trouble to learn it or understand it would
bring the possibility of going astray, misunderstanding it. These
two kinds of errors sum up all kinds of errors.

God is the Creator and author of everything in Islam. All
the dominant Sunni and Shi'a doctrines recognize this, with the
exception of certain sects, such as the Mu'tazilites,[11] who theologically deny that God is the author of evil. Rather, evil is seen

as simply the result of human choice. But the Qur'an is very explicit in some places that you cannot do anything except what God wills, and God has permitted Shaitan, the devil, to do certain things. The Qur'an even says that God leads you astray or allows you to go astray. This is a theological statement. But then there is a question of etiquette. God may say that He creates everything, including evil. But ultimately language is a matter of expression of attitude toward ultimate reality. It is not a description or reduction of reality. That is not possible. That is something that is lost on moderns. The purpose of the Qur'an, and an etiquette that one learns again and again—you see it in conversation between angels or prophets or between good people that are mentioned in the Qur'an—is that whenever something good is mentioned, it is attributed to God. And whenever a calamity or difficulty befalls someone or something, it is not attributed to God. It happens. You lost your children, but God will replace them—rather than saying God took them away but they will come back. Both are ways of saying the same thing, but the etiquette in the Qur'an is the former. So with the expression "those who have incurred wrath," it is unnecessary to say that it is the wrath of God. Wrath is something that God does not prefer to be attributed to Him. There is a hadith, a tradition of the Prophet, that says that when God created the universe, He wrote the final words after everything is created, and this is said on His throne: My mercy has overwhelmed my wrath. This is the slogan of God, if you will. So wrath is there, but it is something that one has to really work hard against God to earn. That's not the normal condition, so that's why it is not mentioned. But in the Qur'anic language it is not inappropriate to say "the wrath of God," because in other places in the Qur'an it does speak of the wrath of God. It is rare, but it appears in some other places in the Qur'an against some specific injustices. All that I have said has to be understood in this context, intertextually. Scholars will look at any of these statements about God's mercy and God's love and understand them in a fuller context. Can one ever say "God's wrath"? Yes, because the Qur'an does use that phrase. But can one say that one of God's names is the Wrathful? One can never say that. One can say that certain people incur

God's wrath. But one cannot say God is the Wrathful. It is not appropriate, because the Qur'an does not say that. One cannot take an action of God and make it an attribute.

When reading this sura, or the Qur'an generally, one feels a sense of the overwhelming presence of God, and when one feels that, then in those moments everything else becomes irrelevant and meaningless, unimportant. Worldly attachments and worldly concerns, almost, one would say, even the act of prayer that one is involved in, become unimportant. It's like you've gotten where you've needed to be. In that language of seekers, it is called *al-jam'a*, the state of union. On the one hand, you don't want to turn back to creation, to anything that is less than divine, so there is a sense of profound *sakeena* or tranquility. You're at rest; you don't want to be anywhere else. You feel a sense of delight which is like nothing else. You are carefree; you feel equanimity. The Qur'an uses a few metaphors. One is *ikhbat* or humility: when you take water and put it in a round cup. The water goes to the bottom and sits there. This is the state of those who are close to God, in the company of God. They are at rest because that's where they want to be.

That's one feeling. There is also a feeling of incredible compassion toward everything else. You don't want anything from anyone. Compassion is different from love, which is bilateral. When I love someone, I need them to be with me. I draw some pleasure from them, as I give them my love. But mercy is something that I simply give without asking for any company or pleasure or anything in return. That's why it is crucial that God is described far more frequently in the Qur'an as compassionate than as a lover.

When one opens the Qur'an and reads the *basmala*, "In the name of Allah who is most merciful and ever merciful," if one does not feel that divine mercy, then one is not reading the Qur'an.

— ۱۲ —

Ovamir Anjum's exposition on the opening sura of the Qur'an invites readers to feel the awe and wonder of divine majesty as well as the intimacy of God's mercy. This is profoundly Islamic, yet members of other faiths can recognize familiar qualities from their own traditions. Upon hearing his tantalizingly enigmatic statement that when "feeling a sense of the overwhelming presence of God" when prayerfully reading this sura, "even the act of prayer that one is involved in becomes unimportant," Christian readers might notice similarities to their own tradition of spirituality. The ancient monk John Cassian, for example, whose words on contemplative prayer exerted a great influence on Western Christianity for many centuries, wrote in the early fifth century that one is not truly praying until one is no longer aware of oneself or the fact that one is praying.[12] At times, when one's conversation partner from another faith speaks deeply from the particularity of his or her own religious tradition, it can sound an echo from one's own.

The Most Beautiful of Stories
INGRID MATTSON

Probably the most widely known of anyone in this book is Ingrid Mattson. She is an established scholar with a long list of publications, is an expert in Islamic law, and for many years directed the Duncan Black Macdonald Center for the Study of Islam and Christian-Muslim Relations at Hartford Seminary, where she also served as professor of Islamic studies and Christian-Muslim relations and founded the first Islamic chaplaincy program in the United States. Ingrid Mattson also served as president of the Islamic Society of North America. Currently she is professor of Islamic studies at Huron University College at the University of Western Ontario. She is a tireless advocate of interreligious understanding and has done much work to promote Jewish-Muslim dialogue. Her book *The Story of the Qur'an: Its History and Place in Muslim Life* (2nd ed., 2013) is a unique, valuable, and altogether readable introduction to Islam's sacred book.

Ingrid Mattson is widely recognized as a scholar of Islamic jurisprudence and a courageous voice for social justice. On this occasion, however, she chose a very different topic and turned to the beautiful story of Joseph in the twelfth sura.

Her words explore story as a vehicle for divine communication, one that yields a different kind of knowledge than, say, the religious legal materials that often occupy her scholarly attention. Ovamir Anjum focused on God as the revealer of knowledge. Ingrid Mattson chooses to focus on Jacob and Joseph as the recipients of divine communication and knowledge. She notes that reality has external and internal qualities, yielding a complex interplay of blindness and faith, of goodness behind hardship. Sadness and grief, therefore, are not incompatible with trust in divine wisdom.

A summary of the lengthy story of Joseph as found in the Qur'an follows.

The tale of Joseph begins, "We tell you the most beautiful of stories." Joseph tells his father of his dream of the sun, moon, and stars bowing down to him, and his father warns him not to tell his brothers, lest they plot to harm him. He tells his son that God will teach him the interpretation of dreams and will perfect divine blessing upon him. Joseph's brothers plan to kill or banish him. One of the brothers advises them not to kill him but instead cast him into a well, where some caravan may pick him up. The brothers ask Jacob to send Joseph with them, and Jacob distrustfully expresses worry that a wolf may eat him while they are careless. They throw him into a well and tell their father that, while they were racing one another, a wolf did in fact eat Joseph. They present him with a bloody shirt. They protest that they are telling the truth, but he responds, "Your souls have enticed you, but patience is beautiful. From God alone I seek help against what you are saying." Meanwhile travelers come by, find Joseph, and sell him to an Egyptian, who notes to his wife that Joseph may be useful, or that they may adopt Joseph as a son. Joseph reaches maturity, and God grants him wisdom, knowledge, and the interpretation of things. But the woman of the house tries to seduce him. He races for the door, and she tears his shirt from behind. At the door, they meet her husband, and she accuses Joseph of dishonorable intentions. A witness from the household, however, suggests that if the shirt is torn at the front, the wife is telling the truth, but if it is torn at the back, then Joseph is to be trusted.

Word gets out, and other women of the city gossip about the wife, who seeks to defend herself by showcasing Joseph, whom they find angelically handsome, to the point of distraction. Joseph is imprisoned, where he earns a reputation as an interpreter of dreams. When the king has a troubling dream about seven lean cows eating seven fat ones, Joseph is freed from prison and brought to court. He explains that seven years of normal yield will be followed by seven years of hardship and advises the king to store up grain for those difficult years. He tells the king to put him in charge of the storehouses because he is a knowledgeable guardian.

During the years of bad harvests, Joseph's brothers come before him but do not recognize him. He tells them to bring him their other brother (named Benjamin in the biblical account). When they return with their brother, Joseph has his drinking cup placed in his brother's bag. They are accused of theft, and the brother is threatened with enslavement. The brothers are told to return to their father and tell them that the brother (Benjamin) has stolen. Again they protest that they are telling the truth, and again Jacob replies, "Your souls have enticed you, but patience is beautiful." He weeps for Joseph until his eyes turn white with grief as he is filled with sorrow. They return to Egypt and eventually recognize Joseph and are reconciled with him. He tells them to take his shirt and cast it over Jacob's eyes so that he might restore his sight. All of Jacob's house travels to Egypt, where there is security, and Joseph's dream is fulfilled.

— ‏الل‎ —

When I interpret the Qur'an, I approach it through different lenses. It is very common for me to approach it to find a legal ruling, for example, but I also read it simply for guidance. The story of Joseph to me has always been extremely rich in spiritual meanings. It's a sura that I return to again and again in my personal life as a touchstone for keeping balance in the midst of great trial, hardship, and adversity. The way I understand Joseph, then, is very much as the word of God speaking to me, but I think I read the Joseph in Sura Yusuf differently than many other parts of the Qur'an because God, as the speaker of the Qur'an, identifies it as a story. Verse 3 begins with the statement "We relate unto you the most beautiful of stories," and the word that's used here is *qasas*. To call this a story gives me the permission to read it as a story. The word *qasas* in Arabic has the meaning of a good story, a tale that we tell about something that happened. A good story is told in a certain way that engages the listener. A good story has symbolism and detail and themes and heroes and villains. It offers vivid images and dramatic, emotional unfolding among family members. We find all of these things in Sura Yusuf, so to me it has a unique role in the Qur'an. There may be episodes of events that are narrated at certain other points in the Qur'an, but this is a complete story that is identified by the Qur'an itself as a story. And I find that this frees my hermeneutical approach to identify the aspects of the sura that make it a good story.

What I identify in that regard as the main theme of this story is the theme of hidden reality. This of course is something that is seen throughout the Qur'an: the difference between the exterior reality and the inner meaning. But here the theme is encapsulated in certain events and objects and symbols in the story that bring us that message in a storytelling way.

The Qur'an talks about *ayat* or signs, and this story contains five signs of the hidden reality. The first is the object of the shirt. The whole point of a shirt is to cover, to put an exterior over what is inside, to protect what lies within. A shirt is an outer skin. What we see in this story is that there are three shirts that play an important role. In verse 18, after the brothers have lost Joseph, after they put him in the well and they come back and they find him gone, they take his shirt. They stain it, as the Qur'an says, with lying blood, or false blood. They present the shirt as hard evidence of what's happened to Joseph, that he's been killed by the wolf. So they're presenting this tangible object—"Here it is, here's the evidence of him being murdered"—but it is a lie. The response of Joseph's father is not to believe it. He rejects this evidence. Even though there's a concrete sign—objective proof, as they would have it, of what they're saying—he doesn't believe.

The second time we come across a shirt is when Joseph is in a situation of attempted seduction. He's in this compromising position with a lady in the house, and as he tries to escape she tears his shirt in the back. Now, in this case the shirt plays a different role. It becomes proof of his innocence because the wise man says in verse 26, "If his shirt is torn in the front, then that means he is lying, and if it's torn in the back, then it means she is lying." Joseph is exonerated with this shirt. We see that an external sign can be a sign of the truth, but sometimes it's not. It can also be deceptive.

The third and final shirt brings us back to the beginning. At the end of the sura, Joseph tells his brothers, who have caused all of the problems, to bring his own shirt back to his father. He says, in verse 93, "Take my shirt and cast it over the face of my father, and he will come to see clearly and come back to me altogether." They bring Joseph's shirt, and it passes over his father's face and heals his sight. Here we have the second theme of the hidden reality, which is Jacob's loss of sight. So here the theme of the shirts links up to the second theme, which is that you can't always believe what you see. Joseph's father loses his sight, and he continues to be lied to. He's lied to about Joseph, and that makes him very sad, and then the sons come and tell him about another situation with the other son, and the other son is being accused of having stolen. Of course, he didn't really steal. At this point all the evidence of the world has failed Jacob. It has lied to him, and at that point he loses his sight. He makes a beautiful statement in verses 83 to 84, where he says, "No, but you yourselves have contrived a story for yourselves, so patience is most fitting." This is such a beautiful statement when he says *fasabrun jamil,* " 'Patience is beautiful. It may be that God will bring them both back to me in the end, for He indeed is full of knowledge and wisdom.' And he turned away from them and said, 'How great is my grief for you all.' Joseph's eyes became white with sorrow and he was suppressed with silence."

Jacob is blind to what's in the world, yet he sees the reality of things. The reality is that the story that's being told to him is not true. He can't see; he isn't able to discover what is externally real. Even though he is a prophet, he can't see through the lies, but he has faith. He relies on the truth, which is the inner reality beyond all of the externals. At this point even to see the world doesn't matter anymore. At the end we have two aspects of the hidden reality coming together. Joseph, who at the end is now made visible or revealed in terms of who he really is, comes forth; his shirt, which is a symbol of the real Joseph who is now public in the world, comes and heals his father.

The third theme of the hidden reality is Joseph himself. Joseph goes through stages where who he is is hidden. The primary hiding of Joseph is when he is in front of his brothers and they don't see or recognize who he really is. They are not able to see this reality because of their own sinfulness. Joseph is able to appear to them as he is, but they don't see him. Finally, after going through the hardship with their other brother and starting to feel regret for what they've done, now there's an opening. They are able to see Joseph, and they say, "Are you Joseph?" in verse 90, and he says, "I am Joseph, and this is my brother." So we have this striking image of Joseph sitting right in front of them, talking with them, engaging with them all of this time, and they don't know who he is. But finally, at the end, it is revealed who he is. At that point the outer and the inner reality are united, and so his shirt is able to bring this healing. Jacob's eyes then are cleared up, and he is able to see. The outer and the inner reality are now brought back together in truth.

The theme of Joseph being hidden only ends with his appearance in the Egyptian court. It begins when he is thrown in the well. The second time he's hidden is when he's thrown into prison. The final time is this metaphorical or symbolic hiding. So there are three times that Joseph is hidden, and each time he is innocent in this. His final unveiling or appearance comes after this cycle of being hidden and brought out twice, until finally at the end the reality of who he is is manifest to everyone around him.

Keeping with this theme of hidden reality, another of the symbols or signs of hidden reality is dreams. The story begins with Joseph's own dream, which he narrates to his father, but his father, who understands the hidden reality, tells him to keep this to himself because his brothers will not understand it. We are informed right at the beginning of the story, in verse 5, that Joseph has knowledge of the hidden reality that his brothers lack. They're unable at this point in their lives to understand what is real. They're too deceived by external appearances. So the dream becomes a prophecy, but it also is a sign of the ignorance of the brothers. At the beginning Joseph is still young, and he himself turns to his father, who is a prophet and a righteous man, for some guidance as to what this dream means. But later, once he's gone through all of these trials, he himself will be able to interpret dreams. In the prison, he rightly interprets the dreams of his fellow prisoners and uses his ability to understand symbolic language and to link what is hidden—after all, dreams are in people's minds when they're sleeping—with external events. Once he's in the prison, we see that Joseph now has this ability to understand both the outer and the inner reality, and it's that ability that turns things around for him. So he gets out of his second imprisonment or hiding—the first being the well—and he comes out into the court. He gives his interpretation of the ruler's dream about the fat and emaciated calves, and his ability to link those symbols or signs of the hidden messages in dreams with what will happen in the world gives him his position of authority in the land.

There are some other, minor signs of the idea of the hidden reality. When Joseph is pulling the trick on his brothers, he fools them by hiding some things in his brothers' packs. He takes something from the court and hides it inside their travel bags, so that when he orders them to be searched, these objects are discovered in their bags. They didn't really hide anything; they are experiencing what they'd done before to Joseph, and this is the beginning of their realization. They begin to understand what they've done wrong. They begin to move beyond their superficial understandings and to consider that there is something beyond what is apparent.

Finally, I would say another sign of the importance of the understanding, the deeper reality behind what is superficial, is in the order Joseph gives to store grain. When grain is stored, it is out of sight until the time that it is needed. So the storage of the grain itself is a symbol of having an essential good that is locked away and hidden until it is needed, when it can be opened and brought out. So there is something in store, waiting for the person who is aware of it, until it is manifest.

Joseph himself asks to be in charge of the storehouses. He says in verse 55, "Put me in charge of the storehouses. I am a knowledgeable guardian," or trustee, *hafiz*. Joseph's ability to guard those storehouses of grain needed for life is a sign of his knowledge of the hidden reality of what is good.

And that, in short, is the story of Joseph, the most beautiful story.

This story teaches me that we need to trust that, behind all of the hardship and difficulty that we face, there is goodness and wisdom. The outcome may be very different from our expectation. Whatever we experience in the external reality is not necessarily the same as the truth of the matter. Like Joseph's father, we have to trust in God throughout all of it.

We are not necessarily going to understand everything. This story has a good ending: Jacob's eyes are healed, and Joseph is reconciled with his brothers and has security. But the story happens in Egypt, in a foreign land. Maybe that foreign land is not the world that we're living in: it could be a sign of the next life. One could say well this story ends too nicely. Very often in life things don't turn out well. I don't see the story as promising us a happy ending in this life. Instead, it shows us that we have to keep faith even when circumstances seem to be terrible and really are terrible. The characters in this story experience suffering, blindness, imprisonment, alienation, and great sadness. Jacob cries so much that his eyes become white; he is no Pollyanna. But he has faith that all will turn out well. He has no idea how that will be, and he's still sad. There is no contradiction in holding those two things simultaneously, the sadness and grief at the external reality that we're experiencing, yet faith and trust in God's wisdom and plan.

— 1ſ —

Where Waters Meet
MARIA DAKAKE

Maria Dakake contrasts the infinitude of divine knowledge with the clear limits of human knowledge. For her this need not lead to mere frustration but can become an occasion of awe. When accompanied by a deep desire to know, which corresponds to God's desire to be known, the result is a desire for divine presence, which can be experienced beyond and despite human finitude.

Maria Dakake is a professor of Islamic studies at George Mason University. She is one of the editors of the forthcoming *HarperCollins Study Qur'an* and is very active in interfaith readings of Abrahamic Scriptures. She has strong interests in women, Sufis, and Qur'anic interpretation. In this conversation, she brings insight into the intriguing story of Moses and the mysterious figure Khidr. Her explicitly mystical readings of this story complement the implicitly mystical dimension of the earlier commentators in this chapter.

— ‖ —

Moses said to his servant, "I will continue on until I reach the place where the two seas meet, even if I go on for a long time." Then when they reached the place where the two seas meet, they forgot their fish, and it made its way to the sea, slipping away. Then when they had passed beyond, Moses said to his servant, "Bring us our meal. We have certainly suffered fatigue on this journey of ours." The servant said, "Did you see when we rested on the rock? I forgot the fish. None but Satan made me forget to mention it, and amazingly it made its way into the sea." Moses said, "That is what we were seeking." So they turned back and retraced their steps. There they found a servant from among Our servants whom We had granted a mercy from Us and whom We had taught knowledge from Our Presence. Moses said unto him, "Shall I follow you, so that you might teach me some of that which you have been taught of sound guidance?" The other said, "Surely you will not be able to bear with me patiently. And how can you bear patiently that which you do not encompass in awareness?" Moses said, "God willing, you will find me patient. I will not disobey you in any matter." The other said, "If you wish follow me, then do not question me about anything before I mention it to you."

They traveled on until, when they had embarked on a ship, the man made a hole in it. Moses said, "Did you make a hole in it in order to drown its people? You have done a foul thing!" The other said, "Did I not tell you that thou would not be able to bear with me patiently?" Moses said, "Do not blame me for having forgotten. Do not make it hard on me for what I have done." They went, and when they met a young boy, the man killed him. Moses said, "Did you kill a pure soul who had not killed a soul? You have done a terrible thing!" The other said, "Did I not tell you that you would not be able to bear with me patiently?" Moses said, "If I question you about anything further, then do not keep me as a companion. You have had enough excuse from me." So they went on until they came to the people of a town and asked them for food, but they were refused any hospitality. Then they found therein a wall that was on the point of collapse, and the man repaired it. Moses said, "If you had wished, you surely could have taken payment for that."

The other said, "This is where you and I part ways. I will inform you of the interpretation of that which you could not bear patiently. As for the ship, it belonged to poor people who worked the sea. I intended to damage it, for there was a king coming after them who was seizing every ship by force. As for *the young boy, his parents were believers and we feared that he would bring them great suffering through transgression and disbelief. We intended that their Lord should give them in his place another child, purer and more merciful. And as for the wall, it belonged to two orphans in the town and beneath it there was buried treasure belonging to them. Their father had been a righteous man, so your Lord intended them to reach maturity and then bring forth their treasure as a mercy from your Lord. I did not do this of my own accord. This is the interpretation of that which you could not bear with patience."* (18:60-82)

This particular sura, the Sura of the Cave, al-Kahf, is the midmost sura of the Qur'an. It is in a sense the keystone, the middle point. Not only is this sura itself the midmost sura, but this particular story is absolutely dead center in the Qur'an. If you were to take a standard Qur'an with six-hundred-plus pages and open to the exact middle, you would come to this story. For me that's somewhat significant, but of course, what's more significant is the story itself. I see this passage as a story that involves a prophet—or two prophets, depending on how you consider Khidr, the other figure in the story—but in some ways it opens a new perspective onto prophethood that's different from every other way that prophethood is presented in the Qur'an. It's totally unique; it doesn't follow any other paradigm of prophethood that we have in the Qur'an. In all the other passages of the Qur'an, prophets are leaders who come to their people and offer them a religious message, a form of religious knowledge, and most particularly Moses. Moses really brings a law, a new way of religious life for his people. In this particular sura, Moses is not the leader. Moses is the follower.

Moses is walking with his servant, who is usually understood to be Joshua, and he says that he's searching for the place where the two seas meet, which is a very symbolic space in the Qur'an and is mentioned elsewhere. It is described as a miracle of God that you have the freshwater of the rivers meeting the seas and they don't interpenetrate. But at this *barzakh*, this place where they meet, there is a brief space where the two do mingle, where the water is brackish, saltier than the river but less salty than the sea. This is the place that he's seeking, the *majma al-bahrayn*, the meeting of the two seas. I think that's a very significant element of the story. The backstory in the commentary is that Moses at one point identifies himself to his people as the most knowledgeable person, and afterwards he's given a message from God that this was not a correct thing to say. God is most knowledgeable, and God was not happy about this claim, and so God told him, "If you go to the meeting of the two seas you will find one more knowledgeable than yourself." Moses, interestingly enough, responds appropriately to this. He doesn't say, "How could there be someone more knowledgeable than myself? I am the Prophet." He says, "I need to go find this person who is more knowledgeable than I am and learn from him." So he's seeking this sea, and eventually he and Joshua go past it; they miss the point. They brought this dried salted fish with them as food, and the fish is partially eaten, and they miss the meeting of the two seas. They keep going, and at a certain point Moses says, "You know, I'm tired. Let's sit down and eat." So Joshua pulls out the basket and the fish is gone. Then he remembers, "Oh! Back there! I remember! I forgot to tell you: the fish"—remember, it's been salted and partially eaten—"came back to life and jumped out of the basket and went back into the sea." Moses says, "That's what we're looking for. That's the point."

So they backtrack, and they return to that point, and that's where they meet this person who is only described in the Qur'an as a servant who's been given knowledge from God's presence. He's not described; he's not named. Muslims unanimously identify this person with Khidr, the Green Prophet, but he's not named. He's just a servant who's been given knowledge directly from God. This compares with Moses' knowledge. Moses has also been given knowledge directly from God, but it's a legal knowledge; it's a knowledge that has to do with this world, and how people behave in this world. So he meets Khidr, and he says to him that he wants to follow him. This is why Sufis love this story. The Sufi finds the master and says, "I'm going to follow you." Moses says to him, "Shall I follow you that you might teach me some of that which you have been taught of sound judgment?" Khidr replies, "Truly, you will not be able to bear patiently with me." You're not going to be able to handle it, he's saying. Moses says, "No, no, no, please, just let me follow." Khidr makes one request of him, "You can't ask any questions." Moses thinks that's fine, of course, until he sees what Khidr does, and then lots of questions come to his mind. So it's also about questioning.

As they go along, they get into a boat, and the back commentary says four people had this boat, and Khidr asks them can we have a ride across the river, for free. They're making a very generous act. They take Khidr and Moses across the river, and there's Khidr making a hole in the boat, nearly sinking it. Moses is obviously outraged, as anyone would be: "How could you do such a thing?" Khidr just says, "Didn't I tell you, don't ask any questions." "All right, all right, I promise, no more questions." They go along and a young boy comes, and Khidr just immediately picks up a rock and kills him. Moses is horrified. After all, "Thou shalt not kill." "How could you do such a thing?" Again, "I told you not to ask any questions." They keep going and, by now they're hungry—here I'm mixing commentary a little bit into this story to help it make sense—and they come to this town, and they ask them for hospitality, for some food. The townspeople refuse; they run them out of town, essentially. As they're going out of town, there's a wall that's leaning and has broken down or is about to fall over, and Khidr stops and rebuilds it. Then—I always think this is funny—Moses doesn't ask a third question. He's the Prophet of the Law. He's the literalist, so he asks a question without asking a question, and he says, "You know, you could have asked for some compensation for that." So it's technically not a question, but it is a question embedded in a comment, and Khidr knows. Khidr says, "That's it. This is the end. This is the place we have to part. We cannot go any further together."

I see this traveling of Moses and Khidr together as that barzakh. Moses is that fresh water. He's the river that moves in a linear fashion, that has defined boundaries, that is lifegiving. You can drink it, and it's a path, of course, that leads to the sea. The sea always represents the eternal. It represents God's knowledge,

God's infinitude. So Khidr really represents the sea, the infinitude of God's knowledge that can't be defined, that isn't clear. For a brief moment, they journey together. They're in that barzakh, that intermediary zone, that meeting of the two seas, but they can't stay that way. Eventually the sea has to be the sea and the river has to be the river. Moses can't really learn, ultimately, what Khidr could teach, and Khidr frankly doesn't think Moses can learn it, and so he's not going to teach it anymore. He says, "This is the parting." But he says, "Before we part, I'm going to give you the interpretation of what I just did." The word that he uses for "interpretation" is ta'wil.

Ta'wil is also used in the Qur'an to mean an interpretation of Qur'anic verses, and the word means to bring something back to its origin, awwal, meaning "first."

In the beginning of the third chapter of the Qur'an, it says, "None knows the interpretation of the ambiguous verses except God, and those firmly rooted in knowledge." Khidr is saying, "There's a ta'wil for you here. I'm going to give it to you." He says that the boat belonged to very poor people, and there was a king who was coming after them and was going to seize all working vessels for his own use. By Khidr's partially damaging it in this way, the king is going to leave it alone because it's not a seaworthy vessel at the moment. That's going to save that vessel for the people. About the boy, he says that he had very believing, very pious parents, and he was going to grow up to be a terrible person and break their heart. He slew him so that a new child could come in his place that would give them great joy. About the wall, he says that there were two orphans in the city, and their father left them a treasure buried underneath the wall, and they wouldn't find it when they were of age unless the wall was still standing, and so he repaired it. And that's it! The story ends right there. One of the things I noticed when I read this and when I thought about it is that I thought, "This doesn't really answer my questions." In fact, it leaves more questions. "You slay the boy, but you're a prophet, so why don't you just teach him? Why don't you reform him?" In any case, new children can come even though the other one is there. It doesn't really answer the question of why this child had to die. Again, with the wall at the end, Moses doesn't say, "Oh! Now I understand! Oh, right! I'm not going to ask any more questions. I know you've got a good agenda. I know you've got it from on high. I know you're doing the right thing. It may seem strange to me, but I'm going to follow along." Instead, they part.

First of all, I think this story says that there are some questions in life that don't have answers, that religion can't answer, that you just have to live with, in a sense. You don't know what the divine wisdom is behind things. Even if that divine wisdom were to be revealed, as it is to Moses, it still doesn't answer your questions. In other words, you can't learn it. It's a knowledge that's so veiled, you might say, that even when it's revealed, it can't be seen. Even when you reveal it, it doesn't penetrate; it veils itself even when it's revealed. It's as if it's saying that there are things that are going to happen, and nothing in the Torah you've been given, Moses, or any Scripture for that matter, is going to answer your questions about it. Even if God were to answer your questions, you still wouldn't understand, living in this particular context. I think that's very important. So they have to part. There's a way in which to live in a spiritually, or even materially, profitable way in this world; you have to set aside certain questions. You have to follow the known path. You have to realize at the same time, while you're traveling down this river, so to speak, that there are things beyond it that you can't understand, that you can't get to, and just learn to live with that. I see it almost as functioning in the Qur'an, if you take it as a whole, very much like the story of Job in the biblical text. The whole biblical text up to that point is really talking about the idea that there's a kind of justice that God has. If the Israelites fulfill their part of the covenant, God will protect them. If they don't fulfill the covenant, God's going to punish them, but then God's going to redeem them. Job questions that whole idea. Job's a good person. His afflictions don't come because God is punishing him for something. Job stands—as does the Leviathan at the end—for that unknowable part of God that can't be explained by everything that comes before it in Scripture. I think in some ways this story serves that same function. Prophets are going to come. Some people are going to follow them, and things are going to be good for them. Other people are not going to follow them, and things are not going to be good for them. It works in a very systematic fashion. This story is saying that there is also another way in which the will of God is operative in the world that transcends human understanding. There's a law, and then there's another law. It's never going to be totally comprehensible to you in that way.

From that point of view, I think it's a very powerful story. The fact that it's set in its context, right there in the middle of the Qur'an, emphasizes its importance. The prophets in this story are not as they are found elsewhere in the Qur'an. As I said, Moses is the follower. People debated whether Khidr was a prophet or not. Most people say he's a prophet, based on the argument that Moses learns from him. As a prophet, Moses couldn't learn from someone who wasn't a prophet. This may or may not be a good argument. But if he is a prophet, he's not a prophet like any of the other prophets in the Qur'an. Prophethood in Islam is really based upon the idea that you come with a public message to a particular people and you deliver that message. Khidr is reluctant even to deliver the message to Moses. His message is not for public consumption. He's working at a different level. I think that the Qur'an is saying that there is a way in which God's power and God's will are working in the world that transcends the limits of religious teaching.

The Qur'an repeatedly invites the readers to ponder and to question. So Moses does the right thing. He finds out that there's someone who has more knowledge than he does, and he seeks it out. He humbles himself and says, "I know you know more than I do, and I'm going to follow you." He does the right thing. Khidr tells him not to ask questions, and he still asks the questions. Yet Moses doesn't become a bad person for asking those questions, and he shouldn't in the eyes of the reader, either, because the reader should have exactly those same questions. We're on this side of the barrier of the water. Moses, in a sense, didn't learn what he thought he was going to learn, but he learned something else. He learned that his questioning cannot exhaust the knowledge of God. Which is not to say that the questioning isn't worthwhile or isn't necessary.

In the context of Sufism, there's a lot of talk about how Sufis are spiritual elitists, that they think that there's a message just for them. I'm currently teaching a course on Sufism. I tell my students that, from the Sufi point of view, what qualifies you to follow this path is not some innate spiritual virtue. It's simply desire. It's what Sufis call *talab*, a desire to seek, to search for something more. That's what Moses exemplifies in this particular context. We can't be Khidr. We can only be Moses, and I think what it tells us is that we should question. Moses is a good example for us, but we're going to come to a point where we realize that even if we get the answers to our questions, the knowledge is going to elude us. It's going to transcend us in some ways.

There are numerous other Sufi understandings of this text. At the most basic level, it's the idea of what is called *adab*— that is, proper behavior. Moses, even though he asks the questions when he's not supposed to, shows his deference. When he asks the question, and Khidr says to him, "I told you not to ask questions," he doesn't persist. He says, "Oh, yes, I'm sorry, I forgot, so we'll go on." He shows first of all talab. He shows that proper attitude of being humble and seeking someone who knows more than he does. He asks questions. He trusts the master when the master tells him to be quiet now, that this is not a question for him to ask. When Khidr gives him the answer, he doesn't respond by saying, "Oh, yes, now I understand," but he also doesn't ask further questions. He may not understand, but he realizes this is where he must stop. He knows his place. Both the talab, the seeking, and the adab toward the master are exemplified for Sufis by Moses in this particular passage. It's also significant because the knowledge that Khidr is given is described as *'ilm laduni*—that is, knowledge from My Presence, knowledge from the presence of God. This is contrasted with the legal and ritual knowledge that Moses has, the exoteric knowledge. Khidr represents the esoteric form of knowledge, and Moses the exoteric.

Sufis take this term. Al-Ghazali and other people use this term continuously, to talk about a kind of knowledge that doesn't come from studying books and doesn't even necessarily come from revelation. It comes directly from above, immediately.

Khidr exemplifies the existence of that kind of knowledge. Sufis say that there is such a thing; there are people who have this in the world. It's juxtaposed with Moses' knowledge, which here appears inferior to Khidr's. He's following Khidr. In the commentary tradition that expands upon the Qur'anic story, at one point Khidr is sitting with Moses, and they see a bird dipping its beak into the water and taking some water. Khidr says, "God has given me knowledge that He hasn't given you, and He's given you knowledge that He hasn't given me, but the knowledge that both of us have, in relation to the knowledge of God, is as the water that that bird is taking out of the river." We do have some knowledge from God, but it's nothing compared to the totality of God's knowledge. That's a very significant element for Sufis. It validates the idea that there is a ta'wil, an inner interpretation, in this case to events, but ultimately, because it's using the same word, to the Scripture. Sufis can say that there is a knowledge that comes directly from God, an interpretation that transcends ordinary means of interpretation, an inner meaning to things. For Sufis it becomes a story that exemplifies their perspective on knowledge as well as a story of proper spiritual etiquette, adab.

Abd al-Razzaq Kashani (d. 1330) was a student in the school of the great Sufi master Ibn al-'Arabi. In his commentary Kashani sees it all as an allegory for the journey of the soul. The meeting of the two seas is the point of origin, and Khidr is associated with eternal life because he goes on and on. He doesn't have a normal human life span, and he's the Green Prophet, green being associated with life.

In the commentary traditions that accompany the story, when Moses sees him, Khidr is wrapped up in a green cloak, and he unwraps himself a little bit to talk to Moses. According to some, he's sitting on an island in the midst of the meeting of the seas. You get this sense of "font of eternal life." Muslims would say he is mortal because no one is immortal, but nonetheless he lives outside of a normal human life span, outside of the normal progress of human life. He represents this prophet of eternal life in a sense, and that's why, when Moses and Joshua pass by the place where he is, the fish comes back to life. It was splashed by some of the water that is the source of life. Even the salted, dried, partially eaten fish could come back to life at this point. Kashani says that this refers to a journey of the soul coming into the world. It originates at the font of life. As Moses and Joshua miss the meeting point of the two rivers and they keep going on, that's where Moses says, "You know, I'm tired. Let's sit down and eat." Kashani says that the soul when it's in the other world is perfectly nourished, and then when it comes to this world it has hunger, and it knows tiredness and weariness. That's the situation that Moses is in as he gets further away from that source of life. He realizes he needs to go back, and they go back to the river and the rock. Kashani says it's like going back to the breast of the mother, the source of infantile nourishment. When he travels with Khidr and he destroys the boat, Kashani says the boat is like the body. It's what you need to get you from this point to that point in this world. It's the thing that conveys you through this life. But the body has to be broken—this is one Sufi interpretation—it must be disciplined and deprived, in order to bring it into line with the intellect and with the spirit. That's really what Moses is doing with the boat. He's breaking it but not destroying it. You can't destroy the body, but you have to break it, to damage it in some way so that it can't be seized by the king, who represents the tyrannical elements of the soul, pride and concupiscence and so on. Breaking the body frees it from being grabbed by the negative elements of the soul. The part about slaying is easy: the young boy represents precisely those negative elements of the soul that have to be slain in order for the better part of your soul to thrive, to grow, and to prosper. As for the wall, he says that the treasure that's buried underneath that wall is *ma'rifa*, spiritual knowledge, and the broken wall is what's called the soul at peace. The Qur'an talks about three kinds of souls: the soul that commands to evil; the soul that blames, the one that wants to be good and is always arguing with the other part of the soul; and the soul at peace, when the negative parts of the soul have been disciplined enough. When there is no longer a fight, you've reached the soul at peace. You no longer have those temptations of the lower soul. It's the highest form of the soul. Kashani says the wall is the soul at peace that's been broken. Only when it's repaired and set back up properly can the knowledge that's underneath come out. When you've disciplined the body, destroyed the negative parts of the soul, and strengthened and rebuilt your truly spiritual soul, then the knowledge can be attained. I find this very beautiful. It takes the story and gives it a symbolic meaning, but in many ways Kashani's reading is allegorical in that it runs parallel to the story rather than being a kind of interpretation of every individual element of the story. It gives the reader a sense of how open this passage is to interpretation. Sometimes allegories can seem to work a little too neatly to be convincing, but in this case I personally find it a convincing allegorical interpretation of this passage. It deepens it and enlivens it. This is a beautiful story about spiritual knowledge.

— ‏۱۲‏ —

Reflection on divine knowability and unknowability is, for these Muslim scholars, an exercise of piety as well as theology. To read their Scripture in this way entails an expectation of layers, of beauty, and of spiritual encounter. Reading the Qur'an is not simply a matter of being told what to do or how to behave. It is to experience a God who is mysterious and unfathomable and yet trustworthy, a God who is beyond the human capacity to grasp fully, yet a Being who reaches out to humankind in a desire to be known and to be in relationship.

The following chapter continues the theme of how to read one's sacred Scripture, with a focus on reading with painstaking attention to the details of the holy text.

2

CLOSE READINGS,
OLD AND NEW

To read a sacred Scripture is to read in company because a holy text is accompanied by centuries of commentary. Reading Scripture with meticulous care within a community of faith brings the reader into conversation with that lively history of interpretive possibilities. Past and present can collide or collude in surprising ways. This chapter is alive with those tensions and unexpected harmonies.

As many of the voices in this book point out, in the past there was robust argument and disagreement among Muslim scholars and teachers. A variety of opinions and positions prevailed on many topics of Islamic theology. The breadth of Islamic tradition comes to life in my conversations with Mohammad Hassan Khalil and Emran El-Badawi in their discussions, respectively, of the fate of non-Muslims in the afterlife and of the Qur'an's response to the Jewish and Christian presence in Mecca in the earliest days of the Muslim community.

Close attention to holy texts can also result in readings that are firmly based in faithfulness to the Qur'an but that are not evident in historical commentary. Asma Barlas finds a thought-provoking critique of patriarchy in the story of Abraham's near sacrifice of his son. Kecia Ali raises profound questions about Mary and the ways in which she does and does not conform to cultural expectations of gender. It is intellectually very lively and stimulating to read the Qur'an with both of these scholars because they constantly focus attention on the details of the text and yet—or, more precisely, because of that acute attentiveness—offer unexpected and exciting possibilities.

Mercy and Salvation
MOHAMMAD HASSAN KHALIL

The first Muslim guide in this chapter shows us that the notion that divine mercy extends the possibility of salvation even to non-Muslims is not a new element in Islam arising from the current defensiveness of Muslims after the tragedies of 9/11. Instead it is a value that was manifest in times when Islam was culturally powerful and therefore in no position of a need to apologize to a non-Muslim majority. What may look like a modern response to contemporary events is in fact a long-held tradition, if neglected in recent times.

Mohammad Hassan Khalil is associate professor of religious studies at Michigan State University. His work *Islam and the Fate of Others: The Salvation Question* (2012) explores how Muslim scholars from long ago and recent times wrestled with the question of whether there was room in paradise for non-Muslims. He finds quite a range of views as he considers historically influential thinkers such as al-Ghazali, Ibn al-'Arabi, Ibn Taymiyya, and Ibn Qayyim, as well as modern Muslim voices such as Rashid Rida, Sayyid Qutb, Farid Esack, Abdulaziz Sachedina, Mahmoud Ayoub, and T. J. Winter.[1] This highly readable book is a captivating model of careful attention to texts and insightful observations. It demonstrates that, while many Muslims may regard the questioning of the eternal quality of hell as dangerously novel, it is in fact a well-documented Muslim tradition. Mohammad Hassan Khalil chose as his focal passage the opening words of the Qur'an, and of all but one of the 113 suras that follow: "In the name of God, the Compassionate, the Caring."

— ﷽ —

There are many different translations of *bismillah ar-rahman ar-rahim*: in the name of God, the Lord of Mercy, the Giver of Mercy; or the Compassionate, the Caring; or the Beneficent, the Merciful; and so on. The majority of Muslim scholars hold that this is the first verse of the Qur'an, and not simply a statement that appears before the opening sura, al-Fatiha. Either way, it comes first, and it is a formula that precedes almost every other sura of the Qur'an, the exception being Sura 9, al-Tawba. Scholars have long debated the reasoning behind its absence from that sura, one theory among others being that Sura 8 and Sura 9 are in fact one sura. In any case, the fact that almost every sura, and indeed the Qur'an itself, begins with this statement is significant.

What does it actually mean? "In the name of God" is clear. *Rahman* and *rahim* are two terms that are derived from *rahma*, meaning "loving mercy," and both are related to the term *rahim*, the mother's "womb," the center of love and compassion and mercy. This idea of rahma frames the Qur'an. When you're reading the Qur'an, even when you're reading some of the more violent passages about torment and hell and so on, everything is framed in this rahma. I find this to be comforting in many ways. My own understanding of the concept of mercy itself has expanded, and my research has allowed me to appreciate how truly expansive this concept of rahma is. There are other verses in the Qur'an that go further in describing the rahma of God. For example, 7:156 indicates that although God's mercy is written for the righteous, it encompasses everything.

During my first semester as a graduate student, I sat in on a philosophy of religion course. I would sit next to a student who had been relatively active in the Muslim community. I remember one day when I was having a chat with him about God, he looked at me and said, "I don't believe in Allah." To be honest, I was surprised. Up until that point in my life, I had never actually chatted with somone who left Islam after having been an involved member of the Muslim community. This led to a series of discussions, and he brought up things that I had always been concerned about but could never fully resolve, including the damnation of non-Muslims and the eternal quality of damnation. I began to research these issues, and I remember one day flipping through *A Reader on Classical Islam* by F. E. Peters. I got to a section that he had titled "An End to Hell?" I was truly shocked. I was always taught that hell was everlasting, and that's that, end of discussion. And here was al-Zamakhshari responding to people who claimed that hell terminates.[2] I thought, "Why would he have to respond to that? Isn't that a nonissue?" That got me thinking that maybe this issue is not as simple as I thought it was. Around the same time, I read Sherman Jackson's book on al-Ghazali, *On the Boundaries of Theological Tolerance in Islam: Abu Hamid al Ghazali's Faysal al Tafriqa*. Here al-Ghazali speaks of mercy being extended to countless non-Muslims, even to non-Muslims who encountered the Islamic message and chose to investigate it actively. Most of humanity being saved? Unbelievable. I remember very clearly that, even as a senior in college, what I was exposed to was a much grimmer outlook: a guest speaker addressing Muslim students on the topic of the afterlife asserted that, according to the hadith corpus, 999 out of every 1000 individuals go to hell. I asked him, "Do you mean they go to hell forever?" and he said, "Yes, forever." I was shocked to hear this. I thought, well, heaven's going to be very empty. But he was a scholar, and I was just a student. So I began to investigate. The book by Sherman Jackson got me thinking about al-Ghazali, and then I read somewhere that Ibn Taymiyya said that hell was not everlasting, and I thought, "Of all people, Ibn Taymiyya would say this? I can't believe that!" It came as a surprise to me that he would say such a thing despite his reputation for being "conservative."

Years later, when I wrote my first book, *Islam and the Fate of Others*, I decided to focus on the writings of four prominent Muslim scholars. Aside from al-Ghazali and Ibn Taymiyya, I chose to include Ibn al-'Arabi because of his enormous influence among Sufis. Then I turned to Rashid Rida because I wanted to look at a major modern figure.[3] Throughout my research, I found that these extremely influential scholars all had a notion of overwhelming mercy, rahma. This goes against the assumption of some scholars that the Muslim emphasis on rahma is a modern trend, a modern apologetic tactic. The medieval scholars I looked at really had no comparable motivation to be apologetic, and yet they espoused a vision of overwhelming mercy, where in the end at least the overwhelming majority of humanity would be saved. The way they spoke about mercy was eye opening for me. They would point out passages that I had never even thought about. For example, the passage I mentioned earlier, 7:156, that God's mercy encompasses everything, or 6:12, which states that God inscribed rahma upon Himself. Then, of course, there is the *hadith* about God's mercy overwhelming or outstripping His wrath. As for the 999 out of 1000 hadith, al-Ghazali states that we shouldn't run with this report because, for one thing, to be "assigned" to hell doesn't mean one is going to be damned. He references other hadiths of people being saved on their way to hell. This is beside the fact that there are variants of the 999 out of 1000 hadith that leave more room for a more optimistic vision. These were all eye-opening discussions for me.

This project allowed me to challenge myself to go further in how I think about mercy. And when you do that, you begin to see the world in a different light. You even begin to interact with people in a different manner. My own conclusion to the book is that all we're really left with is positive ambiguity, and that's, I think, all we really can assert. But with that positive ambiguity, you see everything differently. So for example, when I look at you, the first thing that comes to mind isn't "non-Muslim." Of course you're non-Muslim, but now the first thing I think is, "fellow human being." And when I look at even people who could be considered "evil," I now think maybe there's something there even in these people. Maybe there's some latent goodness. It's not actualized, but there's something there. I approached this topic as an academic, but there's no denying that it also affected my personal life, the way that I see the world.

The three medieval scholars that I looked at are so very different from one another. And yet, I found benefit in the writings of all three. Philosophically, each of them inhabited a different intellectual universe, but they all emphasized rahma and its embracive quality. They agree that rahma is overwhelming; they just don't see eye to eye on how it manifests itself. All this goes back to the idea of positive ambiguity. They know that there's a good reason to be optimistic, even though they don't agree on how exactly everything will play out. They feel compelled to affirm some form of optimism.

Reading the Qur'an under the benevolent shadow of rahma allows one to appreciate Scripture on a different level. I remember as a high school student reading about some of the painful torments of hell. These passages are of course unsettling, and they are intended to be, but when you read these within the frame of rahma, I think it removes some of the anxiety. Still, they force you to think and to ponder, and to reject complacency. There's a sense of urgency in Scripture: you need to change *right now*. That is necessary and an essential part of the Qur'an, but, again, the fact that everything begins with rahma lessens some of that anxiety. There are these very dramatic descriptions, but these descriptions serve a purpose. Parents of young children are very repetitive—I love you, I love you, don't do this, don't do that—and the Qur'an is very repetitive. It is possible to see these dire warnings in a positive light, as an expression of concern.

Again, the terms for mercy are related to the term for the "womb" of the mother. These terms, appearing at the beginning, underscore the concern that God has for creation. They define what follows and allow the audience to appreciate the purpose of the Qur'an. You feel that you can trust the Author; the Author is not out to get you. The motivation is not terror. The motivation is compassion, and realizing this allows one to appreciate the dynamic of the relationship. When someone passes away, we have a saying that comes from the Qur'an: "We belong to God, and to Him we shall return." When we die, we return to the source of mercy.

I found it interesting how all of the main scholars that I looked at repeatedly talk about how there can be rahma even in punishment and in physical torment. I was shocked to read this. How can this be? Some of these scholars present a hypothetical scenario of a child who requires an amputation. The mother is against the amputation, while the father is for it. According to the theologians, the father is actually the one being most merciful toward the child because he wants the child to live. So even though the child has to go through the excruciating pain of amputation—keep in mind this is before the use of anesthesia— it's for that child's own good. Now, of course, the skeptic might ask why God wouldn't save the person from the beginning. Why go through all of that? Here the believers among the philosophers might respond with a discussion of agency. If we are free to choose, then perhaps we have to go through a life of challenges in order to grow. In the Qur'an, Adam and Eve are placed in the garden, and they're told to do just one thing: avoid the tree. That's it; that's all they had to do. Granted, it's an amazing tree, but still it's just one moral task. And they couldn't even do that. By extension, if other beings with agency were to begin their lives in heaven, they too would fail and fall. They need to grow first, and that's what this life is for. That's why the angels bow to Adam: Adam can do things they can't do. The angels are widely presumed to be automatons whose knowledge is limited, whereas humans have some form of agency and can learn more about life—and make mistakes. The point here is that even in life's difficulties, there is rahma, even if we can't see it or appreciate it. It is important to remember that death is not the end. And the Qur'an tells us (31:28) that this life and the next are intimately connected: your creation and your resurrection are like a single being.

When I give my lectures on salvation discourse, my students are usually surprised, just as I was. But I truly think if I had just taken the time to read the Qur'an carefully as these earlier scholars had read it, then I may have also come to appreciate the significance and prevalence of rahma. But I missed that, and I think that many of my students missed that as well, and that's why I think they're surprised to hear about these major scholars, representing different schools of thought, all speaking of mercy.

I've presented my findings in different venues. My research is usually well received. There are some exceptions, though. Some fellow Muslims are disturbed especially by my discussion of the theologians who held that hell is not everlasting. This is seen as a heterodox belief, even though it is represented by significant, recognized scholars, even though it is part of our history. During one presentation, there was some genuine resistance coming from a few people whose concern was that the notion of a finite hell was too lenient. For them, this notion raises the specter of complacency. If hell is not everlasting, why bother to fulfill the obligation to pray five times every day? This, of course, is not a logical conclusion, because those who say hell is finite assume that the damned will only be saved once they have rectified themselves. And the prevailing view in Islamic thought anyway is that God will eventually save all believers, however sinful they may be. In any case, for those who truly experience and truly appreciate rahma, the effect should be devotion rather than laxity or complacency.

When you can find prominent and influential scholars from different eras and regions, who were not minorities in contexts such as our own and were thus not tempted to be apologetic in the way that many American Muslims might be, promoting a vision of overwhelming mercy in the next life, it gives one a sense of confidence in that vision. I think there's something in the Islamic ethos—as these important scholars understood it—that leads to this confidence in divine mercy. Unfortunately, there are many Muslims who promote a message of gloom and doom, and there are many non-Muslims who assume that this message is representative of the Islamic ethos. I think one has to have a balance, but I think what tips the scales toward positive ambiguity is rahma. If you look at the Qur'anic descriptions of God's nature, you see wrath and you see mercy, but what tips the scales toward mercy is the first line one encounters when reading the Qur'an, "In the name of God the Compassionate, the Caring."

— ١٢ —

Remembering Zakariya
EMRAN EL-BADAWI

The Qur'an emerged in a complex historical situation and responded to the presence of Christians and Jews in Arabia. For Emran El-Badawi, therefore, there is no cause for hesitation to explore that ancient context and to bring the Qur'an into conversation with Jewish and Christian texts and theological controversies of that era. For him, a close reading includes a comparative reading with non-Muslim materials.

Emran El-Badawi is a professor of Arabic language and literature and director of the Arabic program at the University of Houston. He is also codirector of the International Qur'anic Studies Association, a new learned society that invites scholars of the Qur'an of all religious, philosophical, and methodological persuasions to examine Islam's holy text together. As he notes, the openness of his method of studying the Qur'an in the context of its Jewish and Christian milieu may strike some conservative Muslims as theologically innovative and unsafe, but in fact he is reviving a neglected dimension of the Islamic tradition in reading the Qur'an in this way. As with

Mohammad Hassan Khalil, what may look like modern novelty is a revival of a time-honored practice.

— ‖ —

The Qur'an has 114 chapters (suras), which were revealed in Mecca and Medina in seventh-century Arabia. A majority of these suras are Meccan, and even within those both traditional as well as Western scholars have detected stages of development. Much of this is somewhat tentative, but I have believed since I first read the Qur'an that Suras 17–20 form a kind of unit, for literary as well as thematic reasons. So, for example, these suras share the same rhyme syllable and demonstrate a sense of progression within a didactic prophetic narrative. I would like to speak a bit about Suras 19 (Maryam) and 20 (Taha).

Sura Maryam begins with unconnected letters, called *muqatta'at*. However, my focus here is on what follows. As I see it, the first verse or second verse of a typical sura sets the mood for the remainder of that text. You see this in the Medinan suras as well as the Meccan. So in Sura Maryam the Qur'an essentially defines the name Zakariya, stating, "a commemoration of the mercy of your Lord is His servant Zakariya" (*dhikru rahmati rabbika 'abdahu Zakariyya*). This may be considered a definition of the term, or a linguistic explanation. Zachariah in Hebrew means "God has remembered." *Zachar* in Hebrew means "to remember." In Aramaic the cognate verb is *dekar*. The Arabic cognate *dhikr* means "a remembering, a commemoration." In these languages, *z*, *d*, and *dh* preserve the same ancient sound. In other words, *dhikr* in Arabic and *zachar* in Hebrew are cognates. The Qur'an connects Zakariya and "commemoration" without recourse to any other text.

The sura carries on from there, speaking about Jesus, John, Abraham, Moses, and the other prophets. The Qur'an mentions in the beginning that there is a path that leads to mercy and that there is another path that leads to damnation, and that through looking at the sequence of prophets, the well-defined prophetology of the Qur'an manifests itself. Prophetology in the Qur'an acts like a sieve for humankind. This idea is important to Muslims in general. To say this differently, prophets are used as examples to remind the Muslim community today, as well as fourteen hundred years ago, who the good guys and bad guys are.

In Sura 19 the Qur'an begins by mentioning the prophet Zakariya and does so in a context where the Christians are being addressed. If you look at the sequence of the sura as a whole, you see that it goes through all the prophets who were relevant for debate at the time. Toward the end it expounds upon the apocalypse as well as good and evil. It concludes by speaking about Jesus once again. So we begin by addressing the Christians, and then come full circle by addressing them at the end. This tells me and other Qur'an specialists that this sura is an inseparable unit. Michel Cuypers and Carl Ernst among others have studied the phenomenon of "ring structure" in some depth.[4]

Whereas Sura 19 addresses the Christians, Sura 20, while it does not directly address the Jews, uses the example of Moses and his people to remind believers today, as well as fourteen centuries ago, about what is good and evil. One striking feature of Sura 20 is that there is a good deal of narrative detail. Although there is little extended narrative in the Qur'an, except for Sura 12 (Yusuf), we find some detail in Sura 20 as well. The sura teaches us showing good from evil; it lets the community know that people have rejected the divine message before, illustrates what has become of them, and even demonstrates that good people can go astray but find their way again—like Aaron. So the sura goes through various permutations of how someone can be saved or unsaved, culminating in characteristic apocalypticism. Ultimately these two suras share the goal of warning and teaching a community of Christians and Jews using *their* stories to argue that this is a divine message and that this is a legitimate prophet in the tradition of *their* prophets. In this respect I agree with the traditional exegetes as well as secular academics, like Theodor Nöldeke.[5]

We can detect in Suras 17–20 that the Prophet's message has partly been articulated already; the Qur'an, in a sense, already exists in some tentative form. It is oral; it is there, but somehow now being *rearticulated* in a way that speaks to Jews and Christians more immediately, using stories and language with which they are familiar. I differentiate these suras from earlier ones that focus more on fire and brimstone, where the message is "repent quickly." These earliest revelations have a strong sense of urgency tapered in didactic narratives of Suras 17–20, or so-called late Meccan suras. An alternative argument holds that the encounter with Jews and Christians occurred mainly in Medina rather than in Mecca. Arguments like this are complex and still hotly debated.

That being said, there is an increased awareness of the Qur'an's Jewish and Christian audience nowadays. There is a growing awareness among Qur'anic studies scholars today that when the Qur'an speaks of *mushrikun*—that is, those who associate the worship of God with another deity—and when it speaks of *kuffar*—that is, unbelievers, folks who are disobedient—that these terms are polemical or heresiographical, rather than informative about the historical identity of such interlocutors. By this I mean that the text is a kind of catalog of those who have committed rebellion and heresy by its standards. This understanding, especially of the situation in Mecca, differs from the traditional view that there was a dominant pagan background with a handful of Jews and Christians here and there. I think that the Qur'an operates in a monotheistic background. That is, I think we are dealing with Jews and Christians primarily. Other monotheistic groups have a place as well. The Qur'an talks about Sabians and Magi, for example. Principally, though, there is such a critical mass of Qur'anic verses talking to Jews and Christians. The text addresses syncretistic pagan cults only a handful of times—Al-Lat, Uzza, Manat, and al-Shu'ra.[6] If, however, we were to record all the instances in which the Qur'an addresses Jews and Christians, we would come up with dozens of references. Both in Mecca as well as Medina, we're dealing with monotheists, primarily Jews and Christians.

That is as much as I can commit to now on this issue, but others have argued that when the Qur'an talks about *nabi*, "prophet," as opposed to *rasul*, "apostle" or "messenger," this points to a difference in the confessional identity of the audience. Although I am tempted to agree with such a hypothesis, I am cautious about the black-and-white designations that have been made in this regard—namely, that nabi resonates with a Jewish audience and rasul with a Christian one. There are surely areas of gray, and I suspect it may be a bit more complicated. At any rate, I think that the Qur'an knows its audience and adapts its fundamental message—strict monotheism, the approaching apocalypse—to speak to its audience in a meaningful way, telling stories that are meaningful to them. This is why I think that Jews and Christians are the primary audience of the Qur'an throughout.

This conclusion both does and does not have implications for how Muslims understand their relationship with Jews and Christians today. It does not in the sense that the Qur'an's conversation with these groups took place a long time ago, in a context foreign to our own, and so in a sense we have to let go of the past. We need to let go of the disputes that may have manifested themselves in the Qur'an's polemic, which I think should be taken in the context of late antique polemic in general. It was an era within which holy men wrote long treatises against the seemingly misguided faith of their interlocutors. Consider, for example, the plethora of Christian Aramaic literature from this time, such as the dialogue between Bardaisan and his student Philippus, Aprahat's *Demonstrations*, or Isaac of Nineveh writing against the Jews, and countless treatises written against the Nestorians and, conversely, against the Jacobites.[7] We find that the Qur'an functions in this context. It works to persuade its audience in this context because they are a sophisticated one, well versed in the intellectual debate and literature of their day. They know full well the kinds of locutions, ring structure, didactic stories, apocalyptic imagery, and legal responsa that manifest themselves within the text. The Qur'an's nonlinear literary form, which can look disjointed to an unassuming modern reader, was completely normal for its time. In this regard, the Qur'an was revealed in a world totally different from the one which we know today.

However, the Qur'an's conversation with Jews and Christians does, of course, affect how Muslims, Christians, and Jews can see themselves today. Not long ago I was speaking to Angelika Neuwirth, an eminent scholar in the field. Among other things, she illustrated (and I paraphrase) that there are no quintessentially Islamic, Christian, or Jewish theologies—just theology. If we appreciate that the Qur'an is part of a larger fabric of religious literature, then we realize that the theological borders that we have placed between us are no longer divisive, and that they are not, furthermore, constructed by Scripture itself or by the message within it. The borders are constructed mainly as a result of political and historical reasons. This realization can imbue a new, albeit ironic, meaning into interfaith dialogue: "We disagree because we have so much in common." We speak in the same terms.

The Qur'an is aware that the word "Zakariya" is not Arabic. The text is "Qur'an-izing" the word by associating it with dhikr. The Qur'an *knows* that this is a technical term, worthy of further clarification. The text hints, perhaps, that its universal message will reach non-Arabic speakers who will find such terminology meaningful. Within the Arabian sphere in which the Qur'an operates, Jews, Christians, and *hanifs*—"proto-Muslims"—were competing with one another at times through Arabic oral tradition, at other times through forms of Aramaic writing. When the Qur'an identifies itself as "clear Arabic language" (*lisan 'arabi mubin*), it acknowledges its existence in a multilingual context, hence the significance of the "Arabic Qur'an" (*qur'an 'arabi*). Why would such descriptions have been significant if all members of its audience simply spoke Arabic? It would have been a nonissue. Such descriptions are a statement that *this* Scripture is in Arabic—a new revelation to be added to Hebrew and Christian Scripture.

Fred Donner has argued that the Qur'anic term "believers" (*mu'minun*) may have included Jews and Christians. I think that the idea has more potential which needs to be developed. The Medinan suras often say, "O you who believe," and then follow with a discussion on Jewish and Christian practices *in the same verse*. So if you're talking to those who believe, and then you're addressing their Jewish law, or their Christian doctrine, then who are the believers? I think that Donner has a point.[8]

It says in verse 34 of Sura 20, "This is 'Isa, the son of Mary about whom they are in dispute," or "about which they speak in excess." Who is "they"? There must have been more than one Christian group. So the text recognizes that there is more than one way of "being Christian."

This is why the Qur'an describes Abraham's faith as "the word of Abraham the puritan/proto-Muslim [hanif], nor was he not one of the associators, that is, pagans." It is a supplement and corrective to Paul's teachings in Galatians, which argue that the gospel he preaches was present with Abraham, and that it was the pure religion of God prior to the Scriptures being revealed. The Qur'an mentions in Sura 3, and then later on in Sura 98, that even before the Scriptures were revealed there existed the pure faith of Abraham—that is, Hanifism. The Qur'an promotes and articulates an updated form of this ancient faith. And so it says that those who argue about the "nature" or "will" of Jesus—that is, the various groups within Christianity—are wrong. Similarly, it polemicizes the Jews in other suras with respect to excesses in their laws, and it proposes Islam as a simpler alternative. Such a proposal would have engaged an audience that included Christians and Jews. Otherwise it would not have been effective; nor would anyone have converted. So the Qur'an proposes Islam as Hanifism recast, partly in order to attract Christians and Jews.

One thing that I argue in the first chapter of my book *The Qur'an and the Aramaic Gospel Traditions* is that there exists some serious sectarian and missionary activity in the environment of the Qur'an. Some Muslims feel uncomfortable when I say that, and fear that I am subjecting the text to a secularizing or even orientalist reading. In such cases I say, "No, I'm reading the Qur'an and you're reading *tafsir*, the commentary that came about later on." The Qur'an discusses the sectarianism of its day explicitly, a small sample of which can be gleaned from such words as *shiqaq* (division) and *ahzab* (parties), and when it talks about groups or sides. The Qur'an is adding its voice to a multiplicity of competing theological and legal schools and proposing its own to be the correct one.

To push this argument further, some Muslims are hesitant to look at such texts as the Infancy Gospel of Thomas or the Protevangelium of James.[9] Muslim tradition is not based, as it were, on such texts but rather on exegetical, prophetic, and biographical literature—tafsir, hadith, *sirah*, and so on—which flourished about two centuries after the Qur'an. However, in the premodern Muslim scholarship of the ninth to sixteenth century, widely accepted authors like Ibn Qutaybah, Tabari, al-Suyuti,[10] and others were looking at and debating the textual context with which the Qur'an is in dialogue. I say "in dialogue" because it is talking to the audience of those texts. In the fifteenth century, in his multivolume *Tafsir, al-Biqaʻi*[11] considers the canonical Gospels— that is, the Gospels of Matthew, Mark, Luke, and John—to be the *injil* referred to by the Qur'an. Most Muslims today would not agree with that. And yet this line of thought was afforded some space within Islam in the past. And al-Biqaʻi was a scholar in high regard. Unfortunately, the difference of opinion that was considered rahma, "mercy," among classical Muslim scholars, has long disappeared today. In some cases this problem has been exacerbated by "postcolonial baggage." And so today we have tremendously bright scholars before the vast sea of knowledge and wisdom that is the Qur'an, but we have discouraged them from plunging their buckets deep into the waters, as our predecessors used to. My instinct is always that much of this problem is informed by political rather than academic challenges.

I hope and feel that I am reviving my own tradition, which has a rich scholarly history. I am not alone; there are others. Within the Islamic world you have someone like Yusuf Zaydan, a historian and historical novelist who has written a number of best sellers in Egypt. He says that as Muslims we need to *truly* study the pre-Islamic world. Otherwise our knowledge of that world is reduced to cheap miracles. For example, if the meaning of a word in the Qur'an is not entirely clear—like the mysterious unconnected letters *ALM*, *HM*, and so on—there is a temptation to identify it as a miraculous utterance. At the same time, when the first Muslim scholars had recourse to such an idea, it followed a lengthy process of research and inquiry.

I am codirecting a new Qur'anic Studies initiative with Gabriel Reynolds. The International Qur'anic Studies Association is a new learned society to be established in 2015. Gabriel comes from a Catholic background, and I come from a Muslim one. Yet the Qur'an is speaking to us both. We want IQSA to be

a place where people of different academic disciplines and confessional backgrounds can talk to one another, agree as well as
have differences of opinion, and revive a tradition which fosters
digging deep and asking bold questions. The work of both Muslim and non-Muslim scholars is essential to this initiative.

I wonder if my ideas are atypical compared to those of your
other interviewees, but I also hope this is a good thing. I hope
that the transcripts of our discussions will demonstrate that
Muslims—in America, no less—are comfortable with diversity.
My work is informed by a thirst to learn more. At the same time,
it is nourished by my aspiration to be the best Muslim I can be,
to my family, to my students, and to society as a whole. Part of
this aspiration—believe it or not—is to maintain my family's tradition of naming our children using prophet names. My grandfa-
ther's name was Musa, my uncle 'Isa, and mine 'Imran. And it is
for good reason that I named my firstborn son Zakariya.

— ۱۲ —

An Open Text and a Critique of Patriarchy
ASMA BARLAS

When Scripture treats a complex topic, such as gender relations, how is one
to determine which verses are central and enduring and which verses are
secondary and limited to a specific context? Christians and Jews who are
committed to gender justice find support for their convictions in the Bible
and then move on to interpret problem passages in Scripture in light of these
ideals. This can result in tension with current readers who resist such a vision
of gender justice and with the history of interpretations of those same passages that have been used in the service of patriarchy. The Bible and the
Qur'an are different texts, but the struggles are recognizably familiar.

Asma Barlas is professor of politics at Ithaca College, where she also
serves as the director of the Center for the Study of Culture, Race, and Ethnicity. She has offered papers and presentations throughout the United
States, as well as from Iceland to Indonesia. Among many other publications,
she is the author of "Believing Women" in Islam: Unreading Patriarchal Interpretations of the Qur'an (2002). This groundbreaking book has been translated into
Urdu, Bengali, Arabic, Indonesian, Dutch, Spanish, and French and offers

a courageous critique of patriarchy in common interpretations of Islam's sacred Scripture.

Courage to speak her truth is nothing new to Asma Barlas. She began her professional work as a diplomat in the Ministry of Foreign Affairs in her native Pakistan but was fired from this position by the order of Zia ul-Haq, the nation's military dictator, whom she had criticized. She then worked for a time as the assistant editor of an opposition newspaper, which resulted in her seeking political asylum in the United States. She is no stranger to controversy, or to its costs.

Her reflections build on an earlier essay of hers, "Abraham's Sacrifice in the Qur'an: Beyond the Body," in *Religion and the Body*, ed. Tore Ahlbäck (2011). In this piece, Asma Barlas analyzes the story of Abraham and the son whom he almost sacrifices. She finds a critique of patriarchy in this story.

─╜─

Here is a translation of a passage from the Qur'an, 37:99-109. As is often the case in Qur'anic retellings of stories found in the Bible, the narrative is very spare, austere in details, almost to the point of perplexity for someone new to the Qur'an. The first speaker is Abraham, though that is not explicitly stated until near the end. His son remains unnamed throughout, though most (but not all) traditional commentary on the story understands the figure to be Ishmael.

> *And he said, "I am going to my Sustainer, who will guide me. My Sustainer, grant me one of the righteous." We gave him the good news of a forbearing boy. Then, when he was old enough to accompany him, he said, "My son, I see in a dream that I am sacrificing you. Ponder, what do you see?" He said, "My father, do what you are commanded. God willing, you will find me one of the steadfast/patient." When the two of them had submitted, he laid him down on his forehead/side of his head. And we called to him, "Abraham, you have fulfilled the dream. This is how we reward those who do good." Indeed it was an obvious test. And we ransomed him with a magnificent sacrifice, and left for him among succeeding generations [the blessing]: "Peace be upon Abraham."*

On Reading the Qur'an

There are so many ways to approach the Qur'an, and I myself have had a different relationship to it over time. I was taught to read it in Arabic when I was a child, and I read the whole text several times, but I didn't know what I was reading. It is almost a fetishization of Arabic, as can happen with other sacred languages. The idea was that I should know how to read the Qur'an, but nobody bothered to teach me Arabic beyond making the sounds. Eventually I got more interested in figuring out what I was reading, so at a fairly young age, I started reading different translations of it. I've been interested in how different translations can give us different senses of the same sura, the same word, the same figure, the same narrative. My segue into exegesis or hermeneutics, into interpretation in Muslim history, is all by way of my interest in how Muslims read the Qur'an as a patriarchal text. Since I wrote the book *Believing Women in Islam*, I have thought a great deal about the argument that I made. I see that I was very empathic in saying that I see it as an antipatriarchal text, and some critics are hardly convinced by that. But by way of a bit of my epistemology, I believe that since the Qur'an is the word of God for Muslims, we have to have a theologically sound understanding of God, so I have tried to explore this link between divine ontology or being and divine discourse. That is in the back of my mind every time I read a passage, particularly passages for which there have been historically either an absence of historical interpretation or where the dominant interpretation has always been in favor of men.

I am bringing the Qur'an into conversation with other parts of me. I am very much a product of a Western education, and I can't draw lines between parts of me: this part of me is the West; this part of me is Islamic. This part of me is authentic; this part of me is hybrid. We are all such mixtures, so I read the Qur'an from the present. Whatever I am is impossible to keep out of my understanding of the text, but honestly, I have never set out to say consciously that I want to bring the Qur'an into the contemporary world. That's way too much responsibility, and it's a burden that I would never assume. But I can say that living in the moment, here and now, is the only way that I know how to read it.

I read Paul Ricouer's work many years ago,[12] and he makes the point about how the hermeneutical encounter always leads to an enlarged sense of self. The hermeneutical movement might be described as a spiral, a constant reengagement. I've sought to be conscious of how I am entering into the hermeneutical experience: What are the assumptions that I am bringing to it? The other part of my work is to question the ways of Muslim methodology. I hadn't really seen my work as centrally methodological until the former dean of the law school at Harvard—who retired prematurely because he was regarded as too Muslim friendly—invited me to coteach a session in one of his law courses. He told me that I basically stood Muslim methodology on its head. I then wrote a paper for a conference in Sarajevo on the changeable and unchangeable in Islamic thought and practice. It is primarily a methodological piece. So I'm very interested in how Muslims become more conscious of the relationship between method and meaning.

For some Muslims this notion is threatening. It is like opening Pandora's proverbial box: Who knows what might happen? But I ask Muslims why are they so afraid that Islam is fragile, why they feel that they must protect Islam because what I have to say will undermine it. For some, the threat might be more deeply personal, that my questions are not a threat to Islam but rather a threat to what they have to do personally, in terms of responsibility and doing the hard work. Even Muslim thinkers who are quite broadminded and forward looking on many issues often draw a hard line when it comes to sexual equality. There are some male scholars who, with their considerable learning and positions of influence, could take far more egalitarian positions, but it would mean having to give up their authority and privilege as men, both in the house and in the community. In Muslim societies, for a man to say what I am saying would carry so much more weight.

Obviously there are people who benefit from the way things are, and this is not just among Muslims. Those who benefit think, if the systems are working for people in a racist society, if white privilege can continue the way it is without being challenged, then why not? If male privilege can continue the way it is in a patriarchal system, then why not? For me personally, the main affront is the abuse of God that results from these systems. As Christian feminists have also said, when we reduce God to our own lowest common denominator of human stance, then what we have is not a divine being but a glorified image of ourselves.

When I think of what is primary in the encounter with the Qur'an, I remember that the Sudanese Muslim thinker Muhammad Taha,[13] the author of *The Second Message of Islam*, who was hanged for sedition, once said that the Qur'an is the methodology of ascent to God. If the Qur'an is the methodology of the ascent to God, if it is a way of knowing God, then it seems to me that all interpretations of the Qur'an, all engagements of the Scripture, are answerable to something higher within oneself. They're not even answerable to the community. I don't feel answerable to the community, by which I mean that when others demand, "Who gave you authority?" my response is, "The text." The text gives me authority because seven hundred times the text says to use your intellect, to engage it. The authority is intrinsic in being a practitioner of the religion. What others think of my authority is up to them.

So I approach these texts both as a Muslim and as someone conversant with contemporary Western intellectual currents. The meeting of intellectual traditions allows for intellectual growth. If we only read what we are familiar with and what we agree with, the result would be Muslim commentary as it mostly looks today. Traditional Muslim scholars dismiss me and say, "Sure, we needed you after fourteen hundred years to come along and tell us what we missed seeing in the text." For centuries there has been more or less a consensus of what commentary on the Qur'an should look like, and what is and is not valid to include, and who is allowed to speak.

A distinguished Muslim scholar who has written on theological tolerance in Islam, and who, in some respects, is a hero of mine, served on a panel with me at a university some years ago. He basically said, "You have all the freedom in the world to read the Qur'an as you wish in the privacy of your own home, but what gives you the authority to bring your readings into the public arena?" I was astounded because his next comment was that Muslim public reason will never accept my interpretation. His point really was, "Who are you? You don't have a formal education in Islamic studies. Who gives you the authority to speak about the Qur'an in public?" This comment was quite an eye-opener for me.

My position is that how the text speaks to you depends on what questions you're asking it. If men are happy with the authority that they think Islam gives them, and they've reached a consensus about what that authority should look like, why should they have any investment at all in alternative readings? Part of my interest in engaging alternative readings is that engaging with other traditions is a way to understand my own. Not in a pejorative way, to say that one is superior—the point is to discover what the differences are and why they are significant.

What brought me to the story of Abraham initially was this whole narrative about the sacrifice of his son. I'm comfortable referring to him as "Abraham" rather than the Arabic "Ibrahim" since English is my first language. (In Pakistan, I was educated in Catholic schools until I was fifteen, where the instruction was in English, and my parents spoke to us in English at home. Having English as our first language can be both a burden and an advantage.)

Traditionally, the story of Abraham is read as a patriarchal parable, but I was interested in seeing if there were other ways to understand it. I had been introduced to the thinking of Søren Kierkegaard, so I read *Fear and Trembling*, followed by various Jewish and Christian commentaries on Kierkegaard and on the story of Abraham in the Old Testament. Then I serendipitously came across a piece by Muhammad Hasan Askari published in the *Annual of Urdu Studies* in 2004 on Ibn al-ʿArabi and Kierkegaard.[14] The Sufi mystic and philosopher Ibn al-ʿArabi (1165– 1240) is a fascinating character. These readings prompted me to try to explore the similarities and differences in the biblical and Qur'anic accounts. How are they different, and do they matter for someone who is Muslim?

Analysis of the Story

The Qur'an tells the story of Abraham and Isaac in minimalist and enigmatic terms.[15] Abraham's son is left unnamed, as is Abraham himself until the very end. If we read it closely, we find what the story says and does not say. While reading the following biblical account of the binding of Isaac, the reader should note that many details from this version do not appear in the Qur'an.

God tested Abraham and said to him, "Abraham." And he said, "Here I am." He said, "Take your son, your only son, whom you love, Isaac, and go to the land of Moriah, and offer him there as a burnt offering on one of the mountains that I will tell you." So Abraham rose early in the morning, and saddled his donkey, and took two of his young men with him, and Isaac his son. He cut the wood for the burnt offering, and set out and went to the place that God had told him. On the third day Abraham lifted up his eyes and saw the place far off. Abraham said to his young men, "Stay here with the donkey. The boy and I will go over there and worship, and then we will come back to you." Abraham took the wood of the burnt offering and laid it on his son Isaac, and he took in his hand the fire and the knife. So the two of them walked on together. Isaac said to his father Abraham, "My father," and he said, "Here I am, my son." He said, "Look: the fire and the wood are here, but where is the lamb for a burnt offering?" Abraham said, "God will provide the lamb for a burnt offering, my son." So the two of them walked on together. When they came to the place that God had told him, Abraham built an altar there, and arranged the wood, and bound Isaac his son, and laid him on the altar, upon the wood. Then Abraham stretched forth his hand and took the knife to slaughter his son. But an angel of God called to him from heaven, and said, "Abraham, Abraham," and he said, "Here I am." He said, "Do not lay your hand on the boy or do anything to him, for now I know that you fear God, since you have not withheld your son, your only son, from me." And Abraham lifted up his eyes and, look, he saw a ram, caught in a thicket by its horns. He went and took the ram and offered it up as a burnt offering instead of his son.

In the more austere narrative found in the Qur'an, God does not explicitly tell Abraham to kill his son. The son is not named. There is no indication of how much time passes between the dream and the proposed sacrifice—and the word "dream" does not appear in Genesis. The Qur'an doesn't mention the place of the sacrifice, Abraham binding his son, the angelic intervention to prevent the slaughter, or of a ram sacrificed in the son's place; nor does Abraham keep his intent to kill a secret from his son as in the Bible. Instead, he consults his son and seeks his response to the dream, and his son plays a role in interpreting it. In the Qur'anic version of the story, the son isn't deprived of moral agency, nor is he the unsuspecting victim of a murderous father; rather, both father and son submit, witnessing to their faith together.

The Qur'an's version of the story of Abraham contrasts strongly with Søren Kierkegaard's influential theological reading of the Genesis account. Kierkegaard's Abraham bears the burden of a terrible secret, withholding knowledge of an inexplicable, tyrannous divine command, which leads to fear and trembling. This reading in turn contrasts with the mystical interpretation offered by the Sufi philosopher Ibn al-'Arabi, who finds Abraham's test to be one of knowledge, not of ethics. In Ibn al-'Arabi's esoteric universe, one doesn't receive a divine command that is in opposition to one's true nature. Because he was a prophet, Abraham's faith was never in question. However, he failed by taking his dream literally, because dreams are on a different plane from ordinary reality. They lie in the realm of imagination and therefore require further knowledge to be understood properly, especially when they oppose reason, such as when they demand to sacrifice one's own child. God saved Abraham's son from the deadly consequences of his father's misunderstanding.

Many Muslims may be offended by Ibn al-'Arabi's reading because its conclusion that Abraham failed in knowledge contradicts the traditional belief that prophets are perfect. Yet the Qur'an itself challenges this notion: as a youth, for example, Moses misunderstands the meanings of the strange acts performed by the mysterious figure al-Khidr in Sura 18. In the Qur'an, God alone has the attribute of perfection.

Ibn al-ʿArabi's reading of the story of Abraham's near sacrifice of his son, for whatever other unpersuasive elements it may contain, holds some elements that are worth considering. Literalism is not the core of faith. Divine will requires interpretation; it is not immediately self-evident. No interpreter can claim infallibility. These are crucial reminders at a time when so many Muslims are given to textual literalism, when they perceive reason and the exercise of the mind as a hindrance to faith, and when male hubris has reached such heights that a handful of men can arrogantly claim to know the truth as it is with God. This claim to authority, which also reveals itself in patriarchal interpretations of the Qur'an, is the point of departure for my own reading of this narrative of Abraham. In Ibn al-ʿArabi's opinion, God's rescue points to Abraham's failure to interpret God's will accurately. In mine, however, this rescue signals a resistance on the Qur'an's part to father-right, or traditional patriarchy.

I approach Abraham's dream mostly from the perspective of the son, because I think his role in assuming his own sacrifice puts a constraint on the rights his father exercises over him. Since my interpretation is the opposite of what Muslim tradition holds, I should note that the lessons most Muslims draw from the story are obedience and its rewards. Some interpreters even claim that the son not only agrees to his own sacrifice, but also asks to be bound, so that he will be unable to attempt to resist. In short, the son is utterly obedient to patriarchal authority. I, however, do not find this patriarchal reading persuasive.

First of all, such a reading inserts many interpretive details into the text. As I noted, the Qur'an doesn't say that Abraham binds his son's body, nor does it suggest the drama and pathos which has been dreamed up by exegetes. For another, the Qur'an tells us that Abraham had submitted himself to God's will while he was still a young man and even risked death as a consequence, so we do not need the story of the sacrifice to prove this. Besides, for Muslims, it is not much of a lesson to know that prophets are willing to obey God: the very word "Muslim" refers to a person who submits to divine will. Most importantly, at no point does God insist on a literal sacrifice. The text explicitly says that this was an obvious test. Elsewhere, the Qur'an condemns the sacrifice of children and family (70:11-14), as well as infanticide (17:31).

My reading differs from traditional interpretations of this story because I also see this narrative in the wider context of Qur'anic teachings about God, faith, and the nature of moral personality—specifically, that God is not Father, that there is "no compulsion in religion" (2:256), that each soul is answerable only for herself, that no soul can bear the burden of another, even if closely related (35:17), and that God tries a soul only to the limits of its own capacity. If Abraham's story is harmonious with these principles, then he cannot witness his son's faith by offering his life to God. Instead, the son must do it himself.

The son's part in his sacrifice challenges the legitimacy of patriarchal norms. The text does not uphold paternal authority for its own sake. In fact, the Qur'an advocates disobeying parents if they strive to make their children join in worshiping anything other than God (31:15). Admittedly, Abraham is not pressuring his son to commit idolatry, but the point here is that in the Qur'an, moral personality is not based on a notion of blind obedience to parents, or fathers specifically.

Further, Abraham does not seek his son's consent or obedience. Instead, he consults his son as to what he makes of the dream. To this open-ended question, the son replies that his father should do as he is commanded by God. Abraham's son takes the dream literally and believes he is obeying God's will. He is submitting to the God of his father, not to his father. Abraham's question also illustrates that, up to this point in the story, he has not yet decided upon the meaning of his dream. Otherwise he could just as easily have asked his son a very different sort of question, such as about how to proceed with the sacrifice.

Abraham is also a son. In the Qur'an he has a confrontation with his father, asking him why he worships these idol images that cannot respond to him. He says to his father, "Follow me." Follow my example. This command is very significant; but in many traditional Muslim interpretations it is dismissed because they can say that the father was an unbeliever. In following his

son, he was following not so much the authority of his son as
the authority of a believer. Yet it is a challenge to father-right by
Abraham himself.

When Abraham has his dream and asks his son about its
meaning, I wonder, "What if the son had said something different?" But part of the reason that one doesn't go there, if one is
Muslim, especially if one is staying within the framework that
Ibn al-'Arabi proposes, is that God gives no command to human
beings that is contrary to their own intrinsic natures. So if Abraham's son is to have any moral authority, then he can only have
it, as Derrida puts it (in another context), by owning his own
death. This task is not something that anyone else can assume
on your behalf. For me, that's where the power of the narrative
is: in the fact that even when you're called by God, you have to,
as a Muslim, be voluntarily submissive to it—otherwise you're
not a Muslim in the descriptive sense of the term, or even in the
religious sense of the term. So what does this say about patriarchal authority, and why does the Qur'an, in my opinion at least,
stand it on its head?

The son's voice is important in this narrative because it
serves to limit Abraham's rights as a father. Abraham does not
have the right to commit infanticide; further, whatever rights he
does have in this instance are subject to his son's moral choices.
But if Abraham's authority is not absolute concerning his son's
sacrifice, can we view him as a patriarch? Is the sacrifice an act
of patriarchal violence? Does it uphold the patriarchal status
quo? This point can be better made by contrasting the biblical
and Qur'anic Abrahams. In the Bible, too, Abraham's will is not
absolute, since it is subjected to God's will, but this relationship
does not detract from his authority as a father; in fact, God's
command to sacrifice Isaac clearly confirms this authority. Even
if Abraham is distressed at doing God's will, his right to kill his
son is never questioned in the Bible. The authority that the two
Abrahams exercise over their sons is therefore very different,
coinciding with differences in Christian and Islamic views not
just of fathers, but of God.

Christian feminists have long argued that patriarchy draws
for its legitimacy on sacralizations of God as Father. While

Abraham himself does not refer to God as Father in the biblical story, given the possibility of patriarchalizing God, one can understand God's rescue of Isaac not as displacing the patriarchal status quo, but as demonstrating that divine patriarchy takes precedence over the earthly one. In the Qur'an, however, God is not father, and it is prohibited for Muslims to refer to God in this way and even to use similitude or images for God (16:74). As the Qur'an repeatedly says, God is uncreated and thus beyond sex or gender. God is also incomparable and unrepresentable.

The Qur'an's refusal to patriarchalize God means that Muslim fathers cannot rely on a model of divine fatherhood to legitimize their own authority. Further, the Qur'an forcefully condemns people who ignored God's messages because they wanted to follow "the ways of their fathers" (2:170), a phrase one can take to mean patriarchy or, more broadly, patriarchal tradition. This hostility to fathers' rule also finds a powerful expression in Abraham's fuller story, especially in the part which deals with his relationship with his own father.

As the Qur'an relates it, after Abraham's search for the one true God eventually leads him to submit himself to God, he finds himself in conflict with his father's people:

> He said to his father, "What are these images to which you are so devoted?" They said, "We found our fathers worshiping them." He said, "Surely you and your fathers have been in clear error." They said, "Have you come to us with the truth, or are you one of those who play?" He said, "No, your Sustainer is the sustainer of the heavens and the earth, the one who created them, and to that I am a witness." (21:52-56)

This exchange demonstrates that the basis of Abraham's father's faith is to cling to patriarchal traditions. Abraham, with God's approval, confronts this practice:

> And mention in the book Abraham. Indeed he was a man of truth, a prophet, when he said to his father, "My father, why do you worship that which does not hear and does not see and does not benefit you in any way? My father, knowledge has come to me that has not come to you, so follow me. I will guide you to an even path." (19:41-43)

Abraham then smashes all the idols except the largest and dares his father's people to get that stone image to identify the perpetrator who shattered the rest. His father's response is to throw him into a fire, from which God saves him, just as God saves Abraham's son from him years later. The condition for Abraham's embrace of God is the break with his own father.

This conflict between God's rule, which is monotheism, and father's rule, which is patriarchy, also finds expression in the Qur'an's admonition to "Fear a day when no father can avail for his son, nor a son avail for his father" (31:33). On that day, "One soul cannot avail for another. No recompense will be accepted from it. No intercession will benefit it. No one will be helped" (2:123).

In the context of these teachings, God's rescues of Abraham from his father and of Abraham's son from him are quite different. Both sons are monotheists, but one is victim to his unbelieving father's assault, while the other submits of his own volition to the God of his father. Both face death, but for different reasons and at the hands of very different fathers. Abraham's father tries to kill his son for his faith, and the son has no choice in the matter; in contrast, Abraham is also ready to sacrifice his son as a matter of faith but can only go forward with it at his son's expressed consent. Without that consent, the story of his near sacrifice of his son would have proved little more than the omnipotence of fathers in patriarchies. One story reveals an outright conflict between obeying God and obeying fathers, especially those who are "without understanding and guidance" (2:170), while the message of the other story is that, in order for God's will to be done, believers must submit to it voluntarily. And, since God is not father, one cannot view God's rule, or monotheism, as a divine endorsement for fathers' rule, which is patriarchy.

The Specificity of Islam

My reading of this text shows some of the radical possibilities of reading Scripture against the notion of father-right. That's where I begin and end, but the tangential theme is the attitude of most non-Muslims toward Islam. The "other"-ing of Islam is something we're very familiar with, where it's completely demonized. It's almost like an exorcism, where it is pushed outside of Western religions. Wherever you have courses in Western religions, you hardly ever have a course in Islam. What makes Judaism and Christianity Western in a way that Islam is not? All three are Middle Eastern. They are all scripturally based. The Hebrew prophets are prophets of Islam as well. The recent tendency of theologians, as I've learned in recent conferences in Iceland and Finland, is to bring Islam into the fold of Abrahamic religions, but I find that embrace too assimilative for me. I do not feel comfortable with it. If exclusion means that Islam is considered completely deviant, aberrant, and other, then the tendency to embrace it too quickly means that you deny what I call the specificity of Islam within the Abrahamic tradition. There's no particular virtue to denying the differences. I love the idea of differences, of negotiating the differences. There is the parable of the tent of Abraham, and the stranger must remain a stranger in order to teach us something. So even if Islam is not strange, it nonetheless must remain distinct from both Judaism and Christianity, though having a family resemblance.

It seems to me that Islam has also become a career for many people. Unfortunately, I've had my share of interactions with people who think that the task of Muslim intellectuals should be to make Islam palatable for Western audiences. Here I am thinking of the whole rhetoric of how there needs to be a reformation in Islam, how Islam and democracy are one and the same, how Islam and socialism are the same, how the Qur'an is essentially this text or that text. For many people, these comparisons and simplifications are a kind of defensive, apologist endeavor.

There may be tendencies toward apologia in my own work, if apologia means some level of defending Islam against vilifications; nevertheless, my aim is not that you, for example, should look at me and say, "I approve of your religion. I think that this is great!"—and that it should be my job to convince you. Instead, my job is to say, "This is my faith. This is how I understand it, this is how I live it, and this is what I want to say about it." My stance can result in my being in a complex situation, both with regard to Muslims and to non-Muslims.

Part of the defensive project is almost unavoidable. When you're pushing against dominant critique, you can't remain wholly outside its framework. There's always the element of pushing from within. But my primary engagement has been with my own community. I don't wish to glamorize that community, because I think there are lots of things wrong with it: there are sexist, misogynistic, and patriarchal interpretations of religious knowledge—and that's a lot to me. So I want to push a conversation, but it is a complicated conversation because I'm kicked by both sides. Many Muslims I meet think that I am too Western, that I'm a feminist. They are suspicious that I am bringing a foreign agenda into Islam. On the other hand, many Western liberal scholars seem to think, "She's too Islamic. She's employing language that is in the Western tradition . . . to the Qur'an. You can't really have both things going on." It is a very difficult place to be, but I am single minded and determined, so I don't let that negativity dictate what I think.

I feel compelled to share certain things. Given my position, I have come to expect a certain backlash when I speak about Scripture, but I'm still interested in engaging people who want to engage me. I have no illusions about conversations with some of the more extreme or even mainstream elements among Muslims. I don't think that they would want to talk with me.

For a very long time, I read the Qur'an with the intention of writing about it, so that calls for a self-consciousness about how I am entering into a conversation with the text. Because that self-consciousness is, hopefully, strident, it is intended to inculcate self-doub—not to speak with a strident voice, because the Qur'an itself is not my word. It is the word of God. I am not a pope, a cardinal, a bishop, a religious leader. I wasn't elected to such a position; I have no constituency. I therefore need not care about critique from others. For me, the basic thing is the ethical encounter with the Qur'an, an encounter that is theologically sound. So I find myself answerable to the text, not to the community.

I read the Qur'an each morning as a spiritual practice. It is an act of worship. It is an act of encountering the text that is ineffable, that is holy and sacred. This kind of reading is a willing suspension of continual analytics, when I am engaged in it. I found that too much of my reading of the Qur'an was purely analytical, and I wanted to create the space to encounter it as God's word, as a method of knowing God. It is a kind of mindfulness of the presence of God, like saying the prayers in Islam. It is a very personal space; perhaps "noninstrumental" would be a way to describe it. But when you write about Scripture as an academic, it is a very different mode of reading.

In both ways of reading, one encounters the text when one does not decide in advance what it means. When there is a consensus about the text, one closes the text. If you and I decide what a poem or a story means, and we pass it on for fourteen hundred years, it is really a closed thing. I cannot see the Qur'an as a closed text. The very act of reading opens it up, but it is easier to rely on whatever dominant interpretation is there than to do the work for yourself. It takes the weight off your shoulders.

Some years ago I made a presentation at the Cardozo Law School of Yeshiva University, and there were two Jewish scholars from Israel. After my talk, they both came up to me and said, "You could have been speaking about the Hebrew Bible. This is exactly the kind of resistance that new readings of the Bible produce." So this is not unique to Islam by any means. That instance brought me some degree of comfort. It showed me that in all our traditions there is resistance to the struggle against hegemonic knowledges. Sometimes the struggle can be disheartening, and it is always good to get some perspective, to see that so many people are doing the same thing in their own traditions. It can relieve you from feeling so beleaguered, because you see that lots of people are in the same boat. They're just doing it elsewhere, with different texts. Patriarchy is pan-Abrahamic, as is the resistance to it.

— ١٢ —

Some Muslims are not averse to bridging traditional understandings from historically Muslim-majority cultures and modern Western thinkers. As Asma Barlas confidently states, Islam is not so fragile. It can endure such an effort. Abraham challenged his father's idols;[16] Asma Barlas challenges her readers' idols, whatever culture is their origin. Islam should no longer be regarded as so foreign, as "the other," in the West, yet at the same time it should remain distinctive, not to be domesticated in the service of any other religion. Even though the Qur'anic account of Abraham differs from that of Genesis, and even though it is crucial for both non-Muslims and Muslims not to allow the distinctiveness of Islam to be blurred or absorbed into other religious outlooks, her method of reading can look familiar to non-Muslim Westerners, and that familiarity can allow non-Muslims an entry point into the Qur'an in a way that in fact honors its distinctiveness. Likeness and difference constitute a repeating theme in this volume, and Asma Barlas illustrates both of them in instructive ways.

Gender and Destabilization
KECIA ALI

As with Asma Barlas, to read with Kecia Ali is to become keenly aware of what is there in the text and what is not. Asma Barlas offers fruitful comparison between the Bible and the Qur'an as each relates the story of Abraham. Kecia Ali for the most part stays within the Qur'an and offers richly complex comparisons of characters and situations within it. These comparisons yield surprises: what may at first look like a male-centered narrative is upon closer examination shown to be prophet centered—that is, focused on who is moving the story forward as the divine plan unfolds. To read with her is to discover that the text is full of unanticipated internal echoes, constantly shifting its angle of vision as characters and consequences are compared. As a result, gender-specific roles are undone: Mary gives birth as only a female can do, yet her story otherwise parallels in many ways those of male figures and prophets and their connections with God. To read with Kecia Ali can feel like undertaking a journey in which one throws away any conventional map. Her insights and questions leave the reader less with a settled determination of the story and more with a desire to explore it again and to encounter the text afresh, if a bit off balance, as perhaps one should be in the presence of what is holy.

Kecia Ali is associate professor of religion at Boston University. She is a specialist in Islamic jurisprudence and has a particular interest in issues related to women. She has written *Sexual Ethics and Islam: Feminist Reflections on Qur'an, Hadith, and Jurisprudence* (2006), *Marriage and Slavery in Early Islam*

(2010), and *Imam Shafi'i: Scholar and Saint* (2011). During our conversation she chose a narrative rather than a legal passage from the Qur'an, and her words show her meticulous attention to detail as well as her openness to new insights, even to a text that she had thought about for years. As Kecia Ali points out, the Qur'an often raises questions and causes its readers to think. Her method of reading is less concerned to persuade her reader of an opinion and much more interested in raising questions that invite further consideration. Just as Mary's gender is not fixed in this periscope, Kecia Ali's reading is not set in stone but instead constantly open to newness. Our meeting was a time of discovery for both of us.

— ⵊⵍ —

Imran's wife said, "My Lord, I have vowed to you what is in my womb as a dedicated offering, so accept this from me. You are the One who hears and knows." And when she gave birth to her, she said, "My Lord, I have delivered a girl." And God knew better what she had delivered, and the male is not like the female. "I have named her Mary, and I seek shelter for her and her progeny from Satan, the rejected." So the Lord accepted her, a beautiful acceptance, and made her grow, a beautiful growth, and put her in the care of Zakariya. Whenever Zakariya visited her in the worship chamber, he found her with provisions. He said, "Mary, from where does this come for you?" She said, "It is from God. Surely God gives to whom God wills without measure." Zakariya prayed there to his Lord. He said, "My Lord, grant me from your Presence virtuous progeny. You are the hearer of prayers." Then the angels called out to him while he was standing and praying in the worship chamber, saying, "God gives you the good news of Yahya, who confirms the truth of a word of God: a noble, chaste, a prophet and one of the righteous." He said, "My Lord, how shall I have a boy when old age has come to me, and my wife is barren?" He said, "Thus God does what He wills." He said, "My Lord, set for me a sign." He said, "Your sign is that you will not speak to people for three days except by gestures. And remember your Lord much, and proclaim God's glory in the evening and in the

morning." And the angels said, "O Mary, God has chosen you
and purified you. He has chosen you over the women of all the
worlds. O Mary, be devoutly obedient to your Lord, and pros-
trate yourself and bow down with those who bow down." This
is from the news of the unseen that we reveal to you. You were
not with them when they cast lots to see which of them should
be the guardian of Mary, nor were you with them when they
quarreled. When the angels said, "O Mary, God gives you
good news of a word from Him. His name is the Messiah Jesus,
the son of Mary, honored in this world and in the hereafter,
and among those near to God. He will speak to people from
the cradle and in maturity, and will be of the righteous." She
said, "My Lord, how can there be a son to me when no mortal
has touched me?" He said, "This is how God creates what God
wills. When God decides a matter, God simply says, 'Be,' and
it is. And He will teach him the book and the wisdom, and the
Torah and the Gospel, and will make him a messenger to the
Children of Israel. He will say to them, 'I have come to you
with a sign from your Lord. I will create for you out of clay
something in the shape of a bird, and I will breathe into it, and
it will become a bird by the permission of God. I will cure the
blind and the leper and give life to the dead by the permission
of God. And I will tell you what you should eat and what you
should store up in your houses. In this there is a sign for you, if
you are believers.'" (3:35-49)

This interesting set of verses reflects on gender and generativity
and reproduction. They're very much about questions of male
and female and reproduction and roles within the context of
family, and yet they're not the typical verses that are turned to
for these concerns. They do not explicitly address questions of
marriage or hierarchy, at least not in the way that, for instance,
4:34 does, or the degree verse (2:228).

I originally looked at these verses in the context of a very
brief reflection piece that I did at least a decade ago now for a
comparative Jewish-Christian-Muslim short article in a little-
known Canadian feminist spirituality journal. The theme was
mothers and daughters in Scripture. There are only two pairs of
mother and daughter in the Qur'an. One is Moses' mother and

Moses' sister, which is the way that they are always addressed. The daughter is not referred to as the mother's daughter; she's "Moses' sister." And the mother is not her mother; she's "Moses' mother." At first glance, that's a very androcentric view, but upon further reflection it turns out to be a very prophet-centric view. It is not so much that the women are bit players in a man's story as that the mother and the sister both collaborate to rescue the prophet figure. So the apparent androcentric tension is resolved by noting that the narrative is always in service to the prophet. The text is very prophet centered because it is divine-plan centered. It's about who is moving God's storyline forward.

The other pair of mother and daughter in the Qur'an is the wife of Imran and Mary. She's sometimes called Hannah or Ann in the Muslim interpretive tradition, and she gets very little air-time. But this is not just the story of the birth of Mary as an analogue and also a precursor to the birth of Jesus; it is also the story of Mary's destiny. Mary, though she ultimately is important because she gives birth to this male prophet who moves God's storyline forward, is herself a more significant player in this story line. We could say again that the story is prophet centered because in fact there is a medieval Muslim argument that says that Mary is a prophet. These writers were not actually interested at all in the question of whether women can be prophets. They were interested in whether someone who receives a particular kind of inspiration from God is automatically a prophet. There are two women who are mentioned as having done so. If you hold this view about inspiration, then you hold as a consequence that women are prophets. It's not that you want to find that women can be prophets and so you read it that way.

The relationship between Mary and her mother is noteworthy. Mary's mother was pregnant with her, and then the infant is not quite what she expected. That is an interesting parallel with the Jesus story, but it's also its own sort of drama, and it's where we get the concern with male and female and consequent roles. The text says,

> Imran's wife said, "My Lord, I have vowed to you what is in my womb as a dedicated offering, so accept this from me. You are the One who hears and knows."

So we have a woman as a religious agent, making an agreement with God. She makes an offer, and it comes to be accepted. Even as she is taking this initiative, she's also acknowledging a kind of lack in herself. It is incomplete. She's able to make the offer, but she doesn't really know how it's going to turn out. It's contingent on God hearing and accepting.

> *And when she gave birth to her, she said, "My Lord, I have delivered a girl." And God knew better what she had delivered, and the male is not like the female.*

She gives birth, which is also agency. Notice here the reference to knowing, which takes us back to the earlier statement that God was all knowing. God was described as one who knows and also hears, and here Mary's mother is talking to the God who hears her. A conversation is taking place.

"And the male is not like the female"—the fact that the Qur'an comments on this suggests that Mary's mother was somehow assuming that she was going to give birth to a male, or that something about temple service or dedicating her to God's service was a role reserved for males. She seems to almost be sort of surprised: "Oh, look what happened! It's a girl!" It's stated as if the expectation was that it would have been a male child. "The male is not like the female" is a very different way of framing things than to say, "Males and females are different." It doesn't also say, "The female is not like the male," which is what one might expect because they're speaking of a female. Here the female is the standard to which the male is being compared. What might that mean?

> *"I have named her Mary, and I seek shelter for her and her progeny from Satan, the rejected."*

This act of naming is interesting. Who names in Scripture? Adam is associated with naming and knowing names and being able to say the names. Where is Mary's father here? Mary's father isn't part of the decision to dedicate what's in the mother's womb to temple service. He doesn't have any say in the birth. He doesn't name. He doesn't appeal to God for "shelter against Satan the rejected" for all of her progeny. If we go back to my statement that Moses' mother and sister (and by the way, Moses' father also doesn't appear in that story) show up in service to the story of a prophet, what we have here is that it's not about male more than female. It's again about who is moving the story forward. It isn't just that Mary is the mother of Jesus; it's that Mary's father is effaced in the story, and Mary's mother, Jesus' maternal grandmother, actually becomes responsible for calling on God for protection for both Mary and her progeny against Satan. There is a Muslim tradition according to which Satan in a way touches everybody at birth except Mary and Jesus. There has been much debate about what exactly that means, but what we have here is again an invocation of a blessing that comes from the mother to the daughter to the grandson. When the grandson is Jesus, that is significant. For all that male lineages are celebrated, here it's not just one exceptional woman: it's a mother to a daughter to a son, again, in the service of moving the story forward.

So the Lord accepted her, a beautiful acceptance, and made her grow, a beautiful growth, and put her in the care of Zakariya.

Recall that when Hannah, or Mary's mother, was making an appeal, saying, "I've made this vow, so accept what is in my womb," it's not complete until her Lord accepts her. And here "Lord" seems to be *Mary's* Lord, who accepted the good acceptance and made her grow. Making *her* grow seems to refer to Mary. The progression is from being Mary's mother's Lord to being Mary's Lord. The worship of this God has become a family business. This transmission also says something, I think, about the way children inherit ties or obligations from their parents. These ties help to move the divine plan forward.

There is then an interweaving of this story again with Zakariya, whose son is Yahya, who is usually identified in Muslim tradition as John the Baptist, who of course figures into the Jesus story. Mary here becomes Zakariya's ward, and she is then folded into a larger story of service to God, a community of prophets—again, an interesting set of connections.

Whenever Zakariya visited her in the worship chamber, he found her with provisions. He said, "Mary, from where does this come for you?" She said, "It is from God. Surely God gives to whom God wills without measure."

This word "provisions" is from *rizq*, sustenance. God sustains and provides for whom God wills. It's not merely that Zakariya found her with food; rizq is much deeper and richer than that. It's a kind of sustenance that's also a blessing. One of God's names is al-Razzaq, the One who provides. And here it is spoken about women again.

Zakariya prayed there to his Lord. He said, "My Lord, grant me from your Presence virtuous progeny. You are the hearer of prayers."

We could say that the model for Zakariya is Mary's mother, though we might also note that Mary is the inspiration for what a child can do. Mary is the model for the virtuous progeny, and it's a female model. He does not say, "Grant me a son." He does eventually get granted a son, and in that way the male is something like the female in the sense that they are both good children. But Yahya becomes, in a way, the bridge between Mary and Jesus because Zakariya is inspired to pray for a child on witnessing Mary and Mary's good act.

Then the angels called out to him while he was standing and praying in the worship chamber, saying, "God gives you the good news of Yahya, who confirms the truth of a word of God: a noble, chaste, a prophet and one of the righteous."

Then Yahya gets a little more airtime here than Mary. You get an annunciation, almost. But rather than exalting Yahya above Mary, what this does is then prepare the ground for a new parallelism between Mary and Zakariya because the way Zakariya gets told about Yahya becomes almost a model for Mary when she is given Jesus. This then puts Mary in a position like Zakariya of being told about this child that she's going to bear, and then Yahya and Jesus come to share some characteristics.

He said, "My Lord, how shall I have a boy when old age has come to me, and my wife is barren?" He said, "Thus God does what He wills."

Zakariya speaks, "My Lord, how shall I have a boy"—and here the word is *ghulam*, which is gender specific, a boy. Here, too, we're setting up an unusual conception. This is preparing for the story of Mary conceiving Jesus. There are clear echoes of the New Testament here, although there's something different as well.

> *He said, "My Lord, set for me a sign." He said, "Your sign is that you will not speak to people for three days except by gestures. And remember your Lord much, and proclaim God's glory in the evening and in the morning."*

Here again is the theme of speaking and listening. The signs are once again about communication.

> *And the angels said, "O Mary, God has chosen you and purified you. He has chosen you over the women of all the worlds."*

The theme of purity recurs. The phrase "of all the worlds," *'alamin*, hearkens back to the first sura, where God is spoken of as Lord of the worlds.

> *"O Mary, be devoutly obedient to your Lord, and prostrate yourself and bow down with those who bow down."*

In Muslim prayer, the word *ruku'* refers to the posture of bending halfway, which is not the same as prostration on the ground, *sajda*, which is also here. "Prostrate and bow down with those who bow down." Who would those be? We don't have firm knowledge of temple practice. Does it mean that Mary is worshiping alongside people in the temple? Or do I ask this because I have woman-led prayer and mixed-gender prayer on my mind? Perhaps it is segregated worship; the plural here, though, is the masculine/inclusive plural. As in many other languages, in Arabic the masculine plural form can refer to a group of males or to a group of mixed gender. More than once in the Qur'an, Mary is included in masculine/inclusive plurals, collective nouns, describing groups of the pious. So here it's "those who bow down"; in another sura it's "among *qanitin*," those who show *qunut*, devout obedience. So Mary isn't among the women who are devoutly obedient; she is among the *people* who are devoutly obedient. *Qunut* is also a term used to describe Abraham.

So she may be chosen among women of more than one world, but here she is included with or is an equal with men, liturgically, and then later in terms of her devotion. Her gender is in a number of places here highlighted, and then it is undone. She is a girl child when that wasn't what her mother was expecting, and yet God knew it all along. And that is good because she needs to be female to do what she's going to do, which only a female can do. That's why the female is the standard to which the male is being compared. And yet Mary's mother is a little like Zakariya. Mary is like the child that Zakariya wants. That child ends up being a boy, but then Mary herself as she becomes a mother is like Zakariya as a father in terms of having the angels come and make this announcement. Zakariya needs a wife, but the wife is barren. It is only through God's agency that this happens. But in Mary's case, she is female, and she has to be female, and there's no man in this story. So it is a miraculous child, but she is analogized narratively to Zakariya, who's the prophet-father. Mary's gender is being destabilized in all of these really interesting ways.

I find a back-and-forth motion between assertions about her femaleness. Mary has been purified and chosen over the women of all the world, and yet she's standing and prostrating and bowing in prayer in a gender-inclusive group of worshipers, or she could be the only woman in that group. We just don't know. She's treated like a man; she's treated like a prophet; she has to be female to give birth; she's compared to other females; she's associated with a mixed group: it's impossible to fix her precisely in terms of gender.

This is from the news of the unseen that we reveal to you.

The phrase "to you," *ilayka*, is masculine singular, so this is a narrative aside that explains that these stories are being told to Muhammad in order to enlighten and enrich. The Qur'an recalls to us that there is a purpose to these stories.

You were not with them when they cast lots to see which of them should be the guardian of Mary, nor were you with them when they quarreled.

This refers to an earlier point in her life. This verse tends to be understood as a response to Muhammad when he was challenged by people both within his community and outside, who said in effect, "If you're really a prophet, tell us. If God is really talking to you like God once talked to the Jews and to the Christians, then prove it to us." The text tells Muhammad, "You couldn't have known this because you weren't there, so God is teaching you." This serves as a proof of his prophethood, in the context of this story of Mary in a lineage of prophecy.

> *When the angels said, "O Mary, God gives you good news of a word from Him. His name is the Messiah Jesus, the son of Mary, honored in this world and in the hereafter, and among those near to God."*

That's a really unusual way to name a child, a matronymic. It's not the only time ever that it happens in Muslim history, but it's certainly the only time it happens in the Qur'an. It does a couple of things simultaneously: it signals the importance of Mary, and it points to the lack of a human father for Jesus. Jesus is unique and original.

> *He will speak to people from the cradle and in maturity, and will be of the righteous.*

Again, speaking is mentioned, implying hearing. In a later passage, Jesus does speak up to defend Mary, so speaking becomes important.

> *She said, "My Lord, how can there be a son to me when no mortal has touched me?" He said, "This is how God creates what God wills. When God decides a matter, God simply says, 'Be,' and it is."*

The angels speak to Mary, but then Mary speaks directly to God. She appeals to a higher authority, and God answers. In fact, all it says here is "He said," *qala*, but the angels were talked about in the plural, and because it's a nonhuman plural the form in Arabic uses the feminine singular. So here it's fair to presume that it's God speaking, unless you posit that the speaker is one particular angel. "This is how God creates what God wills: when God decides a matter, God simply says to it 'Be,' and it is"—*kun fayakun*. The Qur'an talks about creation in a variety of other ways, but here it is simply *kun fayakun*, "'Be,' and it is."

She said, "My Lord, how can there be a son to me when no mortal has touched me?" He said, "This is how God creates what God wills. When God decides a matter, God simply says, 'Be,' and it is. And he will teach him the book and the wisdom, and the Torah and the Gospel, and will make him a messenger to the Children of Israel. He will say to them, 'I have come to you with a sign from your Lord. I will create for you out of clay something in the shape of a bird, and I will breathe into it, and it will become a bird by the permission of God. I will cure the blind and the leper and give life to the dead by the permission of God.'"

The focus now turns to Jesus. Mary disappears from the story. What we have again here is simply that Mary says to God, "How can this possibly be?" and God says, "Well, you know, this is how it's going to be, and this is what's going to happen with Jesus." We don't finish up here with the story of Mary. In Sura 19 we get another account of the annunciation, and her labor and travail, and water and dates. So there again is this image of sustenance. She says that she doesn't want to speak, and if somebody speaks to her she just says, "I've vowed a fast, and I'm not going to talk to anybody." So again there is the topic of vowing, and the theme of abstaining, but she's also being given food and water, which is like the provision that she receives in the temple. When the child is born, she goes back to her family, and people say the sort of thing you might expect people to say: "Sister of Aaron, how could you do this? Your father was a good man and your mother wasn't a whore." And then Jesus speaks and defends her. These two accounts are not perceived in any way as contradicting one another. The story starts here, and it finishes there. The two accounts of Mary complement one another, with many interwoven themes.

Before our conversation, I hadn't thought quite so much about the instability regarding the gender identifications, and about the parallels between Mary and Zakariya and between Mary and Yahya, and how things are not fixed in terms of generation or sex or connections with the Divine. There's a questioning that is going on in the text, which invites further reflection.

— ⇑ —

The voices gathered in this chapter reveal the complex relationships of the act of reading: relationships with the past, with contemporary currents of thought in multiple cultures and religions, with the complicated, multilayered texts that are found in Scripture, with attentiveness to detail and the willingness to entertain ideas that can be new, old, or ostensibly both at once. Reading a sacred text faithfully may involve discerning what is at the heart of that Scripture and then interpreting apparent problem passages in light of that center. This theme will return repeatedly in the pages ahead. Several of the Muslim scholars in this chapter reflected on the complex relationship of text with an inherited tradition of interpretation. That connection with tradition is the focus of the following chapter.

3

LIVING TRADITION

Religious reading takes place in communities, in the midst of methods of interpretation that emerged and took shape over centuries. Even though all interpretations were at one time new, particular patterns of readings become established as authoritative among religions that have sacred texts, as has happened in Judaism and Christianity as well as Islam. Interpretations can change over time, but they often do this gradually and with a sense of obligation to historical precedents.

The voices gathered in this chapter reflect faithful engagement with spiritual and intellectual heritage. "Living tradition" is a fitting description of their work both because they live in tradition by remaining steeped in the legacy of the past and because they keep tradition alive by bringing it into an encounter with the particularities of the present. Whether discussing matters of religiously sanctioned violence, paradise, consciousness of God and divine unity, or the compassion of Muhammad as a messenger of God, they seek to bring together the wisdom of the past with the needs of the present.

An Appropriate Methodology
JAMAL BADAWI

Jamal Badawi has a clear and profound love for the Qur'an, and he does not wish to see its message distorted by extremists who use it to justify acts of horrific violence. He chose to focus on how tradition teaches Muslims to read the Qur'an properly, to avoid such hijacking of Islam's holy book. The method of reading that he proposes here is so rooted in traditional ways of reading that extremists cannot refute it. His reading of the Qur'an celebrates human dignity, honors religious diversity as divinely sanctioned, and rejects dehumanization and senseless violence.

Jamal Badawi was born in Egypt and came to the United States in 1963 to pursue graduate study in management at Indiana University. For many years he taught at St. Mary's University in Halifax, Nova Scotia—for twenty years in the department of commerce and thereafter in both commerce and in religious studies, where he taught courses in Islamic studies. The study of Islam has been his parallel career for most of his life, since studying the Qur'an in his childhood. He has been recognized as a leader among North American Muslims for many years and an influential voice in how North American Muslims interpret the Qur'an. He is much in demand as a speaker in the Muslim community.

His chosen focus is a portion of a single verse, 9:5, in order to show a methodology of reading the Qur'an.

Kill the idolaters [mushrikin] wherever you find them, capture them, besiege them, lie in wait for them at every place of ambush.

This is one of the most misunderstood verses of the Qur'an, and so it offers an excellent opportunity for exploring an appropriate methodology of reading the Qur'an. The Qur'an describes itself as a book of guidance—for example, in 31:2-3: "These are the verses of the wise book, a guidance and a mercy for those who do good."

It tells its readers what to believe and how to behave. Yet there are some verses that can seem, at first glance, to be in tension with or even in contradiction to other parts of the Qur'an. Islamic tradition offers a way to approach these verses and to set them in the context of the larger message of Islam's holy book. Since such passages are misunderstood or even abused by both extremist Muslims and non-Muslim detractors of Islam, it is essential to have an adequate methodology for reading the Qur'an.

First of all, in order to evaluate whether or not a given act or argument conforms to the normative teachings of Islam, there must be some criteria for such evaluations. How are these norms to be identified? In the case of Islam, the primary sources are the Qur'an and authentic or sound *hadiths*, which are reports of the words and actions of the Prophet Muhammad (peace be upon him). The Qur'an, for Muslims, is revelation in meaning as well as exact wording, since these words were spoken by God to the Prophet through the angel Gabriel. Muslims regard hadith as a form of revelation, but in meaning only, because the words were not given as direct divine speech through an angel of God.

These primary sources are supplemented by secondary sources of Islam. The generally agreed to sources are consensus of the scholars on a given issue, or *ijmaaʿ*, and analogical deduction, or *qiyaas*. Secondary sources are not revelatory, even though they are based on interpretations of revelatory sources. Ijmaaʿ and qiyaas are interpretations that involve human judgment, and so they may vary and are fallible as well. This implies that a sound argument based on the Qur'an and hadith cannot be rejected on the grounds that the opinion of a scholar is different from it or inconsistent with it. Errors of understanding and interpretations are possible and do occur. Some traditional scholarly opinions (*ijtihaad*) may be rejected, not because of a methodological error, but because of the fact that such opinions were partly shaped by the special circumstances and historical setting of their times. Such circumstances may differ significantly from those in today's world. In all cases, opinions are to be judged by the primary sources, not the reverse. It may be helpful to note that there is no single person or authority in Islam whose interpretation of any debatable issue is seen or accepted as the only valid one, let alone viewed on par with the texts of the Qur'an and hadith. Diversity in opinion is a long-standing feature of Islamic jurisprudence. Islamic law is of course a much deeper field of knowledge than this brief explanation might suggest; the jurists have many other tools in their work.

Next, a solid interpretation of the Qur'an must be based on a study of the text in its original Arabic form. Translation results in ambiguity. Furthermore, the Arabic language itself has evolved since the seventh century, and some words have changed in meaning.

The Qur'an explains itself. There is a larger consistency in the Qur'an, and what seem to be variations can often be explained by comparing historical examples. In order to understand the message of the Qur'an on a given topic, is it essential to gather all the appropriate verses that treat that topic, as well as materials from the hadiths. One part explains another, as the tradition puts it. An interpreter cannot pick and choose to support a given reading; all the data must be brought into consideration. This can be called the textual context of a verse. The best explanation is based on the Qur'an itself; the next best is based on the hadiths.

Historical context is another tool, particularly what is termed the occasion of revelation of a particular verse. Some verses were revealed to address a particular situation or to settle a particular dispute. A knowledge of this context can help to understand a verse that otherwise might seem to be incoherent with the larger message of the Qur'an.

The historical setting might have necessitated certain revelation or certain measures, some of which were intended to be temporary. Without understanding this, there could be a serious mistake in interpretation. The verse in focus, 9:5, says to kill the nonbelievers, wherever you find them, seize them, and ambush them. Read in isolation, this sounds like an awfully aggressive, intolerant, if not criminal, type of act. It suggests that people who do not accept Islam deserve to die. We cannot say, as some extremists do, that this single verse cancels out all the Qur'anic verses that speak of tolerance and peaceful coexistence. The historical context reveals that the idolatrous Meccans had broken the treaty of Hudaybiyya, which they had made with the Muslims in Medina, and murdered peaceful Muslims. The Qur'an had begun to be revealed to the Prophet Muhammad in the city of Mecca, so it was there that he issued the first call to Islam, but the fledgling Muslim community had suffered years of persecution for their faith. Muhammad had accepted an invitation from the citizens of Yathrib (soon to be called Medina) to come to their city, where the Muslims would be safe and where it was hoped that Muhammad would be a leader who would bring peace to the contentious situation there. So the Muslims migrated to Medina, but the Meccans continued their efforts to defeat the Muslim community. Raids and battles ensued. The treaty of Hudaybiyya stipulated a ten-year truce between the two cities, but not all the Meccans abided by the conditions of the treaty. Some murdered peaceful Muslims. By today's standards that would be considered a war crime. So now the verse is limited to those who had committed that aggression. The verse says to seize them and kill them, so as not to have violent terrorists running amok. Police today, when they are trying to protect innocent people from threat, sometimes cannot avoid killing the perpetrator. To someone first reading this verse, without understanding its context, it may sound like a general principle, but this verse is limited to those who carried arms and killed innocent people.

Another important word to notice in this verse is the word *mushrikin* in Arabic, often translated as "nonbelievers," or even sometimes as "infidels." Some polemical, anti-Islamic writers claim that this refers to Jews and Christians and therefore enjoins a wholesale slaughter of these communities. In fact, the Qur'an never uses the word *mushrikin* as an epithet for Jews or Christians. Of course, the Qur'an elsewhere alludes to there being *shirk* in associating others with Allah, whether it be the Messiah or Ezra (9:30), but as a title, the name consistently used for Jews and Christians in the Qur'an is "People of the Book," which is complimentary. I have searched throughout the Qur'an, and through a concordance of the Qur'an, and it bears this out. So in this verse, 9:5, the term *mushrikin* refers only to idolaters, more specifically idolatrous Arabs, and of those, only the ones who committed this atrocious act. This verse excludes those idolatrous Arabs who respected the treaty and neither fought nor helped to fight the Muslim community in Medina.

Another principle for proper interpretation is that "the few must be interpreted in light of the many." For example, the Qur'an repeatedly affirms freedom of conscience and rejects compulsion in religion. However, we encounter some verses in the Qur'an that allow fighting non-Muslims. To understand these later verses as permitting fighting against others because of their rejection of Islam or in order to force or coerce them to accept Islam is to disregard many Qur'anic texts that are inconsistent with that interpretation. The question then is whether the permission to fight is because of their faith choice or because of their aggression or oppression, with religious choice being incidental, not the cause of fighting.

Among "the many," in addition to many positive references to the People of the Book, are the following verses that speak of toleration and peaceful coexistence:

> Those who believe, and those who are Jews, and the Christians, and the Sabians—whoever believes in God and the Last Day and does righteous deeds, they shall have their reward from their Lord, and there will be no fear for them, nor shall they grieve. (2:62)

> [A]nd you will find nearest among them in affection to those who believe are those who say, "We are Christians" because among these are priests and monks, and they are not prideful. (5:82)

When the earliest Muslim community suffered fierce persecution, some fled Mecca and found safety in the realm of a Christian king in Abyssinia. Later, a group of Christian leaders from Najaran, in Yemen, visited Muhammad in Medina. They disputed theology, especially the Christian teaching of the incarnation. The Prophet invited them to embrace Islam, and they declined. He nonetheless sent them on their way in peace, after permitting them to offer their Christian prayers in his mosque.

These and many other verses show that the dominant voice in the Qur'an is tolerance, respect, and peaceful living together between Muslims and the People of the Book.

Islamic tradition also includes the concept of *naskh*, which is often understood as abrogation but is more properly translated as supercession. A verse that was revealed later in time is understood to replace an earlier verse with which it seems to be in tension. In the case of 9:5, some have claimed that since it was revealed later than the earlier verses that promote harmony and peaceful aspirations with Jews and Muslims, 9:5 instituted a new policy of Muslims toward all non-Muslims. This argument does not hold because there are many verses in the Qur'an that were revealed during the Medinan period that likewise endorse a relationship of respect and peace with the People of the Book.

In addition, the practice of naskh is subject to overuse by some Muslims. Any claim of naskh must be carefully examined. The entire Qur'an is definitively authentic. Any claim of naskh must not be based on mere opinion or speculation. It should be noted that earlier Muslims used the term *naskh* to refer also to *takhsees* or specifying and limiting the ruling rather than abrogating or removing it. This issue is of paramount importance, since the Muslim heritage includes writings that went into unreasonable excesses in their claims of naskh. While a few scholars claimed that hundreds of verses were abrogated, the great majority of scholars rejected these unsubstantiated claims. For example, Jalal al-Din al-Suyuti narrowed down the number of "abrogated" verses to 19; other scholars like Shah Waliyyul-lah al-Dahlawi and Sobhi al-Saleh narrowed them down to even lower numbers.[1] The fact that there are legitimate disagreements about the number of abrogated verses in the Qur'an is itself an indication that some, if not most, of these claims are far from definitive, if not mistaken, based on strong evidence. In sum, naskh cannot be invoked in favor of 9:5.

These and many other verses show that the dominant voice in the Qur'an is tolerance, respect, and peaceful living together between Muslims and the People of the Book. The Qur'an teaches universal concepts and values underlying the relationship between Muslims and non-Muslims. Here are some of them.

Islam is founded on the belief that there is only one universal God, the Creator, Sustainer, and Cherisher of all. He provides for all, including those who reject or even defy Him. Only Allah is the ultimate judge of any person's "theological correctness."

The core teaching of all prophets is peace in submission to Allah. According to the Qur'an, a Muslim must accept, revere, and believe in all the prophets of Allah. There is to be no narrow partisanship that may lead to hatred or violence against communities who perceive themselves as followers of other prophets.

The Qur'an teaches universal human dignity. The Qur'an describes the human as the trustee of Allah on earth, for whom Allah created everything on earth and in the heavens. Sanctity of human life is affirmed in the Qur'an. Rejection of belief in God will surely have consequences in the afterlife, but that is up to God. No human is entitled to dehumanize another because the other is following a different religion or no religion at all. Peaceful coexistence among followers of all religions and respecting their humanity are mandated in the Qur'an. For the believer, justice is a divine command and should be observed even with the "enemy."

All humanity belongs to one family, characterized by both unity and diversity. Humanity is like a bouquet of flowers, in which each flower is beautiful in its own right, yet the combination of all flowers and the rich diversity of their colors is more beautiful. The Qur'an is quite explicit in reminding all that if God willed, He would have made of all mankind one nation (5:48; 11:118). Likewise, the Qur'an states that had it been God's will, He would have made all people believers (10:99). Acceptance of plurality does not mean accepting the plurality of ultimate truths, nor does it preclude sharing one's faith with others and even inviting them to it. The Qur'an makes it a duty on believers to communicate the message of Islam to fellow humans and to be witnesses to humankind.

The essence of Islam and its prophet's mission is summed up in this verse spoken to Muhammad: "We have not sent you, but as mercy to all the worlds" (21:107). A logical fruit of this attitude of mercy is to love humankind as persons and fellow honored creatures of Allah, while dissociating oneself from their erroneous beliefs or even rejection of Allah. This love finds its greatest form by loving goodness and guidance for them.

To sum up, the basic rule governing the relationship between Muslims and non-Muslims is that of peaceful coexistence, justice, and compassion, irrespective of their religious choices.

We certainly live in a world where individuals, groups, and governments commit various forms of violence and terror, committed in the name of ideology, narrow forms of nationalism, and religion. Counteracting violence with more devastating violence enhances that vicious cycle. Little attention has been paid to finding out the root causes of violence, such as gross injustice and dehumanization of others. While religion has been abused to justify senseless and unnecessary violence, it can be constructively invoked to stem the tide of violence. The common values of revealed religions, in particular, can contribute immensely in that endeavor. It is the duty of religious leaders and scholars to clarify these values and clarify misinterpretations of Scriptures not only to others but also for their own religious communities. Intrafaith dialogue is as much needed as interfaith dialogue.

— ١٢ —

For Jamal Badawi, the Qur'an itself teaches how it is to be read: the few are to be interpreted in light of the many. This requires honesty and discernment, in the context of a faithful community that humbly seeks guidance. Faithful readers from other scriptural traditions, such as Christians and Jews, will recognize the family resemblance to their own interpretative stances toward their sacred texts, which also contain language as potentially dangerous, if misunderstood. All the Abrahamic Scriptures have their versions of an injunction to slay the infidels, and all cry out to be read from a place centered in divinely ordained compassion.

Resurrection and Hope
ZEKI SARITOPRAK

Just as religions engage in ethical reflections on violence, religions also reflect on death and what follow thereafter. As with Mohammad Hassan Khalil, themes of mercy carry the day. Zeki Saritoprak emphasizes the abundance of compassion and forgiveness that will prevail on Judgment Day. Because, as he points out, Islam is very much an embodied religion in this life—requiring corporal involvement in the gestures of prayer, for example, or bodily participation in the pilgrimage to Mecca—the afterlife will also have its embodied features. Yet the striking images of the afterlife that the Qur'an offers also inspire this side of the grave. Descriptions of the gardens of paradise, for example, stimulate efforts to make this world a beautiful and happy place.

Zeki Saritoprak holds the Nursî Chair in Islamic studies at John Carroll University. His specialty is Islamic theology, and he has written on eschatology, the role of Jesus in Islamic thought, the twentieth-century Turkish mystic Bediüzzaman Said Nursî, Islamic understandings of peace and nonviolence, and the contemporary Turkish religious leader Fethullah Gülen. He is a committed participant in interfaith dialogue.

— ‏الـ‏ —

If we look at the Qur'an, the holy book of Islam, which is in the Islamic faith known as the final revelation of God, the name of religion is *islam*—the religion of Adam, of Jesus, of Abraham, of Moses. Lowercase "i" *islam* is the submission to the will of God, and lowercase "m" *muslim* is the name of the person who submits to the will of God. No one has the right to limit islam to a certain group or to certain individuals. It is the name of religion in the sight of God, and anyone who follows this tradition is a muslim. To believe in the submission of God is a gift, requiring humility in response.

I did my Ph.D. in Islamic theology. My specialty is Islamic eschatology. My upcoming book examines the role of Jesus in Islam, with a focus on eschatology. Islamic theology is divided into three major themes. One is the concept of God, including God's oneness and God's many names. The second is prophethood and revelation. The Qur'an refers to twenty-five prophets but also states that there are some prophets who are not mentioned, so some figures such as Confucius and Buddha may be considered prophets, if they truly followed the straight path that the Qur'an describes or did goodness for humanity. These constitute a very important part of Islamic theology. The third theme of Islamic theology is death and the afterlife. The sura that I have chosen, Sura 76, deals chiefly with this dimension of Islam, though it touches on the first two as well.

The first creation is even more difficult than the second creation, because, as we'll see, it speaks of the creation of humans as from a drop of liquid fluid. In modern terms you can call it sperm, but Islamic scholars who interpret this verse say this is a process. In fact, it refers to earliest creation of human beings. For example, the food that you have from different parts of the world comes to your body and mixes and then becomes nutrition for you and becomes a part of your body. The sperm is a result of all these interactions, which then comes to the womb of mother, and then from there it comes to this world, where it grows and becomes an evolved human being. And then, step by step, it becomes old, and then it dies. The Qur'an speaks of this process as a miracle, something that is even more difficult than resurrection.

People in this world are temporary. They are here to merit an afterlife, according to Islamic teaching. Every human being is on a journey. All start from the realm of spirits, before life in the womb of the mother, where the spirit receives a house as it comes into this world. Scholars speak of the house of the spirit; mystics speak of the body as the cage of that spirit. For mystics, the spirit is captive in the body, and they would like to open the doors for the spirit to be able to fly. That is the journey.

At death, the person enters the realm of *barzakh*, where the individual stays until the final day of resurrection, when they will be accountable for their actions. Then God will make a decision. In Islamic teaching only God is the judge, and everybody, theologically speaking, will be happy with the decision of God. No one will think that he or she was wronged, because as the Qur'an says, human eyes will be so sharp on that day that they will see the reality of things as they are. So all will be satisfied with the judgment.

It is believed that the mercy of God is prevailing, and so many sins will be forgiven by God on the Day of Judgment. Scholars have debated this, but most Sunni traditions say there will be intercession by the prophets of God. Saints may ask God to forgive others. Because they are valued in the sight of God, who will not want to break their hearts, God will forgive many.

This chapter is called al-Insan, which means "The Human Being." The chapter before this is called al-Qiyama, which means "Resurrection." The last verses of al-Qiyama speak of the power of God and how God will resurrect human beings. It gives evidence, and then eventually it says, "Is this God, the one who prepared this, not able to revive human beings again?" And the answer is yes. God is able to create them again, to resurrect them. So after that, this chapter comes and speaks of the human creation. Again, it shows the power of God. Human creation is a miracle.

> *Surely a time came of a human being that there was no mention of human being at all.*

The Qur'an says that there was a time that I was not there; I was nothing. Mystics speak of *hiç*. *Hiç* in Turkish means "nothing." Eventually you'll be nothing, you'll go underground, you'll be dead, and you'll be in your grave for a long time. To accept one's nothingness is an important principle in Islamic morality. This gives a sense of relationship to the One who made me, who brought me here. I didn't come by my own power or by chance. So I must not become arrogant. Humility is highly valued in Islamic mysticism. There is a saying of the Prophet that says that arrogance is something that God doesn't like, because an individual presents him- or herself as a partner of God. Pride belongs to God alone. God is the Creator; none of the creatures have a right to claim such partnership. Arrogance violates the unity of God and becomes shirk, the great sin in Islam.

> *Surely we have created the human being from a sperm, a liquid drop that is mixed, to put him to the test. We gave him hearing and sight.*

The word *amshaj* means mixed, a combination of many things. All the elements of your body can be found in that small drop of liquid. Why did God create this human being? It was to test him. God made for him ears and sight, because in order for a person to be tested, he or she needs to perceive.

Muslim scholars would say that this test is required for justice. We have two figures in the Islamic tradition: one is called Abu Jahl, the stern opponent of Prophet Muhammad. Prophet Muhammad visited him many, many times and asked him to believe in one God, but he said, "I believe in these idols." He never submitted. But when Abu Bakr, the closest companion of Prophet Muhammad, heard the message, he began to believe immediately. If you had no test, these two people would be on the same level. Diamond and coal are not the same. So there should be a test in order to distinguish the quality of human beings. They need eyes and ears to perceive the test, so that the test is fair. In Islamic teaching, those who do not have what is needed for the test are not part of the test. The insane, for example, go to paradise directly because they do not have it. They are not required even to pray. They are directly going to paradise because God did not give them the means to evaluate right and wrong.

We guide human beings to the way, whether he becomes a thankful person or a denier.

The straight path, which echoes the first chapter of the Qur'an, is shown to human beings. This is the task of prophets, and so we come to the second important theme of Islamic teaching, prophethood. The prophets are righteous people, entrusted by God. They receive revelation from God and convey it to human beings. Some people will be thankful for God's bounties; others will not.

We have prepared for the deniers chains, a heavy burden, and blazing fire.

This verse suggests that human beings should be aware of the consequences of their actions in this world, positive and negative. So the person, individually, in Islamic teaching, is not in a position to make a decision about anyone else's fate. How can you know that someone is going to hell? Maybe in the sight of God he has done something that you are not aware of. Islamic tradition asks, Did you open his heart? So you can say nonbelievers are going to hell, generally, but for individuals you are unable to make a judgment because only God knows who will be in hell and who will be in paradise. The decision is based on what is in the heart, and only God knows what is there.

Surely the pious will drink from a full cup the mixture of kafur, a fountain for God's servants, which gushes abundantly.

Kafur is very fragrant and remarkably delicious water—the drink of paradise, sweet as honey, cold and beautiful. Who are the pious? A description follows.

They fulfill the vow that they make.

The Prophet says that not keeping one's promise is the sign of hypocrisy. Many Muslims have forgotten this.

They are afraid of a day whose evil is widespread.

In Islam there is a balance between fear and hope. You should not say, "Well, I believe in Prophet Muhammad, I believe in God, and that's it; I am done." Instead, you ask, "Was I sincere enough in my beliefs and actions?" Be fearful, but, since as the Qur'an says, God is most merciful, hopelessness is not a quality of believers. This fear is not like a fear of a savage animal. It is much more a fear that you might be losing some good things, like a treasure. You have a treasure, and you want to keep it carefully. How would it feel if on the Day of Judgment I have no faith, and all that I have done is, as the Qur'an says, just foam on the water?

They give food with love to the poor, to the orphan, and to the captives, saying, "We feed you only for the sake of God. We desire neither reward nor thanks from you."

The Qur'an speaks of three groups of people here. The first is *miskin*, the poor, the destitute, those in need of food. The orphans have no father to provide food. The *asir* are captives of the war. Prior to the rise of Islam in Arabia, in many cases they would be killed, but the Prophet suggested that, based on this Qur'anic verse, believers should clothe them from what they themselves wear and feed them from what they themselves eat. The captives are equal to the victors.

The pious give out of their love. They don't think of the poor as a burden upon them. This is a remarkable encouragement to philanthropy. Your intention should be pure. This is a very important principle in Islam. In Islamic teaching, charity became a compulsive duty. Every Muslim is required to give 2.5 percent of their wealth. If they don't find some poor people in their area, they should go to other places and find some poor people and give to them. In the time of 'Umar Ibn Abdul-Aziz,[2] when there was great prosperity, Muslims couldn't find people locally to whom to give, and so they went to Africa to offer charity.

*We are fearful of our Lord, of a day that is frowning, and faith,
a day that is woeful and harsh.*

*God protected them from the evil of that day. God has
warded off from them the evil of the day, and has made them
find brightness and joy.*

This indicates the situation of the Day of Judgment. The book
will be given to some people in their right hands, which means
they are people of paradise. Their faces will shine. If they are
given their book in the left hand, that means they are the people
of hell, and their faces will become very upset. Another Qur'anic
verse says, "Nothing is lost." If you have done a good thing the
weight of an atom, you'll see it. If you have done a bad thing
the weight of an atom, you'll see it. They are all counted. Out
of God's grace, your bad things may be deleted, so you may ask
God for forgiveness.

These are verses in past tense, as though God has already
done this. Scholars of Qur'anic commentary say that it is a part
of Qur'anic eloquence to indicate the truthfulness of something
and the certainty of its happening by use of the past tense, as if
it has already come to pass.

*God rewarded them, because of their patience, with a garden
and silk.*

Silk is regarded as the most beautiful clothing, so the Qur'an
speaks of silk. In fact, the Prophet says that God has prepared
for His servants in paradise a reward unimaginable and utterly
unique. The Qur'an uses beautiful and powerful words to
addresses human understanding, in order to point to something
much greater. But it is not mere metaphor: there is physicality in
paradise; it's not only spiritual. Some philosophers said spiritual
because they held that the body cannot be revived, but generally
the majority of Muslim scholars would say that the resurrection
is both bodily and spiritual because in this world the body is
involved. In prayer, for example, you touch your forehead to the
ground. This is bodily, the ground is physical, so there should
be some reward for these actions that are bodily. In this way
the resurrection is related to body and spirit, and the beauty of
paradise is beyond our imagination. The Qur'an gives us some

reference to those beauties, using words that are familiar, but still it is beyond imagination.

They will be sitting on couches. They will not see neither sun nor disturbing cold.

Paradise will have a mild climate. *Zamharir,* the disturbing, biting cold, is the name of a section of hell that burns by its coldness.

And close to them is the shade of the trees, and clusters of fruits hang low, at their reach.

The branches come closer to them, as in the chapter Maryam, the story of Mary, when the palm tree gave dates to her, dangling them close to her reach.

They will have plates of silver and cups of crystal passed around for them, bright as silver, remarkably designed.

Verses like these inspired the human imagination in Islamic civilizations, such as the Alhambra Palace in Spain. The ideal was to make this planet a paradise for humanity and to beautify it, not only for the enjoyment of humanity but also for the sake of God. So make this earth a paradise, a place where there is peace. That's why the Islamic greeting in paradise is *as-salaamu 'alaykum,* "peace be with you." In this world also the Islamic greeting is as-salaamu 'alaykum. Make humanity happy. So these verses inspire Muslims regarding this world, not only the afterlife.

They are given to drink from a cup; a mixture of it is ginger. There is a fountain in paradise called Salsabil. There are children around this fountain when you see them, they look like scattered pearls. And when you look, you will see blessings and a great realm.

In Islamic teaching it is believed that all children who die in this world before the age of puberty, regardless of their families, will be in paradise, because they were not of an age to distinguish between right and wrong. A person whose young child dies will have an eternal child in paradise. In paradise there's no reproduction, and that's how perhaps love for children, which is a part of human nature, will be satisfied.

Their clothing will be fine green silk and gold embroidery. They will be adorned with bracelets of silver. The Lord will give them to drink of with a pure drink. This is the reward for you. Your actions have been appreciated.

We surely have sent it to you with remarkable sending. Be patient about the judgment of your Lord.

This last verse was spoken directly to the Prophet. Some people say this chapter originally was written in Medina, but this particular verse was revealed in Mecca. Prophet Muhammad was frustrated by Meccan idol worshipers. He and his people were persecuted. The Qur'an admonishes him to be patient and not to make any judgment.

Do not obey those who are sinful and deniers of God.

Be patient, and give your message. But patience is not to be understood as passive. Continue working to make the situation better, but do not become hopeless.

Remember the name of your Lord in the mornings and in the evenings.

Muslim scholars interpret this as referring to the morning prayer and the evening prayer. The best way of remembrance is the prescribed prayer that the Prophet taught the Muslim community, although the Prophet would pray much more, spending two-thirds of each night in prayer.

Surely, these people love this transient world, and they abandon a very heavy day behind them.

Qur'anic commentary says that this refers to the idol worshipers of Mecca, but in any time this group of people might be present. They shouldn't leave behind them a grievous day, the Qur'an says, because this is not good for them. The aim of the Qur'an is for the happiness of humanity. Human beings might be deceived by appearances, mistaking mere glass for diamond. This life is so fleeting. Be prepared for the next life, and do good things. Many people, including many Muslims, are not doing this.

We created them. We strengthened their form. If We wish, We can replace them completely.

This is a reminder. Whoever wishes can take the path to his Lord.

This reminder is given to all human beings, the Qur'an says, but it does not force you. You have the exercise of free will. That is why in Islam it is prohibited to force others to Islamic faith. There is no compulsion in religion.

Your will is under the encompassing will of God. And surely God is the all-knowing and the most wise. And He puts those whom He wills in His mercy as for the wrongdoers—for them God prepared a painful chastisement.

The word for "wrongdoers" can also be translated as "oppressors" or "dictators."

Many Qur'anic verses speak of fire in hell, but they do not give much detail. The Qur'an speaks of fire, but as we have seen, there is even cold. At times it sounds like a ditch that has fire in it and that sinners are put into. Some Muslim scholars speak of hell as the prison of God. Some speak of hell as a land, like a continent, not as a small place. And there are levels of hell: some people say seven levels; some people say even more. Some Islamic scholars say that there is a place for some people who have done some good things and never had a chance to believe, or had a chance but didn't believe, like Prophet Muhammad's uncle Abu Talib. He supported and protected the Prophet throughout his life but didn't believe in his message. He was afraid that to do so would bring him dishonor. Some Islamic scholars say that because of this protection for the Prophet, even if he goes to hell, God will make within hell a paradise-like place for him. One Islamic scholar says that it is as if in the middle of winter suddenly you see the sun come out, and it becomes like a day of spring. That is always possible in the mercy of God. There is a verse in the Qur'an where God says God does not punish any nation to whom God does not send a messenger. They will be among people of paradise because they did not receive any message of God. Scholars refer to the people before Islam and after Jesus. There were people who did not hear the message of Jesus. If they had heard and followed the message of Jesus, they would go to paradise, according to Islamic teaching. But if they neither heard the message of Jesus nor the message of Islam after Prophet Muhammad came, this group of people, called people of *fatrat*, are considered among the people of paradise. Some contemporary scholars ask a similar question about our time. Today people receive negative information, misinformation, and they might never have a chance to get the real information about Islam. Some scholars would say these people are comparable to the people of fatrat, so they will be among the people of paradise. In one hadith, a Bedouin companion of the Prophet prays, "Lord, bestow your mercy upon me and Muhammad only." And after the Prophet finishes prayer, he looks at him and says, "You have narrowed the mercy of God." The mercy of God is encompassing. That is why hope is central to Islamic teaching, as I think it is in Christian teaching as well.

— 1٢ —

Divine Oneness and God-Consciousness
SOHAIB SULTAN

Sohaib Sultan resists dividing the world into easily identified teams of good and bad people. As he insists, the real setting for the conflict between good and evil is in each human heart. This may surprise readers whose images of Islam are shaped primarily from images in the media of extremists eager to slay the infidels. This practice of turning the Qur'anic message inward will be met again later in this volume among other Muslim scholars. Equally new to readers who have a vague sense that the Qur'an is filled with the threatening outcries of an angry deity is his assurance to us that divine warning is cloaked in mercy rather than wrath. To use a term more common among Christians, his approach to the Qur'an is profoundly pastoral: it is above all a book of practical counsel and moral wisdom. His personal warmth and cordiality echoed the comforting message that he finds in his Scripture.

Sohaib Sultan serves as the first full-time Muslim life coordinator and chaplain at Princeton University. He is a nationally recognized writer, the author of *The Koran for Dummies* (2004) and *The Qur'an and Sayings of Prophet Muhammad: Selections Annotated and Explained* (2007). His efforts to promote interfaith understanding have taken him throughout the United States, the

Middle East, and Europe. Sohaib Sultan is a clearly a significant leader in the younger generation of Muslim leaders in North America.

In the interview he spoke of his opportunity to study with numerous teachers over the years. When he reads the Qur'an, he feels that he is in the company of these teachers, as well as the sages of history. He feels a particular appreciation for very early commentators on the Qur'an who felt free to ask all kinds of questions, including many that later Muslims would be hesitant to raise. They were faithful in collecting and preserving what earlier voices had to say, yet open and expressive of their own wisdom. That combination of faithfulness to tradition and openness serves as a model of an elusive balance that all Muslims yearn for. He noted that people often think that later scholars are necessarily more open minded and progressive than the earlier ones, but that is not always so. The earliest commentators often were more progressive, in the sense of advancing the progress of human beings. There are times in history when people feel more politically and sociologically safe to go deeper, and then there are times of turmoil, when conservation seems the most important task, to hold on to something before it slips away. Just as there are "occasions of revelation" for the suras of the Qur'an, there are *asbab*, "occasions" or historical circumstances that shaped the writers of commentary, and these must also be considered. The present is an exciting time for such religious study for North American Muslims. There is an incredible freedom of thought here, he said, as well as ability to mobilize that most Muslims don't have. There is no state support such as is found in other countries, but there is wisdom in keeping the government out of religious projects. Muslims in North America also have a very educated community, who are often able to think beyond the parameters. Finally, he noted, Muslims here live in a very multicultural society in which these separate communities get to know one another instead of keeping apart. This leads to challenge and the growth of new ideas.

— ﷲ —

I think of Sura Luqman as being the heart of the Qur'an and its summation, in terms of the message that it presents. I don't think that this happened accidentally. When I had the good fortune of studying the Qur'an many years ago with a very wise scholar and teacher near the city of Mecca in Saudi Arabia, he began to teach me the Qur'an by opening Sura Luqman. Ever since then

I have felt a great affection and a real closeness to this sura and the message that it has to offer. Just as in many other suras in the Qur'an, there are verses, there are verses that swim in their own orbit, and then there are sets of verses that seem to bring all the threads together. In Sura Luqman, every single verse has its own gems, but for me what I especially connect with is the story of the sage Luqman and his son.

> *These are the verses of the wise Scripture, a guidance and mercy for those who do good, who maintain the prayer, pay the prescribed alms, and are certain of the hereafter.*

This opening passage feels very familiar, similar to other passages in the Qur'an. The Qur'an has been called "an oft-repeating book." Anyone who reads through the Qur'an frequently comes across passages that are very close in story, theme, and expression.

The idea that it is a guidance and mercy for those who do good is a theme that occurs throughout the Qur'an. In the beginning of the second sura, it says that this is a book of guidance for those who are God conscious—that is, people who pray and give charity. There is this fascinating idea at the beginning of both suras that this is a deciding Scripture, a book of wisdom. It talks about itself as being a book of guidance, of wisdom, a criterion, but you have to engage actively with it. You have to live it, not only intellectually, but also in the doing of good, of doing prayer, and giving alms. Then it comes alive. It's asking the reader, the believer, to create the right vessels within themselves to be able to comprehend and internalize the meanings of the text.

> *These are rightly guided by their Lord, and it is they who will prosper. But there is the sort of person who pays for distracting tales, intending, without any knowledge, to lead others from God's way, and to hold it up to ridicule.*

Again, the pattern is so similar to Sura Baqara, which begins with this very moving passage about believers, and then speaks of people who have closed themselves off from guidance, who have closed their hearts. And then it talks about hypocrites, those who mock faith, who turn people away from God, who lead people astray. The Qur'an is often talking about the contrast between the different patterns of being in the world. These contrasts serve as a teaching device. The world is full of opposites: day and night, sun and moon, sky and earth. The moral universe also has opposites. These offer the reader options. I often reflect, as I have learned from my teachers, that when the Qur'an is talking about the God conscious and the hypocrites and those who have rejected faith, I should not be so small minded as to think that this refers to people who exist outside myself. This is a battle taking place within. There is an element within me that is searching and striving to be God conscious; there is an element within me that is withholding itself from the truth; there is an aspect of me that is hypocritical. These are all aspects within a single person. There is a social message, but there is an internal message. So I am not to go around speculating: Is that person a believer? Is that person a rejecter? Is that person a hypocrite? The point is to look within, not to be judgmental of others or self-righteous. The same conflict is inside me.

> *There will be humiliating torment for him! When Our verses are recited to him, he turns away disdainfully as if he had not heard them, as if there were heaviness in his ears.*

For me, this is really about the internal struggle: How many times have I done things when I knew the guidance that God has given us, yet I chose to have heavy ears about it? This calls for introspection, for inward watchfulness, and accountability.

> *Tell him that there will be a painful torment! But for those who believe and do righteous deeds.*

This is something beautiful that I love about the Qur'an. There is always this going back and forth. The Qur'an is chiding, reprimanding, reining in the soul that is inclined toward evil and rejection. Yet then it's always coming back to the "but": but there's hope. There is always a way back. It never leaves you in complete despair.

When I read these verses, they are about me, not about the destiny of other people, or figuring out who are the good guys and the bad guys. And I understand these verses to be very metaphorical. There are many descriptions of heaven and hell in the

Qur'an, but at the end of the day they are describing realities that are beyond the capacity of the human mind to understand fully. And the Qur'an itself says that the heavens have a delight for the eye that is never perceived. It is something completely new. The torment likewise is beyond perception. The greatest pleasure is being in a state of everlasting closeness and intimacy with God, and the greatest suffering is being distant, removed, far away from God. The Qur'an is using these descriptions to explain that this is what it feels like, not that this is necessarily what is going to happen to you, but this is what it feels like.

I don't always like the analogies between parents and God, but we might see a parallel in terms of how a mother looks into her child's eyes and says, "Never put your hand inside the toaster. It's really going to hurt, and we're going to have to take you to the hospital, and you're going to lose your fingers." The mother is not speaking to her child in anger or hatred but out of love, mercy, and a great deal of concern. When God describes to us the consequences of our behavior, God is speaking in similar ways. Sometimes these passages sound sad, and sometimes as though God is complaining, "What a disappointment you have been!" At other times, such passages seem motherly. In verses that to other people may seem angry, I see a mother's stern warning, wrapped in the cloak of mercy. It doesn't feel like wrath to me.

> *But for those who believe and do righteous deeds, there will be gardens of bliss where they will stay: that is God's true promise, and He is the Almighty, the One who decides.*

Once again in this sura we are called to good deeds. Sometimes we can make religion so much more complicated than it needs to be. Moral philosophy and related fields have their place, but we need to have a good heart, good intentions, and do some good to those in need. Don't be morally paralyzed. People know by their very nature what good is. One of the terms that is used in the Qur'an for the good is *ma'ruf*, which means "that which is known." The Qur'an says, call people to that which is known. There are some things that need more reasoning, or more specific scriptural guidance, but there are many things in the moral universe that people know. In the Qur'anic language, that is known as *fitra*.

> *He created the heavens without any visible support, and He placed firm mountains on the earth—in case it should shake under you—and He spread all kinds of animals around it.*

This is another striking aspect of the Qur'an: an apparent change of topic or direction. Where did this come from? Suddenly God is talking about the creation of the heavens and the earth. But the world is a sign. God has created the world filled with signs to point us toward God. One of the major ways in which the Qur'an is often misread is that people fail to see the integrated narrative of the Qur'an. It's not really jumping around from one topic to another. It's rather trying to integrate our moral universe with our physical universe with our spiritual universe. It is all of one piece. The modern mind tries to carve all these apart and becomes disenchanted. The Qur'an is constantly calling us to think in an integrated way and to live in an integrated world.

> *We sent down water from the sky, with which We made every kind of good plant grow on earth: all this is God's creation. Now, show Me what your other gods have created. No, the disbelievers are clearly astray.*

The moral life goes back to the physical universe. Show me what your gods have created. For me, again, this is an internal message. This passage means, show me what your lower passions have created, when you prefer your lower passions to God's higher teachings. These passions tend to be our idols today—and perhaps from the beginning. People in the past carved stones and gave them names, but they are still inside us. So what have these lower passions created? Why would you devote yourself to them instead of God?

Now the beautiful story begins:

> *We endowed Luqman with wisdom: "Be thankful to God: whoever gives thanks benefits his own soul, and as for those who are thankless—God is self-sufficient, worthy of all praise."*

According to the scholars of Islam, the character Luqman is a sage, though not a prophet or a messenger of God. In the time of the Prophet Muhammad, people knew about him; he was a familiar figure in stories. This *aya*, or verse, begins with wisdom and then moves to thankfulness to God, showing how wisdom and gratitude to God are integrally related. This I have always found profoundly beautiful and moving, that the greatest wisdom is being able to see God's blessings and to be thankful for them. The ability to see or identify them is intricately linked to being thankful for them, in good times as well as bad. This is the substance of wisdom.

Whoever gives thanks benefits his own soul, and as for those who are thankless—God is self-sufficient, worthy of all praise.

If you don't want to thank God, it doesn't hurt God. It doesn't diminish the dominion of God in the least. So the value of thankfulness is for your own soul, and the truly wise are able to see that. I feel that I have seen this confirmed in my own life: the people that I have come to know who are truly wise are constantly grateful. They see the good in things. They don't lose hope.

Luqman counseled his son: "My son, do not attribute any partners to God: attributing partners to Him is a terrible wrong."

So the very first lesson that Luqman teaches is one that is at the very heart of the Qur'an. It is the lesson of *tawhid*, of the absolute oneness of God. There is no God but God. This is the wellspring for all moral and spiritual truth. So Luqman teaches his son that this is the first step in a moral and spiritual life: you need to understand the oneness of God.

Next the speaker shifts from Luqman to God. After Luqman tells his son to devote himself to God and respect God, God affirms this and tells Luqman's son that people are to be good to their parents.

We have commanded people to be good to their parents: their mothers carried them, with strain upon strain, and it takes two years to wean them. Give thanks to Me and to your parents— all will return to Me.

God is saying, "Respect Me, adore Me, worship Me, but don't forget your fellow human beings. And that begins with your parents."

If they strive to make you associate with Me anything about which you have no knowledge, then do not obey them.

Respect, in an absolute sense, belongs to parents, but obedience belongs to God. And that extends to other human relationships: respect them, but obedience and worship belong to God.

Yet keep their company in this life according to what is right . . .

Even if parents tell you to do something that is wrong, even if they are taking you away from the straight path, then despite all this keep their company in this life:

Yet keep their company in this life according to what is right, and follow the path of those who turn to Me. You will all return to Me in the end, and I will tell you everything that you have done.

Then Luqman speaks again:

My son, if even the weight of a mustard seed were hidden in a rock or anywhere in the heavens or earth, God would bring it [to light], for He is all subtle and all aware.

Not only is God one, but God is all aware. So live your life knowing that God is all aware, of how you live, of how you worship, of how you act in the world and treat your fellow human beings, of how you treat God's creation. God is fully aware of these things. This is a message that is encountered again and again in the Qur'an. It could be said that the central spiritual consciousness that the Quran is calling people to is *taqwa,* or God consciousness, the awareness of God. So the first lesson that Luqman teaches is tawhid, and then the second lesson is taqwa.

Tawhid and taqwa are metaphysical concepts. So then Luqman moves on to matters of practice. He is not just saying to believe these things or trust in these things. Now he is giving his son a way of achieving them.

Keep up the prayer, my son . . .

Prayer is the way of upholding tawhid and of growing in taqwa.

Command what is right; forbid what is wrong . . .

To this point, Luqman's message seems very individual. Now he moves to the social message of the Qur'an. The summation of the social message of the Qur'an is to command what is right and forbid what is wrong. This line appears again and again throughout the Qur'an. We can see this as an invitation to participate in divine purpose. And it's an invitation to be a social human being, not focused only on yourself. The Prophet Muhammad, peace be upon him, said, "When you see something wrong, try to change it with your hands. If you are not able to, then change it with your tongue. And if you are not able to, then at least have a dislike for it in your heart." When it comes to social responsibility and civic engagement, I need to consider: What am I actively able to do, to change things with my hands, to change things? What am I able to speak out against, or in favor of? And then there are some times when for one reason or another, we are not able to mobilize, with either our hand or our tongue. It may be something living in us, or life circumstances, social circumstances, family circumstances, but at the very least we should dislike it in our hearts. We should abhor that it happens. We should not let evil triumph over us internally.

Bear anything that happens to you steadfastly: these are things to be aspired to.

Just after admonishing to do right and forbid wrong, Luqman advises his son to bear anything that happens patiently. Standing up for what is right and trying to stop what is wrong is never the most popular thing to do. It often requires sacrifice, hardship, and struggle. It requires time, effort, and sometimes a willingness to put your ego aside, becoming subject to other people's criticism and mockery, and at times even physical threat, including losing one's own life. There may be economic sanctions. We see throughout history, from Muslim heroes, as well as Christian, Jewish, Hindu, and Buddhist heroes, that when they stood up for justice, for goodness, for righteousness, they suffered great loss. I think of Gandhi, Malcolm X, Martin Luther King— to name a few from recent times. This is not an easy path. This also reminds me of Sura 90, where God speaks of two paths, the upward and the downward. God complains, why is it that human beings so rarely climb the upward path? Then the sura describes the upward path: feeding the poor, freeing the slaves, and being a person of faith and compassion. That is the upward path, the path that requires struggle and effort.

Then this sura offers a second warning with regard to doing what is good and preventing what is wrong. The first warning is to be patient. The second warning is to avoid arrogance.

Do not turn your nose up at people, nor walk about the place arrogantly, for God does not love arrogant or boastful people.

Once you start trying to do good, it is easy to think of yourself as better than other people, to become self-righteous, to think of yourself as the savior of humanity. If God has given you the opportunity, through your hand or through your tongue, to enjoin what is good, then you may be tempted to think that you are the best person in the world. You can be tested by failure, and you can be tested by success. People start listening to you, and you begin to get a following, and people want to come and rub your feet and treat you like a messiah. So do not turn up your nose at people.

Go at a moderate pace and lower your voice, for the ugliest of all voices is the braying of asses.

This is a call for being humble. To enjoin the good and prevent evil can sound like it requires a very boisterous, loudmouthed personality. But Luqman says not to buy into that hype. Instead, be humble, or walk gently on the earth. Be respectful to the earth. Don't speak loudly; don't be in other people's faces. This passage is teaching how to live the social message of the Qur'an. That social message is to enjoin what is good and prevent evil. How is that done? Be patient; be humble. This is how taqwa is attained, and this is how it's lived.

This is the end of the story of the sage.

The Qur'an has been talking about the spiritual and moral universe. Then again, in its integrated way, it returns to the topic of the physical universe.

Do you not see how God has made what is in the heavens and on the earth useful to you, and has lavished His blessings on you both outwardly and inwardly? Yet some people argue about God, without knowledge or guidance or an illuminating Scripture. When they are told, "Follow what God has sent down," they say: "We shall follow what we saw our forefathers following." What! Even if Satan is calling them to the suffering of the Blazing Flame?

Here again we see that internal struggle within the soul, the struggle to live the spiritual life. But then the focus shifts once more from the physical to the moral sphere.

Whoever directs himself wholly to God and does good work has grasped the surest handhold, for the outcome of everything is with God. As for those who refuse to do this, do not let their refusal sadden you—they will return to Us and We shall tell them what they have done.

Here is another profound idea: don't lose sleep over or become obsessed with how people react to your message. It's all in God's hands. Don't be depressed. This is directed toward the Prophet, who has been calling to his people day and night, and often it seemed that no one was listening. This is a sura from the time when the Prophet and believers lived under persecution in the city of Mecca, when there were only a handful of followers after preaching for thirteen years.

God knows all that hearts contain.

Sometimes you might lose hope in people. It seems that they'll never come back to guidance or to the right way of living. And sometimes this verse can ring true internally. We might feel that we have gone so far that there's no coming back. So this verse instructs us not to be the one who hands out judgment. Don't ascribe to yourself that power of being the judge, because only God knows what is in the hearts. There is a famous saying of Umar, the second caliph of Islam, one of the great sages and saints of our tradition, that God loved Umar even when he was bowing down to idols, because God knew what the end of Umar was to be. And this is true of everybody. Someone might be doing something that makes you want to despair of them, to judge them, but they might be beloved to God because God knows the end. So we cannot try to be in God's place of judgment. Part of tawhid means not to compete with God.

> We let them enjoy themselves for a little while, but We shall drive them to a harsh torment. If you ask them who created the heavens and earth, they are sure to say, "God." Say, "Praise belongs to God," but most of them do not understand. Everything in the heavens and earth belongs to God. God is self-sufficient and worthy of all praise.

So again we are back to the physical universe. And then this next verse is for me one of the most profound in the entire book.

> If all the trees on earth were pens and all the seas, with seven more seas besides, were ink, still God's words would not run out: God is almighty and all wise.

For me this also applies to our understanding of the Qur'an. At times some people say that everything that can be said about the Qur'an has been said, that the sages of our past understood it best and they had the final word. I want to direct them to this verse. The meaning, the depth, the oceans of God's words cannot be exhausted. Part of being a faithful Muslim is being open to how this holy text can take on new meanings as society changes.

There is a paradox for the believer, in Islam. On the one hand, there are verses in the Qur'an and in the tradition that suggest that the best generation was the early generation. Things went downhill from there, until the end of the world. On the other hand, you have something very profound that was among the final utterances of the Prophet of Islam, peace and blessing be upon him. In his final sermon, he talks about God, the equality of human beings—no race or ethnic group is superior—and then at the end, he says, convey this message to a later generation. Then he says, may those who come understand it better than those who are here. So there is that possibility that there might be things about this religion, this Qur'anic revelation, that the later people might understand better than the early believers. They might see things unfold in their lifetime that give them richer meaning and more wisdom.

I think that the reason this paradox exists is that it is intended as a warning against a simplistic, arrogant assumption about human progress in truth and morality. Just because we are later in time does not mean that we are more insightful, or skillful at distinguishing between our preferences and what God wants. There is a tendency for us to confuse the two: "I want this, so God must also want this."

So just as one should not be arrogant toward another human being, one should not be arrogant about one's time and place in history, assuming a moral superiority. They were just ancient, primitive people. The premodern world was necessarily wrong, stupid, and without a proper sense of justice. History was waiting for us to arrive. This is the temptation of modern culture. On the other hand, do not assume that future generations will be inferior, as the final public statement of the Prophet admonishes us.

My love for the Qur'an, if I am to be reflective and honest, comes first from observing my parents' love for the Qur'an. They are two human beings who have taken it upon themselves to read the Qur'an daily for many years, and yet even now, in their seventies, as they read it, you can see in their faces the sense of discovery, of finding some new meaning that they had not seen before. They are for me a model of openness and listening. There are always new gems to be revealed. I feel that even in this conversation with you that—even though I have read Sura Luqman, one of my favorite suras, countless times—I am seeing new meanings. That is what this verse about pen and ink means to me.

Creating and resurrecting all of you is only like creating or resurrecting a single soul: God is all hearing and all seeing.

Once again, the moral and physical universe are integrated.

Do you not see that God causes the night to merge into day and the day to merge into night; that He has subjected the sun and the moon, each to run its course for a stated term; that He is aware of everything you do? This is because God is the Truth, and what they invoke beside Him is false. He is the Most High, Most Great. Do you not see that ships sail through the sea, by the grace of God, to show you some of His wonders? Truly there are signs in this for every steadfast, thankful person.

So here we circle back to the idea of thankfulness, as we saw in the beginning when Luqman was described as a wise person because he was able to be grateful. The effect of these signs is to evoke thankfulness. There is a cycle here. The more you have gratitude, the more you are able to see the signs. This leads to taqwa and to tawhid.

When the waves loom over those on board like giant shadows they call out to God, devoting their religion entirely to Him. But, when He has delivered them safely to land, some of them waver—only a treacherous, thankless person refuses to acknowledge Our signs.

This is really about the internal struggle. I am afflicted with pain or suffering, so I call out to God, who delivers me. Then I return to all those other things that distracted me from God. This verse calls me back to consciousness of God.

People, be mindful of your Lord and fear a day when no parent will take the place of their child, nor a child take the place of their parent, in any way.

Earlier this sura spoke of the importance of absolute respect for parents, but here it notes that there will come a day when parent and child are ultimately responsible for their choices. They cannot take one another's place. There are limits to that relationship, in the context of tawhid.

God's promise is true, so do not let the present life delude you, nor let the Deceiver delude you about God. Knowledge of the Hour belongs to God; it is He who sends down the relieving rain and He who knows what is hidden in the womb.

Again, physical, moral, and spiritual universe are integrated. They all come together.

No soul knows what it will reap tomorrow, and no soul knows in what land it will die; it is God who is all knowing and all aware.

For me, this has always been a really powerful verse. This verse comes to mind when I hear about people passing away. I think about how parents, when they give birth to their child, cannot imagine where their children's lives will end, passing away in a far distant land. I think about the immigrant generation of my parents, who came from India. Many of my friends are from many parts of the world and are the children of immigrants, from Africa, from Asia, and elsewhere. We are now at a time when many of this immigrant generation are getting old, growing frail, and passing away. I think to myself, when their parents gave them birth in Hyderabad, India, or in Timbuktu, Mali, could they ever imagine that their children would pass away in Chicago, Illinois, or in central New Jersey? It seems impossible to imagine.

— ١٢ —

Mercy and Healing
FAREEHA KHAN

Sohaib Sultan's emphasis on taqwa or consciousness of God finds a ready companion in the wisdom of Fareeha Khan. She speaks of how verses from the Qur'an are used to promote consciousness and remembrance of divine presence. Scriptures lead lives beyond intellectual theological reflection alone. The life of devotion can experience the power of Scripture to work wonders. Fareeha Khan is an affiliated scholar at Willamette University. She is a specialist in Islamic law, with particular concerns for gender and for the role of traditional Islamic scholarship in modern times. In addition to a doctorate in Islamic studies, she is deeply schooled in traditional forms of Islamic learning as carried on in women's circles for centuries. She chose to speak not from her expertise in Islamic law but rather from her profoundly personal experience of spiritual practice.

— الله —

The verse that I have chosen is the penultimate verse of the ninth sura of the Qur'an, Surat al-Tawba, the Chapter of Repentance, the 129th verse.

There has come to you from amongst your own selves a messenger. The things that trouble you grieve him and he is ardently anxious for your well-being. And toward the believers he is especially kind and compassionate.

This verse has a deep personal resonance for me. About nine years ago, in the middle of 2004, I had a really bad fall. My husband and I were hiking, and I climbed onto something I shouldn't have. I slipped and fell and had some serious injuries. That moment was one of the most physically trying things I ever faced in my life, but spiritually it was very important and meaningful. Through it, I realized my complete dependence on God. When I got out of the hospital and returned home, I was homebound for about two months. Early on during that time, I received a call from my father-in-law, checking in on how I was doing. He's a pious, spiritual person, and he made a lot of prayers for me. He then gave me a sort of spiritual prescription in the form of the above verse. He told me that the Prophet had once told one of his Companions to recite this verse for mending broken bones. I started reading this verse (in Arabic) as a kind of litany, as often as I could, and it really was in my heart often during that time when I was recovering. And so this particular verse became very dear to my heart.

I'd actually never heard of this verse of the Qur'an being used for healing before. Yet I didn't question it because I knew that my father-in-law was a person of knowledge, and I trusted his piety and his understanding. I had known that the Verse of the Throne (2:255) is powerful in many different ways and is used for different reasons. I had also known about the use of the opening chapter of the Qur'an. There is a *hadith* of the Prophet where some of the Companions were traveling out in the desert and they needed food. They came upon a tribe in the desert and asked if they could be taken in and given some refuge, but the tribe refused them. So they went out and encamped on their own in the desert. After some time one of the members of that tribe came to them and said, "We have someone who is suffering from an illness. We don't know how to treat him. If you can treat him, we'd be willing to compensate you." And so one of the

Companions of the Prophet went back with that Bedouin. He recited the first chapter of the Qur'an (the Opening, al-Fatiha) over the sick person, and he became healed.

Afterwards when these Companions came back to Medina, the Prophet was told about the story, and he said to that Companion, "How did you know that the Fatiha can be used like that?" Apparently, the Prophet had not taught him to use the Fatiha in this way. The Companion had an intuitive understanding that somehow the Fatiha would be a source of healing for that Bedouin. But the Prophet confirmed that the Companion had done the right thing. I'm assuming the verse that I chose for my discussion today has that kind of a story attached to it as well.

So after my fall, this verse brought me a lot of comfort. I was overwhelmed, I think, with the spiritual experience that I'd had when I'd fallen. I had a powerful consciousness of the Divine and of my dependence on Him. How does this verse relate? It is communicating that the messenger of God is someone of deep concern for his *ummah*, for those who follow him, and for those to whom he's been sent to preach. He has a deep concern for all of humanity. There I was, a human being who's utterly dependent on the sustaining and the power and the will of God, but what is it that acts as the connecting factor between that lowly, powerless human and the Almighty? The point of perfect connection is in the being of the Prophet Muhammad. He's the one who directs people, as the prophets before him, like Jesus and Moses and all the other prophets. They were the means through which God, this transcendent being, becomes close to us, so that we can know Him. There's really no other way that we can know Him and have His presence be made meaningful in our lives.

In another part of the Qur'an, God says about Muhammad that he was sent as a *rahmat li'l-alamin*, as a mercy to all of creation. Why is this one individual going to be a mercy for all of creation? As Muslims we believe that God created us so that we could worship Him and adore Him and know Him and love Him. As modern people we rely on our intellects and rational faculty to be able to discern things that are true, but our intellect is extremely bound. We can see through signs that God has placed throughout the universe that He's there. We should get away from our electronic devices for a second, and just look up and expand our field of vision to what's happening outside in the universe. One of my teachers, Umm Sahl, mentioned that they took the Hubble telescope and focused it in on a tiny little section of the visible sky, and the dots that they had assumed were stars turned out to be galaxies. The current estimate is that there are two hundred billion galaxies in the universe. If that is so, then our intellect should lead us to conclude that this didn't come out of nowhere. We can sense that there is something that brought all of this into existence. But in our minds we can't even fathom the creation or existence of two hundred billion galaxies, so what does the Creator look like? The human intellect can't get there on its own. It is these messengers and prophets that God sent who direct us to God and to our true purpose. They show us how grateful we should be for the fact that we have been created and that we have the ability to know God.

In this verse Muhammad is called *rasul*, a messenger. He's bringing a communication from God, reminding human beings that He's there, in case we forget. And we as human beings definitely have a tendency to forget. We become focused in on the difficulties and the trials and the enjoyments of our everyday life; we might forget that there is something more to my life than just having a quiet afternoon with my friend, which is itself a beautiful thing. The messenger is one who communicates what the purpose of life is. And the verse states that he's come from amongst ourselves—he didn't just fall out of the sky. He's not an angel; he's a human being. But he has this directive to help humanity back to God. This messenger could have been someone who was harsh or stern, or constantly berating us for all our faults. But the Prophet Muhammad was not this way. This verse describes his *khuluq*, which is the personality or the character traits of the Prophet. He has a lot of love and concern for the people whom he's addressing. So he's *haris 'alaykum*, "ardently anxious for you," that you get the good in your life, that you realize the purpose of your life, that you don't fall away by the wayside, that harm doesn't come to you, that you don't get turned away from submitting to the divine. Any hardship in your life is a heavy difficulty for him. The suffering of the community brings him pain. He is described as Ra'uf and Rahim, full of kindness, affection, and compassion.

In the Qur'an it says that God has given you signs within the universe and from within your own selves. According to Muslim belief, God is transcendent and completely other than all of His creation. At the same time, the names that He calls Himself most frequently in the Qur'an are Rahman and Rahim, the all-merciful and the compassionate. These divine attributes are very near, and they seem very attached to the human being. This tells us that God wants to be known by the human being, that He wants us to come toward Him, that He wants Himself to be close to us, and that this is due to Him loving us. The theme of love is throughout the Qur'an. Knowledge of God as Creator and of God's Tawhid or oneness was given to every prophet, who then communicated it to his people. However, by the time of the Prophet Muhammad, while there was some idea of Tawhid in some human societies, clear knowledge of God's oneness and God's attributes had been lost. Jesus was the last prophet before him, and he had also brought this knowledge of Allah, but over time what he had taught had been altered and its core forgotten.

So, if God wants to be known, and the knowledge of how He should be properly known is not existent anymore in the world, then the coming of Muhammad is a *huge* deal. It's a really powerful manifestation of the power and mercy of God. There are innumerable signs throughout the universe, but if there's no real way of deciphering them, no translation key, the signs are themselves meaningless. Muhammad is that translator who deciphers what it means that there is this immense, powerful, beautiful, perfectly ordered and rhythmed universe, what it means that your own body has so many thousands and thousands of mechanisms going on within itself at this very moment that keep you up and breathing and being able to talk to me and me being able to talk to you. If we reflect on these things for a second, we know that there's "Something." We'll have a momentary transcendental experience of "Wow, that's just really amazing!" But then where do we go from there? Where do we take that "wow" feeling? We can't, at least according to Muslim belief, get to the ultimate end of that understanding without a proper guide. The fact that the messenger is someone who is loving toward us, who is showing this deep concern toward us, who is worried about us, who is not frustrated or angry with us, not forcing us to do certain things—all of these reflect the way that God Himself is toward us, in a way that no one else can. This verse captures for me some of the essential qualities of the Prophet himself, and that in itself becomes a sign that directs me further toward God.

My being immersed in the study of Islam requires of me that I be a kind of ambassador, willing to talk to people about my religion and clarify for them things they don't understand. Many things are confusing on a civilizational level when it comes to Islam, such as issues regarding women and our roles within society and within family. Muslims living in the West, as well as those who are not Muslim, are wondering, what is it with Islam and the way it treats women? I feel called upon to do something. When I reflect on how to go about teaching and explaining such matters, this verse acts in a way as a kind of tether. It keeps me grounded when I get frustrated with people for not getting what I'm trying to say or what I believe is true. I really need to be gentle, like the Prophet, if my concern is to help someone, to bring them good in their life. The point for me should not be simply to win an argument or to avoid looking like the bad Muslim. I need to be grounded in divine intention. The Prophet serves as a model for this, as a model of mercy and blessing toward others.

— ١٢ —

The voices in this chapter show the spiritual tranquility that can come of being deeply rooted in traditional understandings of Scripture. They radiate the comfort of keeping steady company with those who have maintained the power of holy texts to guide and even to heal. There are secondary themes among these four interpreters as well. Prominent among them is mercy: God's compassion for the Jews and Christians as People of the Book, God's forgiveness for a vast multitude on the Day of Recompense, the counsel not to judge others as evil but to see good and evil at odds in each heart, and the merciful spirit of Muhammad that inspires gentleness in his followers. This refrain of mercy and acceptance is a bridge to the next chapter, which considers Muslim attitudes toward non-Muslim neighbors.

4

ENCOUNTERING OTHERS

Religious communities live within boundaries that define who is in and who is out. Boundaries are protective: they conserve beliefs and practices that might otherwise become extinct. They are also exclusive, and so each community faces how to define its relationship with other religious communities. Are they enemies or potential allies? Are they to be interacted with, proselytized, ignored, or eliminated? Are they to be regarded with pity, suspicion, or compassion? As seen in earlier chapters, there are inclusivist and pluralist strains in Muslim thought. This chapter gathers voices that reflect on the Qur'an's guidance for encountering others.

Repelling Evil with Good
HASSAN AL-QAZWINI

Imam Hassan al-Qazwini is the religious leader of the largest mosque in North America, the Islamic Center of America in Dearborn, Michigan. He is a *sayed*, an honorific title afforded descendants of the Prophet Muhammad, from whom he is removed by thirty-nine generations. His book *American Crescent: A Muslim Cleric on the Power of His Faith, the Struggle against Prejudice, and the Future of Islam and America* (2007) offers many reflections on his own life and on the state of Islam in the Middle East. His words open a door to understanding the faith and experience of the Shi'ite community in the Twelver tradition.

As an immigrant himself—and more than an immigrant, a former refugee who had to flee his native Iraq when young when his family sought safe haven in Kuwait after his father, an important Shi'ite scholar and leader, had been critical of the Iraqi government—he must often counsel other Muslims from the Middle East who settle in the United States on how to adjust to their new social surroundings. Back home it was the norm to be Muslim, but in this North America they must interact constantly with non-Muslims. Hassan al-Qazwini finds support in the Qur'an for mutual respect and cooperation.

In addition to his focus on verse 34 of Sura 41, the imam offered some advice on the Qur'an. One must be wary of translations because they can make egregious errors. As an example, he chose 5:51, sometimes translated as a prohibition against taking Jews and Christians as friends (*awliya*, plural of *wali*). The word does not mean "friends" but, as he said, "my patron, my leader who connects me to God that I pay allegiance to." In essence, here, the Qur'an says (again, quoting the imam), "Don't take your religion from someone other than your Prophet." To translate *awliya* as "friends," he noted, creates misunderstanding on both sides. On this topic he concluded:

> Any translation cannot do true justice to the Qur'an. Yes, some of the translations are good, but there are some linguistic characteristics that are unique to this language and to this style. You cannot transmit this to another language. Every language has its own unique characteristics, including English. So I often struggle when I want to translate something from English into Arabic. Take for example the phrase "It's too nice to be true." I have to say fifty words to translate these six words.

Related to this issue of translation, he pointed out that the true beauty and the power of the Qur'an lies in the Arabic original, not in translation. It should be read, therefore, in Arabic, even if one does not understand the words, because their very power as divine utterance will gravitate the reader toward God. As an example, he referred to 7:143, where Moses asks for a vision of God and is denied that vision as inappropriate but lovingly affirmed in his prophethood. As he compared the original Arabic with an English translation, the room itself resonated with the power of the Qur'an and the persuasive charisma of this gifted spiritual guide.

— ⫘ —

I have chosen chapter 41, verse 34. So, God says, translating from Arabic, "Good and bad are not equal. Repel with the one that is good, so you will find the One between you and him, is turning

him into your friend." Of course, to me every single verse of
the Qur'an is great and astonishing, because we Muslims believe
that the Qur'an is not the words of Prophet Muhammad; these
are the actual words of God, revealed to Prophet Muhammad.
That's why there is a huge difference in the style of Qur'an and
the style of Prophet Muhammad's *hadith*. There is no similarity.
They're both eloquent, but there is a huge difference. Hadith are
the words of Prophet Muhammad, inspired by God, but these
are His words. The Qur'an is the actual words of God, and every
single verse in the Qur'an to me is great and astonishing and
inspiring.

But I have some emotional connection with this particular
verse. It sums up two things. One is that Islam is indeed of the
same essence as that of Christianity and Judaism. Jesus says if
someone slaps you on your right cheek, turn the left, and Qur'an
says repel the evil with good. If someone does a bad thing to you,
you do not treat him in the same way. Rather, treat him kindly,
and you will turn him into your friend immediately, instead of
being an enemy. We sometimes spend time and money to turn
our enemies into our friends, but you cannot always turn your
enemy into your friend through money. But through your kindness, by repelling evil with good, with a noble gesture, you can
turn your enemy into not only your friend, but into your slave
actually. I mean "slave" metaphorically: someone who would
adore you, someone who would love you, someone who would
revere you. And this is what the Prophet himself did, indeed.

You see, there's a big misconception that exists in the way
that the history of Islam and the biography of Prophet Muhammad were interpreted into English. There is this idea that
Muhammad was a man of war and violence. That's not true at
all. Muhammad was the most noble, the least violent person.
Yes, there were violent wars, simply because they were imposed
on him. He had no choice but to defend himself. And I always
tell my Christian and, in general, my non-Muslim friends that
the difference between Muhammad and Jesus is that, from the
Islamic point of view, they were both messengers of God, but
when it comes to the civil order, Jesus was a private citizen, but
Muhammad was a founder of a nation and a statesman. So, being

a statesman, being a founder of a nation, he had to defend his nation and his religion, and when eighty-three wars and battles were imposed on him, he had to defend his land, his people, and his faith. That's why there was often violence. A recent scholar has written that there were only 480 casualties. Compared to other wars, especially those of the last century, this is so little. So Prophet Muhammad was not violent at all. Indeed, his nature was to pardon, to forgive, to not reciprocate with violence to those who showed him violence when he lived in Medina. And you know, in Medina it was different than in Mecca. In Mecca he was a private citizen, a persecuted citizen. In Medina he was in charge.

There was a sizable Jewish community in Medina, and the Prophet's neighbor happened to be a Jew. For some reason that neighbor was very hostile to him, and one of the things he did was to throw garbage on Muhammad's doorstep every day, and the Prophet had to remove the trash every day. The other Muslims were very irritated by the actions of this Jew. Some Muslims approached the Prophet to ask whether or not they should go and teach this man a lesson. The Prophet said, "No, no, no. Leave him alone. He's my neighbor, not your neighbor. Leave him alone." Islam emphasizes reaching out to neighbors, respecting and being kind to them. So he said, "He's my neighbor, leave him alone."

One day the Prophet came out of his house and saw that there was no trash, and he said, "Why is there no trash?" They told him that his neighbor was sick and so couldn't throw out the trash today. So the Prophet said, "Fine. I'm going to go and visit him." So the Prophet went and visited him. The man was afraid that maybe Muhammad had come to retaliate. The Prophet assured him, "No, I came to visit you because you're my neighbor, and my religion teaches me to reach out to my neighbors. I heard that you were sick; I came to check on you."

So, as I said, I chose this verse from the Qur'an because I have this emotional connection with it. First, it reminds me of the ethics of Islam, which resonate in both Christianity and Judaism. And this confirms that these three religions trace their roots to one origin, which is God. These commonalities constitute another proof that these religions were revealed by God. I always say that we—Muslims, Christians, Jews—worship the same God but with different language and different tone. We read different texts, but we are worshiping the same God, and we basically promote the same values. These are, I would call them, the divine values, monotheistic values that we all share. Reaching out to the neighbors, being kind to parents, being kind to others, taking care of the needy and the orphans—these are shared values among these three religions. This proves that there is no contradiction between these religions. These religions complement one another, rather than contradict one another.

The second reason I am emotionally attached to this verse is because there is so much, I would say, injustice done to Islam, and particularly to Prophet Muhammad. The recent video that came out, depicting him as a man of war and violence and a womanizer, is a complete distortion of the truth about Prophet Muhammad. This verse shows how he behaved, how he conducted himself. Once a man came to Aisha, the wife of the Prophet, years after his departure, and he asked her a simple question: "Tell me, how did the Prophet live? What was his lifestyle? How did he act?" She didn't give him a lengthy answer; she gave a very beautiful answer. She said, "His lifestyle was the Qur'an." You want to know how he lived? Read the Qur'an. He would take the Qur'an and implement it, translate it into action. When God says, "Be kind to your neighbor," he would be the first. When God says in the Qur'an, "Reach out to your kin and take care of your family," he would be the first. When Qur'an says, "Do not oppress," he would be the first. When God says to Muslims, "Muslims, you have to forward the trust in your hand to the owners," he would be the first to do that. When he went to Mecca, after he conquered the city, he had to go inside the holy mosque and demolish all the idols. He went to the man in charge, named Uthman, and he asked him to give him the key to the holy shrine, but the man was resistant. He gave the key to the Prophet reluctantly, fearing that the Prophet was taking the key forever. When the Prophet finished his task and completed the demolishing of the idols, some people vied to be in charge of running the holy mosque, including the Prophet's own uncle. But the Prophet said, "No, I'm going to call the same man, Uthman, who was in charge." When Mecca was very hostile to the Prophet, this man was in charge of the holy mosque. The Prophet said, "I'm going to give it to him, because it belongs to him. I'm not going to take it from him. Because God tells me in the Qur'an to return the things that are entrusted to us to their rightful owners. This key belongs to this man; I'm going to give it to him."

So when God says repel evil with what is good so you may find the one with whom you have animosity turning into your friend, the Prophet was the first to translate this verse into action. He would treat his own enemies gently, with dignity and respect. He would forgive those who offended and hurt him. When the Prophet conquered Mecca, Wahshi, the murderer of the Prophet's uncle Hamza, ran away. And someone came to him and asked him, "Why are you running away?" He said, "Because Muhammad is going to get me! I killed his uncle." The other man replied, "Look, Muhammad is not a man who keeps grudges in his heart; he is not a man who seeks retaliation. He is a man of God. He will not retaliate. Go, greet him, and convert to Islam, and he will embrace you." Wahshi then returned and asked the Prophet if he could convert to Islam. The Prophet said, "Of course, of course you can." So he converted to Islam, and the Prophet told him, "I want you to know that I have no grudges against you. This is part of the past. Yes, you murdered my uncle. I'm not going to hold you responsible any more. I forgave you. You just converted to Islam. I embrace you. But tell me, how did you kill my uncle?" And the man told him, "I was waiting for your uncle to pass by. Actually I was going to kill you, but I couldn't reach you. I tried to kill your cousin, Ali. Ali's a very cautious warrior. But Hamza is like a lion. When he enters the battlefield, he does not look back. So I waited for him until he was busy fighting. I came from behind, and I hit him with my spear and killed him."

The Prophet started crying. His tears were flowing on his cheeks, which shows that he was a genuine human being. Some people think that if we don't cry, we are very strong. But not crying is not a sign of strength at all, because if you are a true human being, a normal human being, you cry when you are inflicted with a tragedy like this. This is part of our nature; we are humans, and we are filled with emotions. So, if I don't cry when tragedy like this happens, that means something is wrong with me. So the Prophet's tears were flowing in his beard, and Wahshi asked the prophet, "Do you have any request from me?" The Prophet said, "Would you mind?" He says, "No, I wouldn't mind." The Prophet says, "You're a good man. You killed my uncle, and you repented to God. God has accepted your repentance, and I can tell you that you'll be going to heaven afterwards, but I have one small wish." And the man asked, "What is it?" He said, "Try not to show me your face, because every time I see you I'll remember the death of my uncle, and it hurts me very much. Do you mind if you live somewhere so that I do not see you frequently?" He said, "No, not at all. Indeed, I'm planning to travel to Syria to live there." The Prophet says, "God bless you." So that's all he asked. And by the way, the uncle was a peer to the Prophet. They had grown up together, and he loved Hamza so much that his death was a big disaster for the Prophet. For years tears would come to his eyes every time he remembered him.

The Prophet was a genuine human being, very humble, kind, caring, and loving. Once an insane woman saw him and said, "I've been looking for you. I need you"—and, you know, in the old societies, insane people were demonized. People thought they were occupied by demons, and they were despised by the community. Yet the Prophet said, "I am here for you. What do you want me to do?" She said, "I need you tomorrow." The Prophet agreed to help, and the following day he met her and helped her with her request. So the Prophet was a man who genuinely demonstrated this verse, who translated this verse into true actions.

As a preacher I say this: It is very easy to preach, but it is very difficult to execute what you preach. You know we talk about being kind, tolerant, and forgiving, but all it takes is one small test, and I may fail. But the Prophet passed the test. He showed in a practical way that if you repel evil with good, you will find that you may turn your enemy into your friend. And I think this is the verse that we Muslims need to learn today.

I am embarrassed over what happened after this recent video, when innocent people were attacked and property was destroyed. If the Prophet were alive, he would not tolerate this. Yes, I understand that we Muslims can be angry. I was very angry when I saw this movie! When you know who the Prophet is, how great he was, how affectionate he was, how humble he was, and how closely connected he was with God, to see him being depicted in this very filthy way and called names like "bastard"—I was very horrified, actually, when I saw the movie. But at the same time, violence is not the answer. Attacking innocent people, property, is not the right thing to do. It is a very un-Islamic thing to act in this very violent way. If we Muslims are to follow the Prophet as the Prophet always wanted us to, we are not to repel evil with evil. Rather, repel evil with good, with kindness, with care, with being very loving.

This is exactly what he did when a Bedouin came to his mosque one day. Bedouins don't have bathrooms, simply because they live in the desert. They are nomads and continually travel. They don't know what a bathroom is; their bathroom is behind their tent. So, this Bedouin came inside the mosque with the Prophet, for the first time. After praying behind the Prophet, he needed to use the bathroom. He didn't know city customs, so he removed his cloth and urinated right inside the mosque, or maybe on the side of the mosque. There was no carpet in the mosque, only sand, so in one corner he went and urinated. Soon there was shouting inside the mosque at the sight of a man urinating conspicuously right inside the mosque. People gathered around him and almost beat him. The Prophet noticed the noise, and he said, "What's going on?" They told him, and he replied, "Leave him alone. This man is ignorant. Beating does not overcome ignorance. Instead, teach him." And then, the Prophet rebuked these Muslims who went after him. He said, "Be easy on people. Don't be tough on people. Some of you alienate others from this religion. Do not alienate. The way you're treating this man will alienate others from becoming Muslims. Yes, the man urinated, but in ignorance. He didn't know. So just wash the floor and take care of it that way, instead of beating the man and making a big fuss. That's not the way you invite people to

Islam. You invite people to Islam through kindness, through openness, not by your toughness. Getting too tough with others alienates them."

There are many other beautiful verses in the Qur'an, but this is a highlight for me.

— ٱٮ —

Hassan al-Qazwini's words do not need further comment for a Christian or a Jew to make connections with their own traditions. He himself makes those connections: Jews and Christians are to be regarded as neighbors. Muslims can befriend them. He is convinced that they worship the same God and share the same values, though in different tone, language, and sacred text.

Justice and the Human Family
JAMES E. (JIMMY) JONES

As an imam, Hassan al-Qazwini chiefly serves believers who have centuries of inherited experience being Muslim but are newcomers to North American culture. The following speaker is, among other things, an imam in a community of believers who have been American all their lives but are, relatively speaking, newer to Islam. From different angles, they wrestle with similar challenges of being Muslim in a predominantly non-Muslim setting. From these different angles, they come to similar conclusions, finding common ground between Muslims and others and considering members of other faiths to be neighbors who are to be treated with respect and cooperation.

James E. (Jimmy) Jones wears multiple professional hats. He is a professor of world religions at Manhattanville College, where he holds a concurrent appointment in African studies. He also serves the Graduate School of Islamic and Social Sciences and has been director of the Al-Azhar University Arabic Summer Immersion Program. For three decades he has worked in prison chaplaincy. He serves as imam on the staff of Masjid al-Islam, a mosque in New Haven, Connecticut, where he has also been active in community development. His professional work as lecturer and consultant has taken him to Egypt, Palestine, Trinidad, Bermuda, Saudi Arabia, Bahrain, and Bosnia. Jimmy Jones serves on the national board of the Committee on American-Islamic Relations, is a frequent speaker at the conventions of the Islamic Society of North America, is a member of a national committee to consider how to train imams, and serves with a working group to develop an independent Muslim seminary on a par with the best of nationally recognized Christian theological schools. He is a graduate of Hampton University, Yale University's Divinity School (he also studied for two years at Yale's Law School), and Hartford Seminary, where he earned his Doctorate of Ministry. As a Muslim scholar, he freely quoted from Arabic at length and totally from memory. At the same time, he wore his erudition lightly and spoke with the warmhearted cordiality of a next-door neighbor.

— ‏آل‎ —

I'll begin with Sura 4, An-Nisa, and move to Sura 109, al-Kafirun. The first verse begins:

> O *humanity.*

The point about this is that, contrary to popular perception, the Qur'an is a message to all the world, whether people want to receive it or not. It is not just a message to the Arabs, or a message to the Muslims. It is a message for all humanity. This is the universal dimension of Islam. In this sense it is like the monotheistic message of Judaism and Christianity. They have the same historical, geographical, ethical, and spiritual voice.

> *Be regardful of your Lord who created you.*

The reason why you should pay attention to the Lord is because He created you. So this is another point that is very beautiful about this aya in the Qur'an. First of all, it is a message to humanity, then it gives a rationale. I know a lot of Muslims translate *taqwa* as "fear," but that's only one way to translate this word. Arabic is a rich language. Another way to translate it is "to be regardful," "to be respectful," "to be aware of your duty to your Lord." Why is He your Lord? Because He created you. It says elsewhere in the Qur'an, "I created men and jinn only to serve me" (51:56). So this gives the theological worldview for the Muslims. "O humanity, be regardful, be careful of your Lord and your duty to your Lord." Why? Because "your Lord created all of you." This is the rationale. Now, some people don't buy this. But if you buy the notion that there is a Creator, then you should be careful of your obligations to the one who created your being. This is a very important place to start in terms of looking at the Qur'an because it gives a lot of the theological worldview of Islam.

And the one who created you from one being (nafs).

There are hadiths that explain this more fully, but in its stark reality, it says further that God created you from one being, and from that being created a partner. This is the stark reality, without the addition of hadith and classical interpretations.

I tell my students that if you're serious about understanding a sacred text, then you need to learn at least the rudiments of the primary language of that sacred text. You need to think about what it means linguistically, historically, and socially. You cannot sit here in this time and make an honest rendering by using an English translation. It's just not honest. I think of Leander Keck, who was the dean of Yale Divinity School—I'm a graduate of YDS—and one of my teachers when I was a student there. He wrote a chapter entitled "The Bible Is a Problem." In a book entitled *Taking the Bible Seriously*, he makes the point that it is a problem because it was written so long ago, it was in a different place, and it was in a different language. This makes it difficult for modern people to access it and understand it, but again, if you are a serious believer, you have to spend some time thinking about what it meant linguistically in its original form. So the verse goes on,

And from that pair spread countless men and women throughout the earth.

So this is a statement about humanity. The reason you should be careful about your Lord is that you are all from one family. It is out of this human family that there spread countless men and women throughout the earth. So this is a statement about the Islamic understanding of how humanity began and about the relationships between all human beings on the face of the earth. So this verse is a statement about unity, not only about the unity of God but also about the unity of humanity. And then it goes on,

Be regardful of your Lord, in whom you demand your mutual rights.

Because human beings are forgetful, as it says often in the Qur'an, you find a lot of repetition in the Qur'an, sometimes even in the same verse. So again, it says be regardful of your duties to your Lord, adding "in whom you demand your mutual rights." The rights that human beings have upon one another come from God. John Locke spoke of the social contract and its relationship to the divine in his famous *Second Treatise of Civil Government.*[1] However, here we find it much earlier, in the context of a statement about who this message is for, what is the nature of unity of the human being, and why we should be regardful to God, who created us all from one family and spread us throughout all the earth.

To me, this is a call to justice. If you are not scared of the court, you ought to be scared of your Creator. If you're not scared of the law, you should be scared of the One who set this all in motion.

And reverence those who bore you.

There is a high regard for family in the Qur'an. Some interpret this as a command: don't cut family relations. Family is supported but is also juxtaposed with and related to the ties of all humanity. But those family ties are subordinated to justice. In the same sura or chapter, in verse 135, a verse directed to Muslims, it says, "Stand up for justice, even if it's against yourself, your parents, your kin, rich or poor." Even though family is important, you cannot value it above justice. From a sociological standpoint, this is extremely important for community building. There are many debates today about what "family" means, sociologically. From a theological standpoint, the notion that we are all connected in one humanity is very important. This is the genius of Martin Luther King's theology of mutuality. "We are caught in an inescapable network of mutuality, tied in a single garment of destiny. Whatever affects one directly, affects all indirectly. We are made to live together because of the interrelated structure of reality." I cannot be what I am to be until you are what you are to be. His notion of being Christian, of being "Christlike," was to be concerned about everybody else in the human family. It's very clear that's how he got involved in the protest against the Vietnam War.[2]

And verily, Allah is ever a watcher.

It is not only that God made you. It is not only that you should be concerned for justice because God created you. On top of that, it is God who watches over you. It is not Santa Claus who, as the song "Santa Claus Is Coming to Town" says, "sees you when you're sleeping, / He knows when you're awake, / He knows if you've been bad or good, / So be good for goodness' sake." It is Allah who knows what you are doing. So this is a very powerful statement of the theology of the Qur'an, understanding of human beings, and understanding of the relationships among them. So this is a side of Islam that is often not seen. People see Islam as this foreign entity aimed at Islamic supremacy. This verse says a lot about who we are as Muslims.

This message of justice is absolutely part of what drew me to Islam. I encountered Islam first as a youngster in Roanoke, Virginia, growing up in the segregated South of the fifties, and I used to belong to the Harrison Elementary School boys' choir that used to travel between Roanoke and Washington, D.C., singing in the churches. We would sing in the church and then sleep in the church. In Washington, D.C., I saw my first Muslims, or at least people that called themselves Muslims. It was the Nation of Islam. The women were dressed in white, and the men wore bow ties. I saw them on the streets and wondered who these people were, but I didn't think much about it—I was a kid. And then my next major encounter with Muslims was in college. After I listened to Stokely Carmichael giving a speech in 1967 at Hampton Institute (now Hampton University),[3] in which he told us how little we knew about black history, he recommended reading *The Autobiography of Malcolm X*. That was a life-changing experience. Up until then, I had been an admirer of Whitney Young,[4] who was more of a gradualist in terms of redressing the wrongs of racism in this country. Malcolm X wasn't that. I loved books and still do; that's why it's good to be a college professor. So I started reading what I could on Islam. I didn't know the difference between orientalists and other authors of Islamic books. Like many who read *The Autobiography of Malcolm X*, I was upset over the racial politics then in America. It seemed to me that Islam emphasized justice more than the Baptist Church I was raised in. And reading the Qur'an confirmed this, especially verses like the one we just talked about. The kind of society we are called to be in and about is a just human society. That was clear. The Qur'an didn't mince words about it. The kind of Christianity that we had been taught was the "Turn the other cheek" Christianity. The black church gave rise to Martin Luther King, but there was also much resistance to his ideas. He was seen as a troublemaker. I didn't appreciate him when he was alive, but I grew to respect him, especially after taking a course on him at Yale Divinity School. His theology is a very assertive one: you cannot be Christian just sitting by and watching injustice. It is inhumane to watch people suffer and say that you're Christian and Christlike.

So I started reading the Qur'an, and being a young college kid, I said, "Wow, this seems more fitting to where I am than what I've been taught in the Christian church." So that started my road toward becoming a Muslim. So the message of justice is central to my understanding of what it means to be a Muslim, in the context of a community that cares for one another, that cares for your family, and for all humanity, since you really are one big human family, as the verse we've been discussing says. So it's very sad that much of the discourse both within the Muslim community and outside is about Balkanizing, dividing up the community into various slices, and emphasizing differences. That verse very much emphasizes what is human about us, that we're all created, that we came from one being and spread throughout the earth, that family is important, that God both watches you and watches over you at the same time.

This is where the Sura Kafirun fits in. It is often seen as hostile to non-Muslims. The word *kafirun* comes from a root that has as one of its several meanings "to cover up." So *kafirun* should not be applied generally to everybody who is not Muslim, but to people who would have reason to know what Islam is and deliberately try to distort it or put it in a light that's not true. Yet even in talking to them, the sura is very clear. In my understanding, this sura explains what you should say to such people:

> O *kafirun*, I do not worship what you worship; you do not worship what I worship. I will not worship what you worship; you will not worship what I worship. To you be your way; to me be my way.

To me this is a statement of religious tolerance, even to kafirun. The Qur'an says all kinds of negative things that will ultimately happen to this particular kind of person, but what do you say to them? "I don't worship what you worship; you don't worship what I worship. To you, your way of life; to me, mine." So if we say this to people like that, what do we say to the neighbors who are not trying to cover up, just trying to be good neighbors? There is another example of this in the story that occurs most often in the Qur'an, the story of Moses and Pharaoh. What is instructive in regard to this is that even to somebody who says that he is God, which is a big sin—this is major *shirk* (associating partners with God)—you should go and speak kind words to him and not provoke him. This flies in the face of a lot of rhetoric that comes out of the Muslim community, and a lot of rhetoric that comes against us. At bottom, going back to the first aya of Sura An-Nisa, we are to understand that we are one human family and that justice is ordained by God. And this is where the rights of neighbors come from, according to scholars of Islamic law. Neighbors may have three, two, or one right over us. The neighbor who has three is the person who is a neighbor, a relative, and a Muslim. This person has rights as a neighbor and as a relative, as the aya points toward, and rights as a Muslim. The next level is someone who has two rights over you, either as a neighbor and a relative or as a neighbor and a Muslim. And then there's the neighbor who is neither a relative nor a Muslim. And even this person has rights over you. It's not simply that you should be nice to them because you're nice people, but that you have obligations toward them. This is something that Muslims sometimes don't talk about very much, and sometimes we don't practice very much.

There are lots of writings about the rights that neighbors have. For instance, you shouldn't go to bed if you know your neighbor is hungry and your belly is full. You should visit them when they are sick—again, whether they are Muslim or non-Muslim. If you have food, you should share it with them. This is not something that we talk about or do enough of. If you build a building, you should not build it so high that it blocks the sun from them. These are rights that neighbors have over you. But we often don't talk about them.

Consequently, I am chair of the board of a *masjid* in New Haven, and I'm also cochair of the local block watch, which includes both Muslims and non-Muslims. And we work continually to improve the community. Why? Because we are one humanity, we have duties toward one another, and we ought to be about the business of making a just community for everybody. The masjid is part of a neighborhood coalition (Reclaim Our Community Coalition, ROCC). Like many inner-city neighborhoods, we've been plagued by gun violence, and this coalition is about trying to reduce that violence. So we've been very active in those kinds of efforts. The majority of people involved are not Muslims, and we've tried to take a leadership role.

Most of the people in the neighborhood who know about these activities perceive us positively. We're thinking about reconfiguring the space in our properties. We have some buildings that we own, and I was talking to one of the heads of the local community development organization, and he said, "Do what you need to, but whatever you do, just don't move." From his perspective, the masjid has been a stabilizing force in the community. Since the masjid has been in the block since 1995, clearly there has been a reduction of crime in that square block. Many of us walk to prayer five times a day, constituting a kind of daily block watch patrol. We are people who care about the community. Another example is a parking agreement that we have with a Catholic hospital in our neighborhood. We help each other out. They have a parking shortage, so from Monday through Thursday, they park some of their cars on our property, and on Friday during our weekly services, we park some of our cars in their garage. It's a long-standing, very positive relationship. They are also happy to have us as a safe neighbor on our side of their boundary.

By "neighbors" we don't only mean those who live next door. There is a famous tradition that says that "neighbor" extends forty doors in any direction, the whole neighborhood. These practical aspects are among the things that attracted me to Islam: notions of family, of neighbors, and of relationships among Muslims. As I travel from Bahrain to Bosnia, I've found this to be true.

— ١١ —

Divine Purpose in a Diverse and Messy World
EBOO PATEL

Many voices in this volume speak of the importance of cooperation between Islam and other communities of faith. For such cooperation to flourish, some people need to do that work full time. Eboo Patel has chosen to dedicate his life to that task.

Eboo Patel is in fact a household name in the interfaith community. With an educational background that includes a doctorate in religion and sociology from Oxford University, he is the founder and director of the Interfaith Youth Core, whose story he tells in his book *Acts of Faith: The Story of an American Muslim, the Struggle for the Soul of a Generation* (2007). He served as a member of President Barack Obama's Inaugural Faith Council and writes and speaks widely. His most recent book is *Sacred Ground: Pluralism, Prejudice, and the Promise of America* (2012). He chose as his focus Sura 2:30-34.

— ٣٤ —

*When your Lord said to the angels, "I am going to put a representative (*khalifa*) on the earth," they said, "Will you put on it someone who will spread corruption and cause bloodshed, while we glorify you with your praises and sanctify you?" He said, "I know what you do not know." And He taught Adam the names, all of them. Then He showed them to the angels and said, "Tell me the names of these if you are truthful." They said, "Glory to you. There is no knowledge for us except what you have taught us. Indeed, you are the all-knowing and all-wise."*

He said, "Adam, tell them their names." When he told them their names, God said, "Did I not tell you that I know what is unseen in the heavens and the earth, and that I know what you reveal and what you conceal?" And when We said to the angels, "Prostrate yourselves before Adam," they all prostrated, except Iblis. He refused and was arrogant and became one of the unbelievers.

For me, the whole of everything is in that passage: we are here for a divine purpose. God says that He created humankind with dust and divine breath, to be God's servant and representative. So God is creating Adam, our common ancestor, for his purpose. This reminds me of Abraham Joshua Heschel in his book *God in Search of Man*. "I created you for this purpose." I'm doing a talk next week at Union Theological Seminary on Heschel, and part of what I write about is that I feel like Heschel is doing *tafsir* because Heschel's point is that God needs us to carry on His work on earth. And for me this Qur'anic passage is saying that this is what we were created for. Then God says to His close companions, the angels, "Bow to Adam," and they say, "No"! Then God says, "I know what you do not know." God vouches for us, in the face of the angels saying that this human creature will only fiddle and destroy, which is of course what a lot of human beings do. So the angels are right when God says, "I know what you do not know."

I remember being in Oxford at a time of recommitting to Islam, reading this verse and sitting up straight in my chair late at night, stunned because the angels are saying, "Look, we can see into the future, and this is not going to be good," and God doesn't really disagree. He doesn't say human beings will not shed blood and spread corruption. He says, "But I have made them for other things as well. I know what they're capable of." So for me this is like the second level of meaning in this passage. The first is that we were created by the divine will, and our work on earth is a divine purpose. Frankly, I disagree with a fair amount of religious discourse that claims that religion is about getting back to heaven or *jannah*. I just don't think that's all of religion. A lot of religion is what we do here. God made us with a sacred purpose to steward His sacred creation. What we do here is holy.

So God vouches for our goodness to the angels. I find it very powerful emotionally that when humans don't even know their own goodness, God says, not just to the angels but also to Adam, "I know your goodness. I know what you're capable of." I find that really beautiful. For me, that's part two of this passage.

Part three is that God sets up a contest between the angels and Adam. He says to the angels, "I want you to give me the names." The angels say, "The only knowledge we have is to sing your glory." Then He turns to Adam, and Adam has the God-given ability to do it. I remember reading it over and over again, and what struck me about it is that the word "names" is in the plural form, not "name" but "names." The Qur'an describes creation as diverse. There is a famous line from Sura 49 that God made humanity into different nations and tribes, but here it says that it is the nature of *creation* to be diverse: grass and leaves and trees and fish and birds. What distinguishes Adam from the angels is the ability to name the various names. What makes humans human, and worthy of being God's steward, is our ability to flow with the diversity of creation. So those three things—created for a divine purpose, the vouching for goodness, the special ability that we have to identify the diverse names of creation—for me, everything is an offshoot of that.

The great goodness that God gave us was mercy. The whole arc of the Qur'an is about *rahma*, God's mercy as greater than His wrath. "We sent you, the Prophet, to be nothing but a special mercy upon all the worlds." That mercy characterizes the relationship between the Creator, humanity, and His creation.

God gives us His mercy, and we are meant to steward creation with mercy. But stewarding creation is an impure task. So while mercy has to be the most salient quality, it can't be the only quality. There have to be other qualities as well. There has to be justice, and justice and mercy are not always the same thing. And of course the ninety-nine names of God are a good guide for humans, but the topmost quality is mercy.

So that's where I am. I used to be more reticent about this, but now I just am who I am. I'm a pretty pragmatic person, an on-earth person. This passage gives me what it means to be on earth and what our purpose on earth is. There are other dimensions of Islam that are about how we get to heaven. That's beautiful, but it is not my primary concern right now. I used to feel bad about that. This is not a comment about Islam; I'm making a comment about, frankly, my natural inclination. So reading this passage is an affirmation that my natural inclination to focus on earth is actually also a dimension of holiness in Islam.

I see my work in promoting interfaith understanding as part of naming the names. It is a divinely guided task to engage with diversity positively. An important part of that is the voice that we use. There are many ways that God could have indicated to the angels why He had chosen Adam, a human being, to be the steward of creation, rather than the angels themselves. God chooses a contest that highlights diversity, which is how I'm interpreting names, and the ability of Adam to use a voice vis-à-vis that diversity.

I think that beauty matters a great deal, especially in language. There is a saying of the Prophet Muhammad, "God is beautiful and loves beauty." One of the ways that we express beauty is in language. In the early days, people came to the Qur'an through its beauty, and that still holds true. One of the central Islamic arts is beautiful recitation of the Qur'an.

I love poetry. The Qur'an says several times, "Speak of them in the best of ways." Rumi's *Mathnawi* is called by some the Qur'an in the Persian tongue, and it exemplifies this notion of speaking in the best of ways. Rumi, Blake, and William Carlos Williams changed my life. They came to me when I was in college, and their poetry shows beautiful ways of expressing the names.

So beauty matters, yet the world, which is the focus of my activity, is imperfect and messy. I don't think beauty necessarily means purity. There must be some ugliness for beauty to be perceived. I think purity is a powerful thing, but it's not the path that I've chosen. I feel that Islam as a tradition supports that choice. The Prophet Muhammad was not an ascetic. He was not celibate. He lived in the world. He loved his wives. He loved his children. When he had to go to war, he went to war. But I think what makes his example so powerful is that when presented with a choice he chose paths of mercy and beauty. A striking example of this, for me, is when the Prophet, may the peace and blessings of God be upon him, returns to Mecca to do the hajj, after the treaty of Hudaybiyya. His entourage is a huge caravan of camels and people and much more. He sees down the road that the caravan is going to run over a bitch and her pups, and he changes the course of the caravan. I find it stunningly beautiful that he would change course for thousands of people even on his way to Mecca, a city he's been shut out of for nearly a decade and that has warred against him. He had the consciousness to notice this dog and took an action of mercy. For me, this demonstrates another important part of religion: little things matter. One of the powerful things about religion is that it makes us better.

I'll tell you a story from a week ago. We have a small place in Michigan that we share with my wife's family. We were up there for the weekend, and I was driving to the grocery store to get something, and there was what seemed to me a healthy-looking guy standing in front of the grocery store with a sign, begging. There was a "Help Wanted" sign in the store. My first response was to be mad at him. Frankly, I don't think it's an unreasonable response to roll one's eyes. And then I thought about Sura 93, where it says, "God found you an orphan and provided for you, so do not oppress the beggar." So on the way out I handed the guy a granola bar. Had I not had that verse salient for me, I would have chosen a different response to that person. I chose a slightly more sacred response, one based on a feeling of human empathy, even though the other response—of rolling my eyes a bit—was also reality. This person could both have been lazy *and* hurting. I get to choose my response of which reality to respond to, and in my better moments, I respond within the Qur'an's grand narrative that God created humanity for divine purpose. Maybe you could say that the name that I chose at that point was mercy.

To paraphrase William Carlos Williams: "When they think of us in the time to come, let them say there was a burst of fragrance from black branches." A lot of religion is just that little intimation of beauty, just the little stuff. That brings me back to that story about the Prophet. We know his *adab*; we know how he treated people in the little things as well as the big things. Religion is about both.

There are a lot of people within the world of Islam who could very easily have rolled their eyes at me when I began my work with Interfaith Youth Core, and not a few of them did—when you get down to it, I was a young American kid who's an Ismaili with earrings. But there were people like Professor Ingrid Mattson,[5] Dr. Sayyid Syeed,[6] Shaikh Hamza Yusuf,[7] and others, who took what I was trying to do seriously from a relatively early stage, at a time when the train wasn't rolling. I believe that for them, the little thing to do was to be supportive of me. My job last night, in a discussion with a group of students, was to do a little thing to encourage them. That could have meant listening for ninety more seconds; that could have meant letting them finish their question when they're struggling to think it through and articulate it. I get this wrong often, but I am aware of it because I am a Muslim, because I have a tradition which casts light on little things. When I choose to be better than what I normally would be, I am responding to that tradition. That is what taqwa is, consciousness of God. The great Muslim scholar Fazlur Rahman,[8] whose writings moved me greatly, said that the essence of Islam is taqwa.

I move in some circles that are neither particularly beautiful nor merciful. There is the rat race around the White House, where so much of the focus is on making an impression and getting ahead. Still, as I see it, it is no messier than the years 610 to 632, the public years of the Prophet's life, when the Qur'an was revealed and the Muslim community began. Muhammad lived his life in the world. In the year 610, after he received the first revelation, he didn't stay on the mountain! Islam is not meant for the cave at Mount Hira. Islam is meant for Mecca, for Medina, for the messiness of the world. I don't really like the rat race around the White House, so I'm not that involved in it. But I think that there is holiness in creation, including its messiness. I think that a big part of religiosity is engaging with that messiness.

Hinduism is very wise in its teaching that there are different paths, different yogas. There is the path of prayer, the path of knowledge, and the path of action. One of the things that I've become more comfortable in, although frankly I still feel bad about it, is the realization I'm not a particularly prayerful person. I'm a karma yogi: my path is the path of action in the world. With regard to prayer, I do my best to meet the minimum that is required, but I was given a larger quantity of something else. And I finally have just had to come to terms with that. This is who I am, and being a karma yogi is also holy.

Within Ismaili tradition, service in the world is a central part of being a good Muslim. I take inspiration from the Ismaili theology. Its primary insight is that God's message in the Qur'an is meant universally and eternally, and therefore needs interpretation for the current time and place. I refer to myself as a Muslim with an Ismaili interpretation of Islam, as opposed to an Ismaili, because many Ismailis view themselves as kind of a community apart. I don't think that's wrong; I just don't fit into that. It can lead to exclusiveness, and my work is to be inclusive. Small communities need people who maintain its core, and they need people who go out and encounter others. I'm very proud of my Ismaili-ness, but it doesn't fence me in, as the old song goes.

— ١٢ —

Dignity and Relationality
ZAYN KASSAM

Like Eboo Patel, Zayn Kassam has her home in the Ismaili branch of Shi'ite Islam. The two of them also share a deep appreciation of the faith of other traditions and of the sacredness of the earth. Zayn Kassam is professor of religious studies at Pomona College in Claremont, California, where she teaches courses in Islamic philosophy, mysticism, literature, and gender. Her many research interests include Islamic understandings of gender and of the environment. Her books include *Introduction to the World's Major Religions: Islam* (2005), and an edited volume, *Women and Islam* (2010).

— ⅃⅃ —

*To God is the East and the West, and wherever you turn
there is the face of God. Indeed, God is all-encompassing, all-
knowing. (2:115)*

My story with this verse, the first of the two verses engaged here,
actually goes back to when I was a child. I was born and raised
in a South Asian Ismaili Muslim family in East Africa, in Kenya.
My dad used to say to me that whenever you come face-to-face
with a person, you're not acknowledging the person (*jīva*), but
you're acknowledging the life/soul inside them (*ātman*), which
has been given to them by God. Then he would say, "Whithersoever you turn, you shall see the face of God." In his spiritual
upbringing of his children, he was trying to communicate to us
the fact that psychologically, no matter what trouble we had in
our interactions with various people, we should actually always
remember that they were given the same life force; they were
from the same life force that is within each one of us. My Dad
always used to say that a person's religion is a kind of accident
that they're born into, so regardless of the religious tradition,
you should treat all people as though they were a gift from God
because of the life that they carry within them. He said that it
doesn't matter if a person is a Jain, or a Buddhist, or a Hindu,
or an African Christian. He would use a term from South Asian
culture, actually Hindu culture, which is the idea that the deity
knows no limits and resides everywhere, including within you
(*antaryāmin*). Because we were South Asian Muslims, there was
a lot of crossover between Hinduism and Islam in terms of the
religious lexicon in that although theologically Islam does not
subscribe to the notion of inherence, both religious traditions
can agree on the idea that everything in creation can be, and
indeed is, a locus of divine manifestation, and we see this idea
expressed in South Asian devotional literatures such as *bhakti*
and the *ginans*.[9]

Kenya had been a British colony, and there was some linger-
ing British presence there after Kenya gained independence in
1963. I didn't encounter many British people, but I certainly
encountered Hindus, Buddhists, Jains, Parsis,[10] Sikhs,[11] African

Catholics, and Goan Christians.[12] Dad read an incipient pluralism in that particular verse in the Qur'an, and he taught it to us in terms of how to relate to everyone whether they were Muslim or not. And among Muslims in East Africa, there was a great variety: within the Sunni there were different groupings, and within the Shi'a there were the Nizari and Bohra Ismailis, Ithna 'Ashari or Twelvers, and others. Dad taught us to extend warmth and acceptance to all, despite any religious differences. As I grew older, I understood that it was an ethical relationship that Dad was trying to inculcate within all of us.

Years later I was in college and thinking about the meaning and purpose of life, as students do, and I connected this verse to another verse, 2:164, which speaks of how everything that we see in the world around us is an aya, a sign of God. "In the creation of the heavens and earth, in the alternation of night and day, . . . in the water that God sends down from the sky to give life to the earth when it has been desolate, spreading all kinds of animals over it, in the changing of the winds and clouds that run their established courses between the sky and earth: there are signs in all these for those who reflect."

That verse immediately connected for me with the verse stating, "Whithersoever you turn, you shall see the face of God." And I realized that this essentially means that everything that I see around me is also the face of God. It's not just human beings. That idea then began to extend for me into treating all life forms, whether they're animals or plants or trees or the creatures in the ocean, the birds in the air: everything that carried life was included in this particular verse. Everything in creation is an aya, a revelation, a sign of God. This does not stop at animate things but includes inanimate natural objects such as minerals and mountains. So now, as a college student, I had the language to understand that what was going on in my own process was a sacralizing all of creation, all of earth, and seeing an interconnection because it was all the "face" of God. Subscribing as I do to the scientific worldview, I came to feel that the evolution, growth, and natural characteristics of the world are an expression of divinity. Later on, especially within the last decade, I've become keenly interested in environmental issues.

The environmental crisis that we're in has taken on theological implications for me because everything around us and everything within us is interconnected, and it is sacred. I appreciate the work of Sallie McFague,[13] a Christian theologian who talks about creation as the body of God. This seems to me akin to the Qur'anic statement that wherever you look, you see the face of God. To me, this verse in the Qur'an is calling people to a moral accountability for the actions that we are undertaking, for what humans have done to the earth and its ecosystems in terms of anthropogenic contributions to climate change. We are not fulfilling our responsibility to/stewardship of (*khalifah*) creation, for which, according to the Qur'an, we as human beings accepted the divine trust (*amanah*).

What we do to the environment affects our own viability and sustainability on earth. Carcinogenic pesticides in our foods affect us, and when we adversely affect plankton in the seas through global warming, we extend the damage beyond ourselves ultimately to every element in the food chain. But my focus is not simply to know the harm done to humans by environmental degradation. Because there are sacred interconnections throughout the realm of creation, my question is: What are we doing to the face of God? The whole universe is charged with divine presence.

This has implications for me with respect to how we negotiate and engage difference. Sometimes there is an inclination to go inward and stick with your own community or tribe. This verse blows that insular perspective right open. When I'm engaging with you, I must regard you as a carrier of the sacred, so to speak, although theologically it would be more accurate to say that you, too, are an aya or sign of divine presence. So I've got to find ways to bridge difference. I can't stay focused on keeping out the difference and therefore put up boundaries between you and me. When we're looking at difference—not only just in terms of the different races and ethnicities and religious and class differences that we have, but also differences in terms of mental capabilities or physical challenges—there needs to be a way to build bridges because we are one humanity. From there it extends out to animals and plants as well—we are one world.

Our faith translates into moral responsibility. Relationality is a great part of that—our relationship to creatures of the sea, for example.

Is such a worldview pantheist? I feel much more comfortable with the term "panentheism": all (*pan*) in (*en*) *Theos* (divinity). God by definition cannot be bounded by anything, not even our thoughts or conceptualizations. I'm much more comfortable with the idea that all of this creation is within God, or an expression of divinity, or the locus of divine manifestation. This preserves the Islamic commitment to divine unity, or *tawhid*.

So with all the immanence that I see in "Whithersoever you look you shall see the face of God," there is also a transcendence that I know is beyond my capacity to ken. I like the Hindu conception that Brahman/God is all of creation and yet extends five fingers beyond it. That encapsulates for me the immanence and the transcendence that you have to hold both together in conceptualizing divinity; immanence affords creatures relationality with the divine, while transcendence acknowledges that divinity is beyond human comprehension or conceptualization.

The second verse that is important to me and I'd like to engage here is found in chapter 4, verse 1.

> *Humankind, be conscious of your Sovereign who created you from a single soul, and from it created its mate, and from the two of them spread forth many men and women; reverence God, from whom you seek your rights, and the wombs. God is watchful over you.*

This verse became important to me during my graduate student days when I was struggling with the question as to whether the Qur'an was a misogynist text. I was trying to read all the verses that relate to gender, especially women. When I chanced upon this verse, it struck me very forcefully that the Qur'an does not make a distinction between the soul of a woman and the soul of a male. There are biological differences between the two, but in terms of our souls there is ontological parity. Intuitively, as a woman I knew that my brain's potential for development was as good as that of any male's, and I knew that I could exercise leadership just as well as any male, that I was just as much a contributor to society. It is not the biological sex of a person that defines or limits their contributions and roles in society, but the extent to which a person's capacities are developed. I had political views and ethical views, and I felt myself to be morally accountable to my Creator. So I didn't understand why women were being given such short shrift in Islamic law or in Muslim societies, or even in East Africa, where appropriate behavior for women was defined more narrowly than the freedoms permitted to males. I couldn't understand why society as a whole treated women as second-class citizens. So I began reading about feminism, including Western feminism. I was thinking about the place of women in Muslim societies, North American societies, in societies such as Kenya.

Chancing upon this verse gave me Qur'anic proof, evidence from God, who is considered the Author of the Qur'an, that there was no reason to think that a woman was any less than a man in her potential and capacities for thought and action and moral accountability. This notion of being created from one soul became extremely important to me. It started me thinking: How do I explain the verses in the Qur'an that allow for women to inherit less than their brothers? Why are there so many restrictions for women in terms of divorce and in sexual matters? Reading Leila Ahmed's work *Women and Gender in Islam* helped me see that when you look at the verses that relate to the social conditions and the society of seventh-century Arabia, then these verses make sense. But certainly for the twentieth and the twenty-first century they don't make sense, not if the verses are taken literally. So is there a different way of reading the Qur'an so that you can plug into its eternally valid message on the one hand, but also be able to sift through verses that were socially relevant to the community that was hearing these verses for the first time in the seventh century? Amina Wadud's work and Asma Barlas' work articulated the hermeneutical keys that we can apply as we reread the Qur'an for its gender justice.[14] There are some verses that are socially relevant to the seventh-century context, and there are some verses that are good for all time. To me it felt like this was one of the verses that are good for all time because it provides evidence that God is not a misogynist (to quote Barlas) and opens up the possibility that there does not need to be any gender injustice within Islamic societies, if you can accept the full humanity of women, the full ontological equality of women with men, right from the point of creation.

This verse has become quite important to me in terms of assuring me that, as a Muslim and as a woman, there is no need for any kind of discrimination against men or against women because both are equal partners in creation. Both are morally accountable. Both should give of whatever gifts they've been endowed with, openly and in a constructive manner for the betterment of society and of the environment that sustains us.

These two verses comment on one another, especially the injunction to reverence the wombs and the statement that we see the face of God wherever we look. Carolyn Merchant names early modern scientists for whom the earth is viewed as a gigantic inanimate womb whose treasures should be wrested from her for human progress. People have perceived the earth as a woman whose womb should be harvested rather than as a partner in sustaining life. If the earth is our partner, then there have to be limits and a sense of responsibility toward it. It cannot be asked to give of its fruit in ways that are unsustainable and irreplaceable. In the search for corporate profits, have we gone too far without thinking about the consequences of extracting, for example, oil or minerals beyond their regenerative capacity, or using genetically modified crops in order to farm greater yields than the earth should be made to provide? There are finite limits to what the earth can give us, so there must be replenishment of what is taken from the earth. If we sacralize the earth in light of the first verse, and if we understand from the second verse that the sexes in humankind are created from one soul, then we will not want to impose this image of femaleness on the earth in a manner that suggests that the female is there for our use, or worse, exploitation. We can no longer see the earth—or women, for that matter—as a female subordinate who has no will power or agency of her own. This verse gets at the root of some of the environmental damage that we do. How we view and treat women in a society lies on a continuum with the exploitation of labor, of the earth's resources, of animals, as each of these are feminized in turn and caught in interlocking systems of oppression, as Angela Davis has so famously said.

I see two connections between these verses. I think morality is something that is internal. The kinds of choices we make and the sensitivity that we develop toward relationality are a question of dignity. How we relate to other people and to the environment is deeply connected to how we relate to ourselves. How we hold ourselves morally accountable and morally responsive reflects what it means to us to be fully human. Human dignity lies in making those choices in a manner that reflects our values and our place in the cosmos. As we relate outwardly, we connect that to our own inner conscience. So that's one level.

The second connection is that prayer/meditation/reflection has a unique way of opening up inner perceptions that then allow us to be receptive to and cognizant of what we're seeing on the outside. Our eye for beauty is opened up through prayer, so that when we chance upon beauty there's an inner sense that is willing to receive it with the grace that's all around us. Similarly, the ability to see injustice and be sensitive to it is opened up within us through prayer, meditation, and reflection. Then we want to respond. That's how I see the connection between the inner and the outer because the face of God is not just outside; it's also within. A sense of ontological equality and dignity is something that I want to extend outside as well as to see within, and I think prayer, reflection, and meditation are what enhance that sensitivity.

— ١٢ —

The great warmth in Zayn Kassam's voice is evident, even on the printed page, as she speaks of beauty, justice, human diversity, and the ever-present face of God. Readers of all faiths can find welcome and affirmation in her words, as well as an enthusiastic invitation to participate in the common project of caring for humankind and all creation.

As these Muslim teachers speak about being a faithful believer in a setting with others from many faiths, it might for a Jew or a Christian bring to mind the passage in the biblical book of Jeremiah where that prophet is enjoined to "seek the welfare of the city to which I have sent you" (Jer 29:7). Not that North America is equivalent for Muslims to the exile in Babylon for the ancient Jews, but this continent is an experience of being scattered from one's traditional homeland. A biblical term for this is "diaspora," or "dispersion," which may capture something of the experience of immigration for those coming from Muslim-majority lands. Seeking the welfare of that city requires thoughtful discretion. In the following chapter, Muslim leaders reflect on a variety of contemporary challenges, including the role of women, religious pluralism, the use of violence, and racism within and beyond the Muslim community.

5

CONTEMPORARY CONTEXTS

Earlier in this volume, Asma Barlas, Kecia Ali, and Zayn Kassam focused on matters relating to women and gender justice. Jamal Badawi addressed the topic of religious tolerance, as did Jimmy Jones, Eboo Patel, and, again, Zayn Kassam. This chapter turns to these and other pressing issues, with each speaker offering a different angle of vision.

Just as Muslims developed new expressions of Islam as they moved out from the Arabian Peninsula into North Africa, the Iberian Peninsula, Persia, and beyond, similarly North American Muslims are exploring new expressions of Islam in their setting. In this chapter Fazeel S. Khan, a leader in the Lahore Ahmadiyya Movement, considers how the Prophet Muhammad can be a model for contemporary concerns, including the roles of women, the nature of jihad, and religious pluralism. Ayesha Chaudhry shares from her important research into how Muslims today interpret the contested Qur'anic verse on marital discord in 4:34. Su'ad Abdul Khabeer speaks on racism, bigotry among Muslims, cultural norms within the Muslim world, and the expression of blackness by African American Muslims. Rashad Abdul Rahmaan expounds on a passage that all Muslims could regard as a summary of their faith, yet he directly addresses the context of contemporary Muslims in the United States, especially those of African descent, as he speaks of modern approaches to traditional religious concepts as well as of the social implications of the message of the Qur'an.

The Final Prophet
FAZEEL S. KHAN

One result of this book may be pleasantly to surprise non-Muslim readers with how contemporary Muslim thought can be. In the case of Fazeel S. Khan, the even bigger surprise is that the modernist ideas that he holds forth were expressed a century ago in what was then British India. Unshakably grounded in the timeless essentials of Islam and the prophethood of Muhammad, Fazeel S. Khan's words invite readers to reconsider their understanding of paradise and hell, of human perfectibility, of women's rights, of nonviolence and jihad. Our conversation was characterized by his deep hope in human possibility and an optimism that society can be reformed for the better. If one's image of Islam is one of dismal figures cloaked in antiquated garb trying to turn back the clock, Fazeel S. Khan offers an alternative vision.

Fazeel S. Khan is by profession a civil rights attorney who argues cases at high levels of the U.S. court system. His second vocation is that of a leading spokesperson for the Lahore Ahmadiyya Movement, a movement of spiritual renewal in the Islamic world that began in the city of Lahore in what is now Pakistan in the year 1914. This movement is characterized by its teachings on Islam "as a tolerant, rational, peaceful and liberal faith."[1] Fazeel S. Khan takes this message around the Islamic world, in Asia, Europe, the Americas, and the nations of the Pacific Rim. Such work has been a multigenerational undertaking in his family. His great-grandfather was Maulana Muhammad Ali (1874–1951), author of many books, including a highly influential translation of the Qur'an.[2]

— ﷲ —

The verse that I have chosen to discuss is chapter 33, verse 40. The English translation of the verse is "Muhammad is not the father of any of your men, but he is the messenger of Allah and the last (or the seal) of the prophets." It is a very foundational belief for Muslims that Muhammad is the last prophet. Muslims have had different understandings and interpretations of different concepts throughout the ages, but the one thing that has united all Muslims is this belief that Muhammad is this last prophet. But what does being the "last prophet" mean? What does it signify? Well, in order to understand this concept of finality of prophethood in Islam, you first have to understand the premise underlying the institution of prophethood in Islam. Who are prophets, and what is their function? And in order to understand what this institution of prophethood entails, it is necessary first to comprehend the significance of the concept of divine revelation in Islam. That is, what is the purpose of God communicating to prophets? And comprehending the significance of divine revelation requires one to appreciate the question of what is the purpose of life. So, let's start from the beginning.

The purpose or object of life in Islam is outlined in the very first verse of the Holy Qur'an. It says, *al-hamdulillahi rabbi 'l-'alamin.* "All praise is due to God, or Allah, the Lord of all the worlds." The specific Arabic words that are used in this verse are very telling. The word *hamd*, which normally is translated as "praise," actually means having so much appreciation for something that you want to incorporate it into your own being. The word *Allah*, normally understood as "God," really means the Being that necessarily exists by Himself, meaning He's One, and the possessor of all the attributes of perfection. And the word *rabb*, normally understood as "Lord," actually means that Being that not only creates but fosters, nourishes, and sustains its creation from lower to higher stages until it reaches a stage of perfection. When we take a look at the deeper meanings of these key words, this first verse seems to imply that our purpose is to identify, understand, and emulate the divine attributes of God, who is the Creator and nourisher of the entire universe. We're to strive to know God, so that we can live a life that is godlike with others, thereby developing the divine attributes within us and ultimately becoming close to God. That is my understanding of the grand question from time immemorial of what is the purpose of life: trying to understand what God is, and trying to emulate the attributes of God in our daily lives so that we become close to God in the spiritual sense.

Now, in order to know God and acquire these divine attributes, man is in need of some guidance, and this is provided in the form of divine revelation. In the Qur'an, in 2:30-38, we're given the story of Adam. Adam symbolizes man in general, or humanity. This story explains why revelation from God is needed and the purpose that it fulfills. Here are the relevant verses:

> And when thy Lord said to the angels, "I am going to place a ruler in the earth," the angels said, "Wilt Thou place in it such as make mischief in it and shed blood?" And God said, "Surely I know what you know not." And He taught Adam all the names. That is, He gave Adam knowledge of all things. . . . And when We said to the angels, "Be submissive to Adam," they submitted, but Iblis [the devil] did not. He refused and was proud, and he was one of the disbelievers. And We said, "O Adam, dwell thou and thy wife in the garden, and eat from it a plenteous food wherever you wish, and approach not this tree, lest you be of the unjust." But the devil made them slip from it, and caused them to depart from the state in which they were. . . . Then Adam received words from his Lord, and God turned to Adam mercifully. . . . We said: Go forth from this state all. Surely there will come to you a guidance from Me, then whoever follows My guidance, no fear shall come upon them, nor shall they grieve.

I understand this story of Adam and his wife, and of their relationship with the angels and the devil, as an allegory for the status and nature of man in general. Adam, or man in general, is given knowledge of all things, meaning man is endowed with the capacity to acquire a deep understanding of the environment in which he lives. And with this knowledge, man will be able to conquer the forces of nature. This is what is meant by the angels, the controlling powers of nature, submitting to Adam. Yet despite having the capability of controlling the physical world, man is unable to master the lower desires within himself. And this is why Iblis or the devil, the being that incites the lower desires in man, does not make obeisance and causes him to fall prey to his suggestions. So the moral of this story is that man is powerful against all, but weak against his own self. In order to make man perfect in the complete sense, guidance was provided from God to man in the form of divine revelation. With the help of divine revelation, man can overcome the fear of the devil's temptings and remove this hindrance to his progress to perfection.

Now, this guidance comprising divine knowledge for spiritual progress is communicated by God to persons known as prophets. The Arabic word for prophet is *nabi*, which is derived from the root word *naba*, which means "an announcement of great utility" or "imparting knowledge of a thing." One lexicologist explains the word *nabi* as meaning "an ambassador between God and rational beings from among His creatures." And another lexicologist says *nabi* is "the man who gives information about God." In addition to delivering this divine knowledge that God desires to convey to man, prophets also serve as a model that is to be followed, to illustrate how these divine messages are supposed to be practically implemented. The prophet's example inspires a living faith in the hearts of people and can bring about a real transformation in their lives. The Qur'an tells us that God—as the Lord, the Rabb, the Creator and fosterer of all creation—sent prophets to all people of the world. Just as God granted everything required for our physical sustenance—the air, water, soil, sunlight, animals, vegetation—so too He provided all people with what was required for their spiritual development as well, by sending prophets to all people. In 35:24, it says, "There is not a people but a warner has gone among them." In 10:47, it says, "For every nation there is a messenger," and in 2:136, it states, "We believe in God and in that which is revealed to us and in that which was revealed to Abraham and Ishmael and Isaac and Jacob and the tribes, and that which was given to Moses and Jesus and in that which was given to the prophets from their Lord. We do not make any distinction between any of them and to him do we submit." In addition to Israelite prophets, the Qur'an makes specific mention of Hud and Salih of Arabia, Luqman of Ethiopia, a contemporary of Moses (generally known as Khidhr) of Sudan, and Dhu 'l-Qarnayn of Persia. There is a saying of the Holy Prophet that God had sent 124,000 prophets in all.

In addition to receiving and conveying this guidance, prophets by their personal example showed people how to live a righteous life. And although these prophets appeared in every nation with the message of how to achieve closeness to God, the Qur'an tells us that the message that was given to the prophets prior to Prophet Muhammad was limited to a particular people and for a particular time. They were, in a sense, national prophets, and their work was for the moral uplift and spiritual regeneration of one nation or one period of time. The Qur'an states that Noah was sent to "his people" (7:59). Hud, Salih, and Shuaib—each one of them was also sent to "his people" (7:65; 7:73; 7:85). Moses is spoken of as being commissioned to "bring forth thy people from darkness into light" (14:5). Jesus is spoken of as a "messenger to the children of Israel" (3:48).

In the past, when nations lived in isolated states, confined to distinct geographical areas, national prophets were ideal. However, when humanity progressed to the point that nations no longer lived constrained by geographical boundaries, and communications and mixing between people progressed immensely, this divine scheme of the institution of prophethood required a means by which the entire human race could be spiritually unified. And, because each nation was somewhat ignorant of the fact that others were also blessed with these divine favors—communications, and revelation—nations started thinking of themselves as chosen ones, recipients of divine favoritism.

So the pinnacle in the divine institution of prophethood was the coming of one prophet for all nations, and the Holy Qur'an states that Prophet Muhammad was this final prophet in this long chain of messengers sent to humanity. It says, "Muhammad was not the father of any of your men, but he is the messenger of Allah and the *khatam an-nabin*," meaning "the last or the seal of the prophets." Being this last prophet signifies being a universal prophet, not a national prophet but one for all people and for all times. What criteria would a universal prophet need to satisfy? Here are three. First, a universal prophet would have to deliver a universal message. Second, the prophet would have a comprehensive model of life experiences. Third, this universal message and this comprehensive life experience must be preserved for later generations. So, based on those three criteria, I see how the Prophet Muhammad satisfies this model for being a universal prophet.

As we know, the Holy Qur'an illustrates the universality of its message by distinguishing the scope of the mission of the Holy Prophet. Unlike prophets before him, the Holy Prophet is not described as being sent to a particular nation, race, or people, but rather for all of humanity. There are several verses establishing this: "Blessed is He who sent down the discrimination upon His servant [i.e., Prophet Muhammad], that he may be a warner to all nations" (25:1); "Say: O Mankind, surely I am the Messenger of God to you all" (7:158); and "We have not sent thee but as a bearer of good news and as a warner to all mankind" (34:28). Moreover, the Qur'an itself is repeatedly referred to as "a reminder for all nations" (68:52; 81:27; 38:87; 12:104).

And the universality of Prophet Muhammad's message is further illustrated by the fact that not only did he declare that prophets of God appeared in every nation, but that it was mandatory for anyone who believed in Him to also believe in these other prophets of God. So certainly we see that he brought a message that wasn't meant for a particular people or particular time, but really was supposed to be universal in scope.

Now, concerning this criterion of being a comprehensive model of life experiences, the Holy Qur'an says that "certainly you have in the Messenger of Allah, that is Muhammad, an excellent exemplar" (33:22). And this verse points to the distinguishing characteristic of Prophet Muhammad. We see that the Holy Prophet's life was so multifaceted that he was able to provide a model of virtue for mankind under all types of circumstances. He could provide an example for a general, for a soldier, for a legislator, for a judge and a magistrate, because he served in these functions. He can serve as a model for a husband and a father, for a laborer, and also, through his trusted companionship, for a good friend. His life was a model for all of mankind. It's not really through his sermons and his teachings that we estimate his character, but rather through his actions and his deeds.

We understand the Holy Prophet to be the perfect human being. He was able to display the divine attributes in a perfect way, and that's why he's a model for us. Take, for example, the divine attribute of forgiveness. God is forgiving and we're supposed to emulate this attribute. We need a model of someone who's being ruthlessly persecuted at first. But then events change so that the persecutors eventually fall at the oppressed person's mercy. And the oppressed person must have the power to mete out the punishment if he wants to. The Prophet Muhammad was ruthlessly persecuted in Mecca, fled to Medina, and then returned to Mecca with ten thousand followers. The city surrendered without resistance. There was a completely bloodless conquest, without revenge or punishment. This is what for Muslims distinguishes Prophet Muhammad from other prophets. He had these comprehensive life experiences that gave a model for all these types of divine attributes. Again, it's not through his teachings or lessons that we estimate his character, but rather through his practical example.

Pious Muslims want to imitate the Prophet. Many show this externally, through physical appearance. The Ahmadiyya Movement tries to revive the spirituality of the faith as opposed to simply focusing on the ritualistic parts of it. The purpose of a *mujaddid* is to revive the spirituality of the faith. We believe that the founder of this movement, Hazrat Mirza Ghulam Ahmad, who we believe is mujaddid of this past century, had the qualities of Jesus, the Messiah. Jesus was sent as a messiah to revive the spirit of the Jewish faith because, at that time, the Jewish faith was being practiced very ritualistically. We believe the same thing is needed today for the Muslims. The objective of the founder of this movement was to revive the spirit of the faith, just like reformers or mujaddids did in the past. Sure, if having a long beard or wearing clothing a certain way helps you model the virtues and the morals of the Prophet, that's fine. But if that's all you're concerned about and you're forgetting about how the Prophet acted and how he dealt with people, then there's no sense in such superficial admiration. The goal is not just to emulate the Prophet ritualistically. The Qur'an is very clear that prayer is not to be performed unmindfully, or the doing of good simply as show. The goal when praying is not simply to go through the motions ritualistically, without understanding that this is an opportunity to communicate with God. And the doing of good should be done with no expectation of receiving anything in return, but rather with the understanding that this brings one closer to God. And these are complementary. There's no sense in praying if you're not going to be doing good to your fellow man. I think at some level every religion is based on this two-part formula of belief and action. You believe in a supreme being, that's the faith part, and the action part is doing good to your fellow man. Repeatedly in the Qur'an, prayer and charity are mentioned together. That really shows us the true spirit of prayer. Prayer is an opportunity to try to develop divine attributes within yourself, so that you are able to do good to others. In fact, each of the established practices in Islam—prayer, hajj, fasting, forgiveness, and charity—is an opportunity to help develop those attributes.

This recent trashy little film on the Internet is very disrespectful to the Prophet and therefore very hurtful to Muslims. However, the violent response by some Muslims is even more damaging because Muslims are supposed to emulate Muhammad, and this is not at all what he would have done. We know how he responded to ridicule in his own life: he forgave. We have no examples of the Prophet retaliating because he was simply insulted. So the violent and impulsive reaction by some Muslims is in fact more insulting to the Prophet than the offensive material itself.

This verse, 33:40, says Muhammad is not the father of any of your men, *but* he is the messenger of Allah and the last of the prophets. The use of the word "but" leads us to expect some type of logical response or rebuttal. So what is the connection between the two clauses in this verse? He's not your physical father, but by being this seal of the prophets, he is the spiritual father of mankind. It is through his example that others will be given spiritual life by becoming close to God.

Being the last prophet signifies being a universal model for all of mankind, the model that most perfectly manifests the divine attributes on earth. We're all on this journey toward perfection, and most of us are not going to reach there in this lifetime, but this is a training ground for us for the hereafter. We don't perceive heaven and hell to be two physical places that you go to afterwards, one very pleasant, one very hot. Rather, heaven and hell are conditions or states that people find themselves in. There's a verse in the Qur'an that talks about the heavens extending throughout the entire universe. So someone asked the Prophet, "Well, if heaven is everywhere, where's hell?"

He responded, "Where is the night when the day comes?" This shows that these are not physical places; they are conditions. So when one is close to God, not physically but spiritually—having developed the divine attributes within himself—one is in a heaven-like state. When one is detached from God, which is the meaning of sin, one is in a state of hell. We have all the images of fire when thinking of hell, but in every language we see expressions like "burning with envy," "burning with rage," "burning with jealousy," and so on. This is what hell is. It's a state of your soul. So when your soul is close to God because it's reflecting the divine attributes, you're in a state of heaven. There's a verse in the Qur'an (2:25) that says people in heaven will say, "We ate of this fruit before." They tasted in this life the happiness or that feeling that people get when they help another, or when they show forgiveness or mercy. So this process of spiritual development doesn't stop after we die. One continues to develop the soul afterwards, in different stages of heaven. And hell is not for punishment, but for reformation. The most common attribute of God in the Qur'an is being merciful, *Rahman* and *Rahim*. Everything that God does is based on His mercy. In the Qur'an, we're told God made mercy binding on Himself. So it's the one thing that limits God, that He has made binding upon Himself. So even hell is to help someone reform so that they can be in a better state, and we can try to apply that lesson to our lives in this life as well. Sometimes bad things happen, and we may think this is horrible, or we're getting punished for something, yet in reality it may be an opportunity for reflection, understanding, and change. Many times we have devastating things happen, and we think years down the road, "What a blessing!" What hell entails is based on the same concept.

We don't believe hell is forever. Now, the term used in the Qur'an is "a very long time," but then if you ask someone to put their finger in a fire, three seconds can feel like a lifetime. This is what hell really is: seeing a reflection of being detached from God. In our very materialistic world that may not seem like a lot, but in a spiritual sense, it could be the most painful thing to see how detached one can be from God. God says that He uses His hand to lift up people from hell. Obviously we don't think

God has physical hands—this is a metaphor. So hell will not be forever. There will be a point where Allah will take everyone out of hell, out of that spiritual condition, when they are ready to progress to the next stage.

And, just as hell is not physical burning, the joys of paradise are also symbolic or metaphorical. In many instances the verses in the Qur'an describing heaven actually start off by saying "a parable about paradise," and then it offers the examples. We are in a materialistic form right now. So we have to be given examples that we can relate to, and these are just illustrations of things that people find appealing in this world. They are just symbolic of spiritual rewards. The whole concept of *hur*, as we understand it, just means "pure," and its linguistic form is feminine. A lot of people think that this means you can have virgins in paradise and so forth. But if it's not a physical place, you don't gratify yourself with your physical desires. An analogy to better understand this concept may be the expression "virgin land." We don't mean anything sexual in this term. It means "pure." Likewise with regard to the hurs of paradise, these are simply pure blessings that one would receive. In verse 3:51, Prophet Jesus refers to his disciples as *hawariyyun*. The term is derived from the same root, *hur*. No one believes that Jesus called them his *virgins*; we believe that he called his disciples the *pure* ones. So this isn't just whitewashing this concept. When you look at the root word and how it's used in the Qur'an, it is clear it has no sexual connotation whatsoever.

Islam is a religion that's based less on rituals and more on the cultivation of one's soul. The Qur'an states that titles really have no significance. It doesn't matter if you're a Christian, a Jew, a Muslim, a Sabian,³ and so forth, but what is important is taking care of the orphan, and the widow, and being true to your promises, and praying. Belief is supposed to help facilitate the doing of that good.

In the Qur'an we're told that God breathes His spirit into each one of us, and that's what our soul is. So we all have the divine attributes within us. It's analogous to a seed. A seed has the potential to grow into a tree, but it has to be cultivated, and it needs certain ingredients in order to progress. It needs water, it needs sunlight, it needs cultivation, it needs proper minerals. Life offers these ingredients for the soul. It provides opportunities to cultivate your soul so that you can progress along this route to perfection.

Similarly, there are misunderstandings about women and their rights. In Islam, women should be free to become educated and to carry on any work they choose and live as equals to men in society. There is no practice of concubines in Islam. This is another concept that some Muslims believe in that has no basis in its authoritative sources. With regard to marriage, mutual consent is an essential aspect.

The status of women in a lot of Muslim-majority countries is second class. They're restricted in multiple ways, under the guise of religion. Much of this is cultural. The Qur'an does have rules for both men and women with regard to how to intermix in a society without falling into the trap that we see happening in most societies over time. There is absolutely no difference between the genders when it comes to one's spirituality. The highest form of divine gift is becoming close to God by God communicating with you. We have examples in the Qur'an of women receiving revelation. Mary the mother of Jesus received revelation intimating the birth of a child. The mother of Moses was given clear instructions about what to do with her child. So spiritually there's no difference whatsoever between men and women, but in many places in the world today this is neglected, and the focus is only on the externals. Dress becomes more about politics than piety. I'll give you a story. Many years ago I was in Turkey, in a mall in Istanbul, a city that I love. I saw women with the hijab in miniskirts, and I thought that was so strange! I'd never seen such a thing, and it made me realize that the hijab for many is a political statement about Muslim identity, especially in a country like Turkey when there is friction with a secular government. Wearing the hijab was a way of saying, "You can't force me not to wear this. I am a Muslim woman." But the real purpose of the hijab is modesty. Here is another example. I was in Florida once, in an area where there is a large Arab population. I would see a man and his wife walking together, and the wife would be completely covered in a burka, but the guy was in really short shorts and a sleeveless shirt, pretty openly looking around at all the other women, who were wearing very little. Islam is about modesty, and both sexes dressing appropriately and both sexes lowering their gaze. Again, the reason is so that one does not get caught up in some of the social ills that are destroying a lot of societies.

Here is a final point about prophethood. There will be no more prophets appearing, as Prophet Muhammad is the last prophet, but that does not mean that God has stopped speaking to humans. One of God's attributes is *kalam*, which means "speaking." There's a hadith from Sahih Bukhari saying that the Prophet said that prophethood has ended except for *mubashshirat*, "good news," meaning there will still be communication by God to people. As Prophet Muhammad is the last prophet, there's not going to be any new *law*. The Qur'an is the final revelation, and Prophet Muhammad is the universal prophet that everyone is supposed to try to use as their model and follow in terms of virtues. But that doesn't mean that people still do not receive some type of revelation from God. It can be through visions; it can be through dreams. Some saintly people hear the word of God. This is not a new concept. Established Sufi leaders who are recognized by the majority of traditional Muslims write about these saintly, nonprophetic revelations.

We believe that people can still attain this high spiritual state where they can receive communication from God. That doesn't make them prophets. There are Sufi terms relating to spiritual stages called *baruz*, or "manifestation of the Prophet," and *zill*, or "being a shadow of the Prophet." When you reach this high state of emulating the Holy Prophet, you lose your "self" in the person of the Holy Prophet. God then communicates with you, but it is not due to your person but rather due to the person of the Holy Prophet. You simply are a reflection of that great soul. And this is the status that the founder of the Ahmadiyya Movement reached, being a *baruzi-nabi* or *zilli-nabi*, a prophet in a metaphorical sense. Unfortunately, after the death of the founder of the Ahmadiyya Movement, a segment of the movement started claiming that the founder was an actual prophet in his own right. That is unfortunate because if you read his writings, what he states is no different from what you see many Sufi leaders in the past have written. But because of the interpretation that the Qadian section of the movement gives to his status, he is denounced as a heretic by some Muslims. But this is completely wrong, for he went to great pains to explain he was not claiming actual prophethood for himself. And most Muslims who denounce Ahmadis on this basis do not distinguish between the Lahore and the Qadian sections. It is ironic that the reason they condemn Ahmadis is the very reason for the split in the movement—the Lahore section was created in response to what it considered an erroneous un-Islamic belief in prophets being able to appear after the Prophet Muhammad that was being preached by the Qadian section.

One of the principal objectives of the reform advanced by Hazrat Mirza Ghulam Ahmad was to rebut the understanding that Islam is a violent religion. He called attention to the true character of Prophet Muhammad, as a mercy to all nations, as very caring and compassionate and loving. He also argued that all of the wars that the Prophet engaged in were defensive battles. And this is exactly what the Qur'an permits. When you are oppressed, and the example given in the Qur'an is when you see houses of worship—not only mosques, but churches, synagogues—being destroyed, then it is time to stand up and stop that type of injustice. But the Qur'an very clearly states that when the aggressor stops, you also must stop. When the other side inclines to peace, you must also incline, even if they're trying to trick you. You should never be the aggressor. One of the principal objectives of this reform was to show that Islam is not a violent religion. The Qur'an does not allow Muslims to engage in aggressive warfare. One of the biggest obstacles for the acceptance of Islam was that people, including many Muslims themselves, believed it to be a violent religion. Hazrat Mirza Ghulam Ahmad said that in these times the attacks on Islam are not physical. No one is attacking Muslims because of their religion per se. Yes, Muslims face a lot of problems in the world and many injustices, but it's not because of their religion. There are other reasons, whether it's land, resources, or politics. Today the attacks against Islam are through arguments. Whether it's attacking the Holy Prophet's character, whether it's exploiting certain verses of the Qur'an, the correct response is to defend yourself through literature, through argument, and reasoning. So he coined this phrase that this is not the time of jihad by the sword, but jihad by the pen.

So this movement has been engaged in this jihad through the pen for the past hundred years. We not only try to educate non-Muslims about the faith, but we also try to correct some of the misunderstood beliefs of our fellow Muslims. Despite being the victims of terrorist attacks in Pakistan and in other places, both segments of the Ahmadiyya Movement have refrained from responding with any type of revenge. A couple years ago, there were two Ahmadiyya mosques from the Qadian group that were attacked, and a hundred people were killed, but there was no thought of retribution. Ahmadis really do believe that the example of the Prophet Muhammad was to forgive and that you're successful not by engaging in some type of war and winning, but by transforming the hearts of others. The verse about the truce of Hudaybiyyah, in the Qur'an 48:1, calls it a great victory. What a concept! Not making someone subservient through your military force and then saying it's a victory, no. Coming up with a compromising deal and saying, we're going to settle and resolve things peacefully—that was the great victory. We believe that's the example we should be following.

— ١٢ —

Domestic Violence and Idealized Cosmologies
AYESHA S. CHAUDHRY

Ayesha S. Chaudhry blends personal narrative with acute insight into past and present commentary on the "wife-beating verse" of the Qur'an. Her keen perceptions on the interplay of tradition, "idealized cosmology," and authority within the community result in a fourfold scheme that acknowledges the complex relations of present and past. Her taxonomy of traditionalist, neo-traditionalist, progressive, and reformist invites readers to reflect on their own idealized cosmology and relationship to tradition and to reflect on the dynamics of interpretation that thoughtful believers bring to their Scripture.

Ayesha Chaudhry is a professor of Islamic studies and gender studies at the University of British Columbia. Her research interests include Islamic law, classical and modern exegesis of the Qur'an, and feminist hermeneutics. All these come to the fore in her book *Domestic Violence and the Islamic Tradition: Ethics, Law and the Muslim Discourse on Gender* (2014). Ayesha Chaudhry kindly spoke about her research that led to this important volume.

— ⚭ —

First Encounters with 4:34

The focus of my work has been the Qur'anic verse 4:34. I was introduced to this verse before I ever read the Qur'an. I was born in Canada, where my parents migrated from Pakistan. I heard this verse mentioned in religious settings where women would ask, "My husband beats me. Is there a verse that permits him to do this, and will I be sinning against God if I call the police to protect myself from domestic violence?" Husbands would argue, "Why are you calling me to account for hitting my wife? The Qur'an allows me to do that." So I knew from conversations in my religious community that this verse existed somewhere. It disturbed me as a child, but I did not really think about it much until later on.

The first time that I really read the verse was in high school. I had learned to recite the Qur'an in Arabic by the time I was five, but I did not learn its translation at that time. In grade 9, I bought a copy of the Qur'an in the shop at our mosque, mostly because I thought it was cute. "Cute" is not a word that is typically used to describe a Qur'an, but it looked cute to me. It was small and had gold-leaf edging around the pages, and it had parallel Arabic and English texts. I was reading this Qur'an when I came across Q. 4:34.

Here is a translation of the verse. I am supplying the Arabic for several words, along with the traditional rendering of those terms. In the modern period, these words have become highly contested amongst Muslims. In the precolonial period, however, these were ubiquitous interpretations that everyone agreed on.

Men are qawwamun *(in authority) over women because God has preferred some over others and because they spent of their wealth. Righteous women are obedient and guard in their husbands' absence what God would have them guard. Concerning those women from whom you fear* nushuz *(disobedience or rebellion), admonish them, and/or abandon them in bed, and/ or* wa-dribuhunna *(hit them). If they obey you, do not seek a means against them. God is most high, great.*

I was really disturbed by this verse the first time I read it. Muslims hold that the words of the Qur'an are literally the word of God, and it bothered me that God had said this. Religious scholars in my community would interpret this verse by assuring us that it was not as bad as it sounded. They claimed that the "Islamic tradition" had resolved any problems this verse raised.

The Islamic tradition that they referred to was always a disembodied, vague concept that was never clearly defined. It was, however, always precolonial. It was vast, full of amazing and illustrious scholars with encyclopedic memories of the Qur'an, with immense knowledge of prophetic practice (*hadith*), and of all the sciences and scholarly disciplines related to Islam. These scholars were persons of virtuous moral character. They debated and disagreed with one another about the interpretation of every verse, and they were able to maintain a multiplicity of opinions within their ranks, never imposing one interpretation on everyone else. The religious scholars in my community would say that any question about Q. 4:34 was answered in the precolonial period, but they would never say precisely which individuals formed the "Islamic tradition," what "answers" they had offered us, and why this verse should no longer pose an ethical challenge.

Muslim Feminist Interpretations

After these dissatisfying experiences in conversation with my community leaders about this verse, I went to university, where I started reading works by Muslim scholars who were committed to a gender-egalitarian vision of Islam. The scholars who especially influenced me were Leila Ahmed, Amina Wadud, and Asma Barlas. Both Amina Wadud and Asma Barlas, as well as other female scholars, were trying—as believers—to promote an egalitarian vision of Islam, much like feminist scholars in other patriarchal traditions who sought to remain members of religious traditions without ceding to patriarchal norms. Of course, Q. 4:34 would come up as a thorny problem in gender-egalitarian visions of Islam. Muslim scholars interpreted this verse in ways that tried to remove its patriarchal and violent connotations, so that it would no longer pose an ethical problem.

For example, the phrase "men are in authority over women" could be understood as a descriptive rather than prescriptive statement. In this case, it referred to conditions in seventh-century Arabia but not to contemporary society, in which men are no longer the sole breadwinners. Women are now members of the labor force all over the world, and so men are no longer in authority over women. These female scholars also note that the phrase "God has preferred some over others" is not specific. Rather than meaning that God has preferred men over women, it could mean that God has preferred some *people* over other *people*, regardless of gender. In the precolonial period, the term *nushuz* was understood to mean "disobedience or rebellion," but scholars promoting gender-egalitarian visions of Islam restricted the meaning to sexual disloyalty. "Admonish them" was understood as having a conversation between equals about the issue at hand. "Abandon them in bed" could be understood as "separating beds," which is not necessarily a hierarchical move; this could be a mutually agreed upon decision. The word *wa-dribuhunna* could not possibly mean "hit them" because that does not solve any problem. Since hitting cannot contribute to the resolution of marital conflict, the word must mean something else, such as "walk away from them" or even "have sex with them." The nature of Arabic words, as derived from three-letter roots, allows for malleable interpretations. While some Muslim scholars have been able to remove the violence from Q. 4:34, they cannot do this without breaking from the Islamic tradition.

I, however, had never heard nonviolent interpretations of Q. 4:34 until I studied the works of Muslim female scholars. In the mainstream Muslim communities that I interacted with, these female scholars had no traction. I was puzzled as to why

Muslims did not latch on to such nonviolent meanings for this verse. I was also interested in the competing claims about tradition: the community in which I had grown up said that the Islamic tradition was characterized by multiple viewpoints on this verse, but many Muslim feminists regarded the tradition as misogynist, patriarchal, and uninterested in an egalitarian vision. So I took these nonviolent interpretations to the scholars in my community and asked them what they thought. I asked them if the tradition was really as vast, complex, and sophisticated as I had heard, or if it actually offers us very little in terms of nonviolent readings of Q. 4:34. The response was always vehemently negative: "These women do not know what they are talking about. They do not understand Islam. They have a shallow understanding of the Islamic tradition, which is pristine and uncorrupted. The tradition is so valuable, why would they want to cut themselves off from it? By doing so, they have no authority."

The Precolonial Tradition

During my doctoral work, I decided to study the tradition to discover what it had to say about Q. 4:34. I wanted to discover the promised multiplicity of voices and to share it with others like myself. In particular, I examined Qur'anic exegesis and Islamic legal works.

Qur'an commentaries were usually multivolume endeavors, in which scholars would consider every word in the Qur'an and offer multiple interpretations, including their own. They would consider linguistic, social-historical, legal, mystical, and other perspectives on each verse. I examined these commentaries and legal works to uncover the various conceptions of an ideal marriage and the resolution to marital conflicts. I restricted my study to Arabic sources because this was the language of the scholarly elite, and the sources I studied spanned from the ninth to the fifteenth century, covering vast geographic and historical contexts.

To my dismay, which may suggest my naïveté, I found that these sources were almost completely uniform in their patriarchy. Precolonial scholars agreed that men were in authority over women because God had preferred men over women. They offered religious, social-historical, cultural, and philosophical reasons for men's superiority, saying things like men were better than women based on essential and nonessential characteristics. Men are more intelligent and physically stronger. The legal witness of one man equals the witness of two women. Men can marry four women, but a woman can marry only one man. Men receive double the inheritance of women. Men go to war, while women have to stay at home. Men lead Friday prayers, but women cannot. Men are better at archery and horsemanship. Men have beards and turbans. There was some disagreement as to whether some of these arguments were valid, but there was no dispute about men's superiority. They understood the phrase "righteous women are obedient" to mean "obedient to God and to their husbands." A woman obeyed and pleased God by obeying and pleasing her husband.

Nushuz literally means "rising," and was understood by these scholars to mean any sort of rising by a wife, out of her place in the marital hierarchy. These scholars recommended phrases of admonishment, such as "Fear God, and remember my rights over you," which did not invite a conversation between a wife and husband as equal partners. The phrase that appears later in this verse, "if they obey you, do not seek a means against them," was seen as emphasizing that nushuz generally referred to disobedience. Many scholars understood nushuz to be sexual disobedience, referring to occasions when the women did not want to have sex. This led to a problem with the next imperative, "abandon them in bed." In sexually abandoning wives who did not want sex anyway, men would only be punishing themselves and giving their wives exactly what they wanted. One scholar, al-Tabari, solved this problem by saying that the second imperative was ordering men to tie their wives in bed, like a camel, and then have sex with them. Another scholar, al-San'ani, concluded that this phrase actually means the opposite of what it seems: instead of "abandon them in bed," it means "call them to bed." This is important methodologically for modern scholars because it shows how the tradition itself was open to nonliteral interpretations of the Qur'an.

As for the phrase *wa-dribuhunna*, no one disagreed about its violent connotations. Discipline of one's wife was viewed as a basic marital right for men. Although there were ethical debates about this prescription, they were about the procedure and extent of permissible hitting. Men were exhorted not to break their wives' bones, or leave bruises or open wounds. According to the legal tradition, there was no retaliation in marriage. Wives could not sue their husbands for abuse unless they could show broken bones or open wounds as evidence of abuse. Even if a man were to kill his wife, many jurists argued that he was not liable with his life but only had to pay blood money, which is a lesser punishment. The same applied to slaves and children. This mindset is far from extinct. Very recently in Saudi Arabia, a man tortured and killed his five-year-old daughter, and the court fined him *diya* (blood money) rather than requiring capital punishment. This penalty reflects classical Islamic legal tradition and a precolonial cosmology.

I was disappointed to find these attitudes in the precolonial Islamic tradition. Some people might regard my disappointment as naïve: How could I have imagined that this tradition, steeped in patriarchy, would promote an egalitarian vision of Islam? Yet, as a member of the believing community, I wanted to find someone from that glorious past who was opposed to husbands hitting their wives. I wanted there to be someone who was influenced by the strong women around him and would say, "No, you cannot hit your wives." I felt dismayed; I wanted my tradition to have been better than that. I wanted to reconcile the modern concern for nonviolent interpretations of the verse with premodern voices, which did not offer anything helpful toward a gender-egalitarian vision of Islam. What were the reasons for the radical differences between these two conversations? Why weren't Muslim scholars who were committed to gender-egalitarian visions of Islam more influential within the mainstream Muslim community?

Idealized Cosmologies

I find that there are two different idealized cosmologies at work in the pre- and postcolonial conversations. An idealized cosmology is an imagination of what the world should look like, a view of the world that does not necessarily reflect the social-historical context. Of course, the two are related, but an idealized cosmology is concerned with how the world *should* be, not how it *is*. In the precolonial period, I found a single idealized cosmology: there was a hierarchal arrangement which was crowned by God first, and was followed by husbands, and then wives. The relationship of wives to God, therefore, was mediated by husbands. Husbands were "demigods" or "shadow deities" to their wives, and wives pleased God by pleasing their husbands. Husbands regulated the moral behavior of their wives. When women committed nushuz and rose out of their place, they violated this idealized cosmology and had to be kept in line. Thus, husbands had disciplinary authority over their wives, and were provided with tools to enforce that authority. One of those tools was hitting. In this context, the precolonial conversations around Q. 4:34 begin to make much more sense. There is no interruption of expectation. Legal and exegetical explanations support this cosmological framework. The scope of the ethical conversations reflects and adheres to this cosmology.

To examine the postcolonial period, I studied materials in Arabic, Urdu, and English. I chose English because it is a global language spoken by many Muslims around the world, Arabic because it is still a scholarly language in the Muslim world, and Urdu because it is the largest Islamicate language, understood by 500 million Muslims around the world. I considered printed sources, including the Internet, as well as audio and video sources. Together, these sources represent a wide geographic range.

I found that in the modern period, a new egalitarian idealized cosmology has arisen and taken hold among many Muslims. The postcolonial idealized cosmology is still hierarchical in that God is at the top, but husbands and wives are now considered to be on equal footing with one another. They both have independent relationships to God. They can aid each other in getting closer to God, but they do not regulate or have disciplinary authority over each other. It therefore makes no sense for either of them to have the right to hit the other. Because modern Muslims already believe this, when they come to the Qur'anic text, their expectation of a just God is interrupted by a violent interpretation of this verse. Their ethical conversations, therefore, are not about the procedure for hitting one's wife, as they were in the precolonial period; they are about why husbands have disciplinary power at all. The idealized cosmologies of the pre- and postcolonial scholars are radically different, and this accounts for why the ethical conversations are so dissimilar.

The Egalitarian-Authoritative Dilemma: Four Modern Approaches

In addition to the matter of cosmology, there is the issue of who gets to speak with authority among Muslims and how. I believe that Muslims who promote a gender-egalitarian Islam must necessarily confront the egalitarian-authoritative dilemma. If someone wants to promote a new vision of Islam, the way to do so with authority among Muslims is to show that this position is linked to the pristine, uncorrupted precolonial Islamic tradition. But if that tradition is unashamedly patriarchal, how can someone promote a new egalitarian vision of Islam? One approach is to root oneself in the precolonial tradition but then compromise on the egalitarianism: "The genders are not really equal. They are more complementary. It is better to think of the genders as apples and oranges. Both are fruit, but very different. Women are better at nurturing; men are better at aggressive activities." The other approach is not to compromise on the egalitarianism, but then one loses connection with Islamic tradition, and the result is that one loses authority in the very community that one is trying to reform.

Muslim scholars deal with this dilemma in different ways. I have identified four modern approaches to Q. 4:34, which I call traditionalist, neotraditionalist, progressive, and reformist. I divide them into these categories based on their answers to three questions: Is it ever ethically good to hit your wife? Which idealized cosmology is ultimately privileged, the patriarchal or the egalitarian? Is religious authority rooted in the precolonial Islamic tradition, or is it moved to the living community?

The traditionalist approach answers the first question positively. It is ethically good to hit one's wife for disciplinary purposes. The Qur'an is the literal word of God, and God would never prescribe what is unjust. If one reads the Qur'an and finds something that is unjust, the problem is with the reader's perception of justice. So hitting one's wife for disciplinary purposes is ethically good, and Muslims should not be ashamed of this, unless such hitting extends to the extremes of broken bones and open wounds. However, although some precolonial scholars considered hitting with a whip or stick appropriate, some traditionalist scholars restrict the hitting to a toothbrush (*miswak*). Hitting with a miswak was a minority opinion in the precolonial period, and though it is interpreted to mean "toothbrush" in the modern period, my research indicates that it likely meant a "switch." Traditionalists privilege a patriarchal cosmology, but unlike in the precolonial period, they feel the need to defend and justify this cosmology against an egalitarian one. They claim, "Men are better than women because they are more intelligent. Of course there are exceptions to this rule, but in general the rule applies to everybody." In their minds, there is an interlocutor who disagrees with them from an egalitarian perspective. Despite this internal dialogue, religious authority for them remains rooted entirely in the precolonial tradition, which supports their own authority within the community.

Neotraditionalists argue that it can be ethically good to hit one's wife for disciplinary purposes, but they try to restrict the beating as much as possible, even making it symbolic. They say that a husband can hit his wife only under severe and very restricted circumstances, but they do not explain what those circumstances are. Hitting is meant to be symbolic and can only be carried out with something like a toothbrush or perhaps a rose. Neotraditionalists privilege a patriarchal cosmology over an egalitarian one, but this is an extremely uncomfortable fit. They tend not to dig in their heels as much as traditionalists, but they also do not acknowledge that men and women are equal. The husband still figures into the woman's relationship with God; she does not have an independent relationship. Religious authority for them is still rooted in the precolonial Islamic tradition, but that tradition is made to look more harmonious with the modern world.

Progressive Muslim scholars argue that it is never good to hit one's wife, not even symbolically. They privilege an egalitarian idealized cosmology over a patriarchal one, but this is also an uneasy fit because they root their religious authority in the precolonial Islamic tradition. However, since scholars in the precolonial period uniformly upheld the right of husbands to physically discipline their wives, progressive scholars engage the precolonial Islamic tradition in new ways. Often this involves misrepresenting the precolonial Islamic tradition—making it sound more egalitarian than it really was—in order to make their case for a more egalitarian vision of Islam.

Reformist scholars agree with the progressives that it is never ethically good to hit one's wife. They differ from progressives in that they privilege an egalitarian idealized cosmology over a patriarchal one without qualifications. Religious authority for them is moved from the precolonial tradition to the living community that is interacting with and living with the consequences of various interpretations of the Qur'anic text. Whereas a traditionalist scholar might say to a Muslim feminist, "You are Western or modern and therefore corrupt," reformist scholars own those identities. They readily acknowledge that they are modern and Western. They say, "The Qur'an is a universal text and as such should speak to us." They root their interpretations in those subjectivities and do not pretend to be otherwise.

One of the primary conclusions of my study is that religious texts do not have meanings independent of the communities with which they interact. Recall what I said about al-San'ani interpreting "abandon them in bed" to mean "call them to bed." Methodologically, reformist scholars are probably doing something similar, taking the Qur'anic text and mapping it onto their own social-historical context, in order to find meanings that are relevant to their own communities. In doing so, however, they are breaking from the content of the tradition. I think that progressives and reformists do this mapping with greater self-consciousness than was likely or even necessary in the past because they are working within the egalitarian-authoritative dilemma. Reformist scholars recognize that although the pre-colonial tradition may have value in the discussion of other topics, it does not have anything constructive to offer when it comes to gender-egalitarian visions of Islam. They therefore give themselves permission to break from that tradition on matters of egalitarianism—or, to put it another way, permission to *continue* the tradition, which need not be limited to the precolonial period. For them this rich, multiply opinioned tradition that is held to be so complex and sophisticated on many topics is actually flat, monotonous, and unhelpful for devising a gender-egalitarian vision of Islam. If, however, the "Islamic tradition" is extended to include modern Muslim conversations, then the tradition becomes enriched. Progressive and reformist scholars differ with regard to how they seek authority. Reformists are willing to move the center of that authority to the living community, while progressives are really doing the same thing, but doing it by appealing to the tradition. Because progressive scholars appeal to tradition, they sometimes have to be creative with it, even to the point of misrepresenting it.

This fourfold conceptual pattern can be mapped onto other issues of debate among contemporary Muslims as well, such as hijab or jihad. I believe that it is a useful heuristic device, if applied flexibly, as a way of expressing the range of Muslim opinions on various topics. I find that it works much better than a simple division into liberal and conservative Muslims, which misses the subtle combinations of relationship to past and present that the four-part scheme offers. It can help us witness the performance of the polysemic nature of the Qur'an alongside the multiple ways in which Muslims can be believers and adherents to the same religious tradition.

— ١٢ —

Divine Care, Dignity, and Cultural Norms
SU'AD ABDUL KHABEER

Rooted in the African American experience and in her identity as a woman, Su'ad Abdul Khabeer brings the realities of racism and sexism to her interpretations of the Qur'an. As a result, her readings emphasize honesty, pain, dignity, liberation, racial justice, and kindness. She challenges definitions of Islamic ideals that exclude blackness, and she identifies bigotry as *kufr*, a form of disbelief that denies gratitude to God. Despite all difficulties, her words reveal a hopefulness of spirit.

Su'ad Abdul Khabeer is a professor of anthropology at Purdue University. As a lifelong Muslim and a social scientist, she brings stimulating perspectives to her faith and her community. As we met, the depth of her commitment to Islam was palpable, yet it was expressed in a new idiom, not dominated by the traditional model of jurisprudence. Her powerful expression of the personal and social dimensions of her faith felt like a glimpse into an emerging articulation of American Islam that will shape the years to come.

— ‏الله‎ —

I chose three verses. The first is Sura 28, verse 13.

This verse follows the story of Moses. Pharaoh has been killing the men, keeping the women; Moses' mother is concerned and doesn't know what to do, but she's inspired to put him in the river. His sister then goes after him and recommends to Pharaoh's family, "I know someone who could be a wet nurse for this child." The verse that I've chosen reads:

So we restored him to his mother, so that her eye might be comforted, and not grieve, and so that she might know that the promise of God is true, though most of them do not know.

I'm struck by this verse on a number of levels: as an individual believer, but also as a Muslim woman who exists in a world in which the discourse is "Islam versus women."

As an individual believer, I am moved by how monumental it is that God restored Moses to his mother so that she might be comforted and wouldn't have grief. To me, this woman represents the least of us. Aside from the fact that she is the mother of Moses, we know almost nothing about her—not even her name—but God makes a substantial effort to return her son to her. In the Islamic tradition, God is larger than everything you can imagine: the Creator, without beginning or end. In comparison, we as individuals are insignificant. *Yet*, we're significant enough for Him to care about whether we are happy or sad. That's phenomenally powerful, the notion of God loving you, caring about you, and being concerned about you, even though you are nothing compared to His everything.

As a Muslim woman, I think that this passage is also significant given the popular conversation that argues that women don't have rights in Islam. However, this was a *woman* that God decided He wanted to make happy. In the narrative of this prophet and of his message of liberation to the children of Israel, this woman's happiness is important enough that God attends to it. I am reminded of the story of Mary in childbirth in Sura Maryam (19:23), where she says, *yallaytani mittu qabla hadha*, which literally means "I wish I had died." Then she is told not to worry, and God provides water and dates for her. As in the story of Moses' mother, this narrative validates pain as something that is real, something that hurts. It's not as though she suffers through the pain and then announces that she is on a higher plane. No, she cries out, "This is hurting!" So the Qur'an validates the fact that we have pain and says it's okay for us to acknowledge that pain.

The Euro-American tradition has this weird notion of motherhood where the woman is supposed to do everything: clean, cook, raise the children, everything! One person is not meant to do this job alone, but that's how we envision it, so when a women can't do it all, we think she has somehow failed. This verse about Mary acknowledges that motherhood is hard, being a parent is painful, and that's okay. Ultimately, she gets respite. She gets what she needs. God responds to her because of her character and devotion. Her mother dedicated her to service in the temple, before Mary was born, before her mother knew that her child was a girl. So I think all those instances of women's prayers being answered speak to the individual experience of suffering and pain and difficulty; it is real, people experience it, and you don't have to pretend like it doesn't hurt. Your pain and suffering don't go unanswered or unnoticed, even though you're such an insignificant being in comparison to the Creator. These stories serve a variety of purposes, and they bring up questions about the centrality and the importance of women to God, and to the Islamic tradition. When we think about figures of women in the Qur'an, I see them as emblematic of this individual experience of pain and suffering, but they also speak back to a notion in which women are seen as secondary, or somehow inferior to men in Islam. So it's hard.

This verse about God's care for the mother of Moses fits into that wider sense of affirmation of life, and affirmation of women's value, dignity, worth. I've always been struck by that story and how it relates to how we think about God and how other people think that Muslims think about God. Some of the myths and stereotypes about Muslims emphasize a uniquely harsh, conservative, angry demeanor. Muslim-rage. Of course, for me, as a black woman, all of my various rage issues run parallel to one another. Speaking sarcastically, for all the rage I have—my Latino-rage, my black-rage, my Muslim-rage, my woman-rage—it's no wonder I can't get anything done! So if the Muslim community is enraged, then they must serve an enraged or vengeful God, right? But I think these instances, particularly the one with Musa's mother, speak to sensitivity, kindness, and intimacy rather than rage. When you love or care about someone, you know their intimate needs, and you respond to them. This feeling of intimacy is true in my own experience as well: I don't feel a victim of rage when I'm done praying. I may feel inadequate in a spiritual sense vis-à-vis God, but not a victim of anyone's rage.

I think the possibility of this intimacy with God can be elusive because we're distracted by so many things. It's often hard to maintain that kind of close connection, but the option of having it is always there. There's a verse in the second sura of the Qur'an that says, "If my servant asks about me, I am near." Someone else I know once translated this verse from the Arabic as "Because as immediately as you need me, I'm there." This interpretation reflects that closeness.

This divine permission to express pain relates to my research into hip-hop as an expressive culture. It has been motivated, in all of its iterations, from the basest to the loftiest, by speaking truth to power. In part, it's about identifying and acknowledging your pain and suffering, and not apologizing for it. I can see a way in which marginalized, oppressed people have had religion used as a tool to placate them—"You'll get it better in the next life." That may be true, but Allah also says in the Qur'an not to give up your share of this world either. In the Qur'an, the Prophet teaches a prayer that says, "Give us the best in this life and the best in the hereafter. Protect us from the punishment of the fire." It requires a delicate balance to want your share of the world but not be completely consumed by it, but that's part of who we are. So thinking about liberation or suffering in hip-hop is thinking about how to talk about your pain, how to be honest about it, how to illuminate and identify it, how to put it out there and not ignore it or cover it up. Your suffering is part of your experience and identity, and a major emphasis of hip-hop as expressive culture is about announcing, "I'm here, I'm not invisible, I exist, I take up space, *I'm here.*" So, in that way, I can see a connection between hip-hop and this verse from the Qur'an.

Another passage I want to talk about is Sura 60, verse 5.

Our Sovereign, do not make us a trial for those who disbelieve, and forgive us. You are the all-mighty, the all-wise.

The Arabic word *kufr* is about peoples' disbelief, but disbelief is about denying truth, and it's about ingratitude. This is because to be a disbeliever means you're not grateful for what God has given you. And it also means you deny the truth that He exists. Racism and bigotry are kufr because they deny not just the truth that God exists, but also what have been God's laws about the equality of human beings—that we are all born and created with the same capacity to be good, to be bad, to be who we are as created beings. If you deny that truth, then you're also denying God, because it's His truth. I think this verse is a prayer of the people. It's the prayer of Abraham, talking to his father before they tried to burn him. This is a prayer that Muslims in the United States should take seriously and incorporate into their lives because what they're praying for is to become something that people who deny truth can't trifle with, or dominate and control. All these people, who are trolling absurd ideas about Islam and Muslims, are doing is kufr. We need to acknowledge that bigotry as what it is, and not kufr in that they're not Muslim, because that's beside the point. The point is how dangerous that kind of kufr is for us, in terms of our ability to exist and be who we are. So we need to identify it for what it is, and then ask God for help, because ultimately we can't control anything. We can put up billboards, and we can hold press conferences, and we can do other things to respond to this vitriol; but ultimately, because God controls everything anyway, you have to ask Him to do this service for you, to help you in this way. For me, it was a powerful moment to recognize that there is always a spiritual level to all the things that we deal with on the nonspiritual plane. Yet there's a way in which, since we believe in God, all the press releases in the world aren't going to do anything because they usually consist of the white-American prototype talking about this brown-Muslim mad person, asking, "Why do they hate us?" But when *I* ask why they hate us, I'm wondering, "Why does this white-American prototype hate *us*?" They hate us because we're not white, we're not Christian, and we're never going to be, so press releases be damned. That's not going to do anything for us anyway.

So there's a level on which you have to identify racism for what it is. It's denying truth, it's denying God, it's denying His love, and you have to ask Him to fortify you as you come up against it, because you will come up against it. This kufr can be really pervasive, and it's fueled by ignorance, but it's not just people don't know who Muslims are; there are power interests who are invested in creating these hierarchies and binaries in order to maintain a particular kind of status quo. Therefore, by revealing the way in which the Qur'an here is speaking to the condition that American Muslims find themselves in (that is, that racism and bigotry are kufr), you also then are identifying how the experience of American Muslims in the twenty-first-century United States runs parallel with experiences of other groups who are Muslim too. I'm black, and we've been Muslim for a long time, but these struggles against white supremacy are connected, so what American Muslims of all ethnic or racial backgrounds are experiencing is connected to what African Americans, Latinos, and Asians all experienced. So the Qur'an in this way, to me, is saying that prayer in that sense is not just a prayer that Muslims can make. It's a prayer that a lot of people can make because ultimately we are agents and subjects, not objects, and our struggle is to resist the denial of our humanity.

The last one I chose is Sura al-Hashr, which is chapter 59, verse 10. This is more what I think about a lot in my work dealing with hip-hop because part of what my scholarship has been focusing on is the way in which young American Muslims use hip-hop as a way to be Muslim. One of the primary techniques or results of using hip-hop to be Muslim that I see is this notion of "Muslim Cool." This idea of Muslim Cool is a response to white-American normativity, as well as the ethnoreligious norms of the South Asian and Middle Eastern Muslim communities. Blackness becomes a tool or medium through which to construct a way of being Muslim that pushes back against these kinds of norms. What's significant about that for me is that the American Muslim community struggles with a number of things, one of them being antiblack racism within the community itself. Part of what makes Muslim Cool powerful is that it flips a dominant narrative that seeks to keep blackness at a distance, keep it away in order to be both upwardly mobile and spiritually or religiously authentic. The further away you are from blackness, the more successful you are as an American and the more authentic you are as a Muslim. This belief is the result of antiblack racism; Muslim Cool is a response to that.

I picked this verse because the verses preceding it talk about the relationship between the *ansar* and the *muhajirun*. When the Muslims move from Mecca to Medina, the ansar (helpers) are the people who live in Medina, and the muhajirun (emigrants) are the people who left Mecca. The relationship between them develops, and the ansar open up their homes, and the two peoples welcome each other, saying, "You are now part of my family." They establish institutions to create bonds between people so they may see each other as brothers and sisters, not strangers. So the people who open their homes and the people who left Mecca out of conscience for God are blessed:

And those who come after them pray, "Our Sustainer, forgive us as well as those of our brothers who preceded us in faith, and do not let our hearts be angry toward those who believe. Our Sustainer, indeed you are kind and merciful."

Muhammad Asad, citing Razi,[4] notes that "those who come after them" refers to all those who attain belief in the Qur'an and its Prophet. When I think about this verse, it reminds me of the relationship between these American Muslims, primarily African American Muslims and Muslims from South Asia and the Middle East. We don't have exactly the ansar and muhajirun's relationship in the same way, but the idea is that Muslims from South Asia and the Middle East, in a way, preceded us African American Muslims: whether we're reclaiming or reverting to our original faith, we're rediscovering Islam while they already have it. Yet, when they come to the United States and we get mixed up in all these U.S. racial logics, it results in animosity and enmity between different groups of people. So I think this prayer is really significant for American Muslims to think about because it's imperative to resolve these kinds of racial issues. We have to identify this as something that's real; we can't pretend like it's not happening. We have to respond to it, referring to or asking God to help us remove those kinds of feelings because those kinds of things emerge or come in those conflicts.

This subject is dear to my heart and close to my own work. Muslim Cool itself is positionality. It's being an American Muslim responding to these cultural norms—white-American normativity, and the ethnoreligious Islam of South Asian and Middle Eastern Muslim communities—and it's grounded in blackness and the history that Islam and hip-hop have with each other. I and many others have argued that from its inception, hip-hop has been informed by Black Islam. "Black Islam" is a term that I use to describe iterations of Islam in African American communities, whether that's the Nation of Islam or the Five Percenters or Sunni or Shi'a Islam. The major takeaway is a sense of consciousness and knowledge of self, and an ethical positionality vis-à-vis the Divine, other people, and the natural world. That is in hip-hop music because of the influence of Black Islam on the progenitors and communities that developed hip-hop. So, knowing that, it's not really surprising that hip-hop would speak to young Muslims today, right? Hip-hop music deals with the same ethic that they are also being taught to understand in their religious community, but it surprises people because they have these images of who they think people are, or what they think is possible. And it's not uncontested. Brother Ali, a hip-hop artist who's also a friend of mine, really believes that all the debates about music and whether or not it is appropriate for Muslims are really a fear of blackness. These debates are older than America and older than the formation of blackness in our modern period. It is a fear of black people and desire to distance yourself from blackness that leads people to dictate what kinds of music and images are allowed or not. There's a scene in the film *Deen Tight* by Mustafa Davis where Amir Sulaiman, an African American Muslim who's a poet and emcee, talks about how when you go to shows, they tell you, "You can't put your hands like this, you can't go like this, and you can't move like that." He says it's as if what makes you black is *haram*. They're policing your body, not just policing what you say and what instruments you use, but they're policing the very way you move. The ways you use and move your body are very much natural to you and culturally appropriate, but to some people, certain movements are associated with blackness and therefore we want to distance ourselves from them.

Muslim Cool is really implicated in all of these different issues of race and culture. Because the practitioners of Muslim Cool aren't just Black Muslims, but they're also Pakistani and Arab American, there are further questions of cultural appropriation and minstrelsy and how to mitigate and mediate that, given that we live with this history and we can't escape it. It is what it is, but how do I not pretend like it doesn't bother me when someone Pakistani says, "Yo, bro"? I say, "Let's talk about why that bothers me, and figure out how and when it will not bother me. Because when you know that black people are more than caricatures and when you're as committed to my liberation as I am, then it won't matter as much anymore."

— 11 —

Belief and Deed
RASHAD ABDUL RAHMAAN

Like Su'ad Abdul Khabeer, Rashad Abdul Rahmaan reads the Qur'an centered in the African American experience. This is reflected in his discussion of orphans, of the need for education, and of slavery.

Rashad Abdul Rahmaan is an imam and serves a Muslim school in Milwaukee, Wisconsin. When he was a young man, Imam Warith Deen Mohammed, the leader of the many predominantly African American mosques, recognized his talents and chose him for special instruction. Imam Abdul Rahmaan is also very active in interfaith dialogue in numerous settings.

Before turning to his chosen Qur'anic verse, Rashad Abdul Rahmaan spoke briefly on the relationship of the spiritual heirs of Warith Deen Mohammed to the classical sources of Islamic thought. His words help to clarify his understanding of how the Qur'an speaks to contemporary concerns.

Many Muslims take as their starting point the classical orthodox Sunni tradition, while we begin particularly with the teachings of Imam W. Deen Mohammed, whose works include commentary on the Qur'an, theology, philosophy, and religious law. There is much agreement between his ideas and the classical tradition, but Imam Mohammed went further in that he spoke specifically to our time and circumstances as descendants of slaves, African Americans, and converts. Consequently there are dimensions to our perception of the religion that we don't find addressed by our scholars of the past. We don't reject searching out what our best minds in the *ummah* have had to say, but I think we have a more liberal approach to their ideas, and we don't see ourselves as being bound to this or that position. We see ourselves as a new group of thinkers for Islam in the world, yet we're members of the international ummah of our Prophet Muhammad.

We find ourselves in very different circumstances in modern America. What was thought and written by Muslim thinkers five hundred or one thousand years ago is not sufficient for us to root our lives in and give us the direction that we need today. This is not only the opinion of our community. Many Muslim leaders in the world are now advocating that Muslims look again into their knowledge sources and rethink their positions in light of all of the changes that have occurred for the world community. The classical tradition was born out of the effort to understand and live Islam properly in past circumstances. Those scholars were true to the spirit of the religion when they were thinking freely, and we believe that this should continue.

— ‏آل‎ —

Righteousness does not consist in turning your face toward the east or the west. The truly righteous is the one who believes in God and the Last Day, in the angels, the books, and the prophets. The righteous person gives from one's wealth, in love, to relatives, to orphans, to those in need, to the traveler, and to those who ask. The righteous one frees the neck of those in bondage, and establishes the ritual prayer and gives the required charity. The righteous fulfill their covenants that they make. They are patient in hardship, in adversity, and times of distress. They are the ones who are truthful and regardful of God. (2:177)

I chose this verse because it really highlights for us what Muslim life, or any religious life, should be, as God wants it to be. We see the Qur'an not as a book that is separate from what was given to the Jews or the Christians. We see Scripture as one stream. And God tells us in our own holy book, the Qur'an, that the Qur'an itself is a continuation, a correction, and a completion of what was revealed before. So we believe that the essential purity and light of what we call the Bible today—in Qur'anic language, Torah and *injil* (Gospel), one stream of light—and we are not to separate ourselves from the People of the Book, though in practice that hasn't been respected by all Muslims. But the spirit of the Qur'an is that we are one in our focus with the children of Abraham. Abraham we call our second father, meaning that he's the one who was blessed to see where the human family is to go. Adam is our first father because he's the flesh, the natural life. He is the pure, innocent nature that God created. Abraham is our second father, the intellect or the enlightenment of that nature. So that's why our religion is after the *milla* or religion of Ibrahim (Abraham). *Milla* has been translated various ways: religion, way, etc. We would also say "hope." It was the hope or the direction that Abraham wanted for humanity. Imam Warith Deen Mohammed taught it to us this way: the Qur'an is *tafsir*, or commentary, on all that came before. God has explained this by saying the Qur'an is what makes clear. The Qur'an is an explanation, a *hadith*, a report. We would say that it is the clarification and explanation of what came before, to the People of the Book. God is addressing the concept of righteousness in this verse, first saying what righteousness is not, and then explaining what righteousness is. It is not righteousness that you turn your faces in the direction of the east or the west. True righteousness is not religious rituals alone, such as prayer, washing, or other formalities. Righteousness is deeper than that. This has been a problem for human beings, as we see when we look at the history of religious communities. Even today we see that religious life has been reduced in many instances to forms without substance, like an orange with no juice inside of it, just the dried flesh. We don't like to attack any particular group, but we know that there are some denominations in all three Abrahamic faiths, as well as other faiths, that put emphasis on chanting or praying, and the people don't even know what the leader is saying. In the Muslim world, it's very common to emphasize recitation of Qur'an without emphasis on understanding and applying it. When we recite our prayer, we're reciting Qur'an, so what's the use of reciting the words five times daily if the Muslim society itself is not a reflection of the word of God? This is empty ritual. God is saying that the ritual for us is just discipline, to establish it for the conscious mind so we can regulate our life and to put our focus where it should be. The substance of the ritual is when we disperse. God says in the Qur'an that when the call to prayer is given on Friday, leave off your business, leave off your interests in the world, and rush to the remembrance of God; and then when the prayer is concluded, go back out to the world. So this verse addresses the *Jumah* prayer. However, it's also addressing the nature of ritual worship itself, which is to give us the tools, the spirit, and the correct thinking so that we can go back into the world and express the content of those rituals.

So what then is righteousness? First, God talks about belief and then about works. This was given to the People of the Book in earlier times: faith without good works is dead. The Qur'an confirms what was given to the People of the Book. Almost every time God says, "Those who believe," He follows it with "and those who work righteous deeds." This verse contains all the articles of faith given by our Prophet, with the exception of one: to believe in God and the Last Day. That means not only that we believe that there is a Cause behind the creation and an Authority over the creation. But we also believe that we're responsible to that Authority. The Last Day is when we face the Supreme Authority over the heavens and the earth and account for how we lived. As God tells us in our holy book, "Is not the creation as well as the command for God?" (7:54). Who could guide us better into the fullness of our creation than the One who created us?"

There are other beliefs. We believe in the angels, in the books, and in all the prophets. We can never say "our messengers" because we did not give the message. God gives the message. But we can say "our prophets" because we believe that the prophetic nature is inherent in every human being. All of us have the ability to tap into that depth of our own self, but only a few of us are blessed to do it. So when we say, "Our Prophet," we are acknowledging the nature that is a part of our own makeup.

We believe in the angels, in the books, in the prophets. There's a logic to this progression. We believe in God, whose will is operative in every aspect of the creation. Angels are the carriers or the keepers of the will of God. Some Islamic scholars will even say the forces of nature are actually the activity of the angels, keeping the creation under God's command. Angels perform different functions. The angel Jibril was the medium through which revelation came to the prophets. So angels are also messengers. When Mary, the mother of Christ Jesus, peace be upon her and him, was growing under the care of Zakariya, the angel came to her with a message announcing the birth of a man-child who would be a leader for their people. The same happened to the mother of Moses: angels came to deliver the message that the child that she was going to bear would also be a leader and a liberator for the people. So the angels are the medium through which the will of God is expressed throughout the universe.

We believe in the books. Human beings are really the only creatures that have the freedom to get outside of the will of God, at least to some degree. Now, some Muslim leaders will say that jinn also have that ability, and we do accept that, but that needs explanation. Some believe, and we accept, that jinn begin in human form. So human beings have free will. Everything else in the cosmos—the sun, the animals, the plants, even the angels—can only remain within the parameters that God has set for them. Man is free, so when he loses contact with the will of God for his life, he needs guidance, revelation, light, and redemption. So that's why the books come next in the list: the will of God for man comes in the book.

The will of God for man is first in his own nature. We don't believe that God has to impart revelation for man to be good. We believe he's born pure. But in time, circumstances and natural forces will eventually put it upon the spirit of man to cry out to God for help and seek God as a higher authority. So the books are sent to lead by the light of revelation. Revelation opens up to him not only what he has lost but also what he never would understand if God had not come to him and assisted him. But we can't just have it as a teaching, we also need human models to express and actualize those teachings. So the belief in the books leads to the belief in the prophets, who not only receive the revelation but also exemplify the message. So we believe Jesus Christ not only taught God's will, but also he was the embodiment of it. We believe the same is for Moses, and for Muhammad, whom we see as the last or seal of the prophets. And again, we wouldn't say "last messenger" because angels are messengers. Messages can also be given in dreams, and in other ways.

The prophetic nature really represents the unfolding of the plan of God for man. Man begins as a seed in Adam, and the growth and development of that seed into a full-blown tree are the different stages in one prophetic movement. So we don't say our prophet is superior to any other. These are stages in one movement, just like the growth of human life. The potential for Muhammad's prophetic reality already existed in Adam; it just wasn't time for his expression to come about. But in time it did.

Each prophet is a stage in the movement toward a particular destiny. The destiny is the ideal, perfected human life in society. So the Prophet himself is a model, not just for our individual behavior, but for the promised human community. The People of the Book were given different ways of expressing this vision. We have the language of a land flowing with milk and honey, of the kingdom of heaven, of a city of light. All of this points to the particular destiny that the prophetic nature is moving toward.

So the books come and need to be embodied and lived by men and women, and this is our belief in the prophets. So now we have to establish that life in the world, not just as individuals but in the context of community life. So the rest of the verse says, "the giving of wealth out of love for God to the near of kin, to the orphans, to the poor, to the wayfarers like the travelers, those who ask, and in the freeing of the neck," or freeing of the slave.

First, we must see that wealth is more than just material substance. Our Prophet, praise and peace be upon him, said that true wealth is the richness of the soul. God tells us in the Qur'an to spend of our material means as well as our human means—what the modern world terms "human resources." People with creative and productive ideas, with energy and a desire for a better life, should contribute what God has blessed them with. So the giving of wealth is not limited to the material realm. The most important wealth is the giving of knowledge, correct education.

This wealth is to be given out of love for God. We love him by serving him. God wants us to serve him by performing the duty He created us to perform: to be responsible for the creation. So the first step is to alleviate the burden on those who are suffering. This begins with our nearest kin; family is first in the book of God. Family has first rights, but then we help address the needs and alleviate the burdens and look after the interests and assist with the empowerment of others. Orphans are those who are not connected to their lifeline. An orphan is not just someone who doesn't know his mother or his mother and father; it's a person that's disconnected from his nature. Adam and Abraham are our true fathers, and when we find human beings on the planet earth disconnected from that lifeline, they are the true orphans. Adam was given the responsibility to be a productive intellect responsible to God. So when we find a people who are not responsible for their own life, and they're not responsible to God, they're orphans. They have been separated from their true purpose that God created them for. We should be educating and helping those people stand on their feet so they can manage their own life. The term in Qur'an is *khalifa*, which has reference to inheritance; one who comes behind and takes up the responsibility for something. Every human being is an inheritor of the human life and purpose that was given to the first man. When we are separated from that, we become orphans from our own reality. Scripture—Old Testament as well as New Testament—addresses this in terms of birthrights. Our birthright is Adam, not as a historical person but as a nature. We inherit the nature and purpose that was in that flesh.

Then we spend to help the poor. These are people who are not totally orphaned in the sense that we discussed, but still lack the means to establish their life as God intended. And we help the traveler, and those who ask. "And the freeing of the neck"—I'm looking at the Arabic and translating it literally, but it means the freeing of slaves. Slavery is on two levels. There is physical slavery, but the worst slavery is the slavery of your own psychology. Your thinking can be enslaved by culture, by false beliefs, by lusts, and by vanity. This is the slavery of our world. We know that slavery exists in other parts of the world, and Americans tend to see themselves as being so free. But the public life shows us that many of us in our society are some of the biggest slaves on this planet, although their chains are invisible to the eye. One of the greatest forms of slavery is to make people think that they're free. How do we change this? Correct education—and this is what Abraham represents for us. He is the first liberator. Moses is a liberator, to take the people to a Promised Land. We don't necessarily see the Promised Land as a physical space on a map. We see the Promised Land as the destiny God wants for us in our heart, our soul, and our thinking. If we can reach that place, where God wants us in our spirituality, then wherever we live on this planet Earth can become a promised land, a paradise. So the expression of our righteousness is the effort to alleviate the social burdens, to uplift those who are oppressed and downtrodden.

This verse then says to uphold the ritual prayer and to give the *zakat*, and these are expressions that are often given together in the Qur'an: those who establish the prayer and give regular charity. God tells us in the Qur'an that every creation knows its mode of prayer, or *salat*. The term *zakat* comes from "purification." It means "to augment or increase" but also "to purify." In the Qur'an, God says ·that He did not create the jinn or man except to worship or serve God. Salat is an expression of that. To serve someone is to work for them, which takes us back to man's original role. God made man a worker. Our salat is work. Our zakat is the giving of the wealth, to protect ourselves from becoming decadent and from giving in to the forces of greed and corruption. That is why zakat is connected to the concept of purity.

The verse then speaks of covenant, and the most important covenant in Scripture is the covenant made with God. To keep that covenant is to remain true to the life that God created us for. The verse then speaks of the patient in hardship and affliction and in difficult times. When we are on the path of God, trying to do the work of God in the world, this results in opposition. Our Prophet's history tells us that very clearly. They had no problem with him as a human being until he became a prophet and messenger and began to teach his people and to speak against the odious practices that they were engaged in. Then they brought on the afflictions, the punishments, and the pain. That's the history of most of the prophets and messengers of God. We're told in our holy book that Abraham, when he was making efforts to awaken his people and bring them away from idol worship, was thrown in the fire. We see that as a symbolic expression: whenever a person is raised up by God to bring about change and enlightenment for people, those who want to keep the power and authority try to put that person into fire, figuratively speaking. The same happened to Socrates, for example. Our modern world is no different. This verse also addresses the patience of those who are living their average, normal lives, trying to serve the will of God.

Then God says that those are the truthful. Those who live according to the description of righteousness in this verse are the truthful ones—not those who are just concerned with ritual worship, not those who have the knowledge and keep it within a small circle of learned men, but those who take the light and seek to broadcast it for all people. These are the true and sincere worshipers of God. They are the *mutaqun*, from the root *taqwa*, which means "regardfulness," sometimes translated as "God-conscious" or "God-fearing." The best translation into English is "regardful." As we grow and become more educated, our natural regardful nature increases. God tells us in the Qur'an to have sacred regard. This is taqwa, and we are to have it for God, for family, even for the fire, which means that we should have regard for our moral behavior. The mutaqun are those who are truly living out the best urges of their own human soul.

— ١٢ —

The array of voices gathered in this chapter give witness to the hope, honesty, creativity, rootedness, and sophistication of contemporary Muslim interactions with the Qur'an as they consider the challenges faced by Muslims both within and beyond their religious communities. In some other chapters in this book, reigning elders are represented, but all the voices in this chapter are relatively young, suggesting the kind of vitality and ingenuity that will characterize North American Islam in the decades to come.

Yet another theme that binds the Muslim scholars in this chapter is a common concern with justice. That concern takes center stage in the following chapter.

6

JUSTICE

Justice is at the core of the message of the Qur'an, and in this chapter three voices explore justice from different perspectives. Dawud Walid finds in the Qur'an and in Islamic jurisprudence a solid foundation for human rights and an unambiguous call to social justice. Amina Wadud, whose influence on other Muslim thinkers included in this volume has already been acknowledged, roots her commitment to gender justice in her great love for the Qur'an. She finds harmony between Islam and feminism and therefore refuses to compartmentalize them. As sadly so often happens for pioneers whose thinking is ahead of many others, she has been criticized by other feminists for being a faithful Muslim and by other Muslims for being a committed feminist. She speaks here of love and intimacy in marriage, and her words seem to imply a loving and intimate marriage as well between the inward work of piety and the outward work for human justice. Like Dawud Walid and Amina Wadud, Mahan Mirza sees a close bond between devotion and service to others. Prayer without care for the marginalized is empty and heedless.

The Heart of Guidance in the Qur'an
DAWUD WALID

Dawud Walid is an imam, a widely known human rights advocate and activist, and the executive director of the Michigan chapter of the Council on American-Islamic Relations. In addition to serving as imam to a historically African American mosque, he was also imam to an ethnically Bosnian congregation in the United States. He has studied widely in the classical Islamic tradition, including Arabic morphology, jurisprudence, and creed, and he is completing his work to earn the *ijaza* (formal qualification granting authority to teach) in *tafsir* (exegesis of the Qur'an). In addition to his depth of knowledge of traditional Arabic sources of wisdom, he looks particularly to Imam Warith Deen Mohammed as a guide for a method of practicing Islam in the context of the United States—a method, he noted, that speaks to the needs of this historical setting and does not allow Muslims overseas to dictate how Islam is to be lived out in America.

— ﺍﻝ —

By the time, humankind is surely in loss, except those who believe and who do righteous deeds and enjoin one another to truth and enjoin one another to patience.

One of the foremost early scholars of Islam was part of the fourth generation of Muslims. His name was Muhammad Ibn Idris al-Shafi'i.[1] He was one of the jurists of the four schools of Sunni thought. This chapter is called "The Time," or ʿAsr. Al-Shafi'i said that if people contemplated this chapter deeply, it would suffice to guide them. This is the second-shortest chapter in the Qur'an, with only three verses. It says that God swears by time that surely man certainly is in loss or losing, except those who believe and work righteous deeds and are involved in the mutual enjoining of truth and the mutual enjoining of patience. This chapter is very short yet profound. This chapter really speaks to me because it is a call for social justice: it lays out the parameters and the mechanism for seeking justice. So first, if we turn to the third verse, it speaks of those who believe, which means trust in God's authority and in the authority that God placed in man as well. One of God's names in the Qur'an is al-Mu'min, "the one who believes." So God is the believer: He knows that He is God, and He believes and trusts in the authority and the free will that He gave man. God created us in the likeness of our father Adam, whom He commissioned to be the vice-regent of this earth to take care of this creation and to deal justly with the entire creation, but especially to give particular attention to human beings. The verse speaks first of faith, then action, "those who work righteous deeds." Al-Shafi'i said that faith is in speech and in deed, and that speech is part of the deed. So faith is a profession with the tongue, but the authenticity of one's faith is mirrored in deeds. These deeds aren't just ritual worship like prayer, or fasting, or making pilgrimage; these deeds are also to be reflected in the social world. Social justice is a central part of this chapter. The verse goes on to speak of those who are enjoining a mutual truth. Now, al-Haqq, which is "the Truth," is actually one of God's names. Truth, first of all, concerns what we believe God decreed as moral and ethical parameters. This is the foundation of what the truth is. But in general, truth is also anything that holds up to the rules of logic, because we believe that God created this creation through His divine order and wisdom with logic. Anything that is true will not contradict that order. "The truth," *al-haqq*, also means "the right." Its plural, *al-huquq*, means "rights," so those who enjoin the right are those who enjoin human rights. So it's al-Haqq (God) who gave human beings al-huquq, or human rights. Finally, the verse speaks of those who are involved in the mutual enjoining of patience, of *sabr*, and one of God's names is Sabur. God is the patient one, patient with His creation and patient with human beings. He knows in His divine wisdom that there will be faithful people who will eventually come and execute His will on earth. From a philosophical perspective, of the sequence of these four things, sabr, or patience, is the last in the sequence. The reason for this is that once a person stands up for faith, and then begins to work righteous deeds, and then enjoins human rights, then the people who don't respect these three things—the oppressors, the corrupt people, those people who try to exploit people out of greed and who take people away from their best lives—are going to go challenge those people who do those three things. This is what we believe all the prophets and the saints experienced. It happened with Moses and Aaron under Pharaoh, with David by Goliath, with Jesus under the occupying Romans in Palestine. Muhammad the Prophet met this in Mecca as well. So those who follow in the way of the prophets or the saintly people, such as Daniel, another example, need to remind each other to be patient and stay the course. Those tests are going to come, and so do not give up hope or faith in doing what is right, even if the status quo comes against you to try to stop what you're doing. In many cases when fighting for righteous principles and justice, there are people in the status quo who may be against what you're doing, to the point that you can start second-guessing your own values and your own work. So this is why, philosophically speaking, enjoining of patience is very important in this verse.

In other passages in the Qur'an where the Prophet Muhammad is told the stories of earlier prophets, he is reminded both that it is difficult to be a prophet and that God enabled them to persevere for the sake of righteousness. This offers comfort to those who speak for justice.

There is a prophetic saying that Prophet Muhammad said that none should say that they are better than Yunus, or Jonah. Jonah was the one prophet mentioned in the Qur'an who basically gave up hope in his mission for a short period of time. He was instructed to be a caller to faith in Nineveh, in Iraq, and the people didn't come and embrace his message. He went out to the boat, and then went overboard, and got swallowed in the belly of the big fish for three days. He then realized that he was the reason why he landed up in that fish. He confessed that he had made a mistake, and then he came out of the fish and came back. He then saw the people of Nineveh embrace faith and monotheism. This is the Qur'anic narrative, telling us that none of us should think that we're better than he was. He lost patience for a moment and gave up hope, but he understood his mistake, he confessed, and then he later saw the results that he wanted to see.

Human rights to Muslims are similar to what Thomas Jefferson said in the Declaration of Independence: we hold these truths to be self-evident, that all men are created equal, endowed by their Creator with certain inalienable rights; among these are life, liberty, and the pursuit of happiness. So there are certain basic human rights that we have, and the scholars have called these the *maqasid*, or the objectives, of the shariah. The first is the protection of the *din*: our people have the right to practice religion and not be compelled to practice religion. So in the second chapter, the 256th verse of the Qur'an, it says, "Let there be

no compulsion in religion, for right guidance is clear from error."
"Let there be no compulsion"—*la ikraha fid-din*, in Arabic. The
root of the Arabic word for "compel" means "to despise" or "to
hate," so this means that if you force anyone to worship or do
something against their will, they will intrinsically grow to hate
it. So freedom of religious practice is a human right to worship
as one sees fit—is a human right. The second human right is
protection of the soul or the body, to protect one's own life and
to protect other human life from physical injury and death. The
Qur'an speaks about this too: "Whoever kills a soul unjustly is
as though he is killing all of humankind."[2] Another one of the
human rights is the protection of the *aql*, which is "human intellect." We have the right to think freely and a right to our intellectual property. Another human right that we have according
to Islam is the protection of *al-mal*, which means "property" or
"wealth." We have a right to own property, and we have a right
to have economic dignity. This is why the Qur'an and certain
hadiths speak of the merits of freeing people from slavery. One
critique of Islam that is heard is that the Qur'an does not give
a complete prohibition of slavery. I don't see a complete prohibition of slavery in the Torah or the Gospels either, so I don't
understand this critique. There are verses in the Qur'an and sayings of the Prophet that urge people toward freeing slaves. This
was exhibited by Muhammad and his Companions. There were
so many people who were in slavery who were freed, of different nationalities, from Africans to Persians to even Europeans
because the Arabs were equal-opportunity slaveholders.

Another one right is the protection of one's posterity or lineage: people have the human right to not only marry but to protect one's offspring and to be able to leave something for their
offspring as well.

These are some of the basic human rights—there are more.
Anything that violates the intrinsic dignity of the human being
is a violation of human rights. Torture, for instance, is strictly
prohibited in Islam. There's a story of a man who used to slur
the Prophet, named Suhail Ibn 'Amr, one of the chief people
who fought against the Prophet. He later verbally professed
Islam, but before then he was captured during a war, and one

of the Prophet's Companions, Umar, said, "O Muhammad, O Prophet, O Messenger of God, let me take this man and break his teeth and rip out his tongue so that he won't speak against you anymore." And the Prophet swore by God and said, "Don't harm him. Don't mutilate him, because if you do, I fear that God will harm me even though I'm a Prophet." So he commanded his companion not to harm him. The Prophet Muhammad proclaimed that in times of battle—I believe these are the first rules of engagement that humankind had ever seen—the elderly and women and children cannot be attacked. If someone is held prisoner of war, they have to be clothed with proper clothing and fed similar food to their captors'. So, for instance, a prisoner cannot be humiliated and be made to stand naked, or inadequately dressed, or put in a special outfit that makes them feel humiliated. Likewise, feeding captives lesser foods is considered demeaning and therefore a violation of their dignity.

In the Qur'an there's a verse that says *i'dilu huwa aqrabu lilt-taqwa*.[3] It means, "Be just, and this is what is closest to piety." And there's another saying of Prophet Muhammad that says, "Implementing justice for one hour—or it can mean one moment—is better than a year of ritual worship." So I believe that while of course it is important to pray and to fast, the higher worship is serving man, enjoining justice and trying to place roadblocks in front of injustice, promoting what's good and just, and forbidding the evil injustice.

There's a verse in the Qur'an, 3:110, "You are the best of people brought forth from mankind, because you enjoin what is right and you forbid what is wrong and you believe in God." In the same chapter, verse 104, it says, "Let there be among you a group who invites toward good," meaning who calls toward faith, "and commands what is just and forbids what is evil and they shall be amongst the successful people," *muflihun*. The Prophet himself also said in a very widely known saying, "Whoever sees an evil or injustice, let him change it with his hand. And if he's not able to do so, then resist it with his tongue. And if he's not able to do that, then resist it with his heart, but that is the weakest form of faith." This saying of the Prophet is first recognition that people have different levels of faith and that there are some people who will feel bad about injustice, but they're not going have enough moral courage to actually try to change it or to speak out against it. Some people feel bad about it, but they're scared, and this doesn't mean that they're bad persons. They just haven't developed the amount of certainty, or maybe they haven't been able to push aside their fear to take action. Also, it means that—reflecting back to that verse 3:104—there has to be a certain group of people in the Muslim community to raise the flag for justice. It is an obligation that the community must support those people who do that—they must. In the language of jurisprudence, it is called *fard al-kifayah*, which means that it is a community obligation, not binding upon everyone but that must be done by some, and therefore if there is a group in the community that is meeting this obligation, it covers the whole community. But if there's no one in the community doing this, then this will cause God to remove some of His protective mercy from those people. In other words, they are inviting their punishment in this life if they don't stand up for justice. This makes sense, because if a group of people do not stand up for justice, then obviously they're going to get punished for their nonaction by those who perpetrate injustice, the oppressors. It is going to happen; it is cause and effect. This standing up against injustice however is not just for the sake of other Muslims but for the wider human community. We don't live in silos unconnected from other human beings, so standing up for the rights of non-Muslims is in fact standing up for our rights. We're a human family, and in America in particular we're all citizens, and if there are certain laws or certain policies that affect one group, they'll affect the whole. That's been articulated by so many people, including Dr. Martin Luther King and others. The Christian tradition reflects the same idea: faith without works is dead.[4] God is saying that man is spiritually dead if what he professes with his mouth is not reflected in deeds. There is another saying of Prophet Muhammad that I quote sometimes in my sermons that says, "Prayer is light, and charity is its evidence." It's called *sadaqa*. But in Islam sadaqa means more than just giving money. The Prophet said that any act that brings about goodness in society is a sadaqa, a charity. That can be moving something out of the road that could cause a vehicle to get into an accident. That's a charity. The Prophet said that a good word, or a word of justice, is charity. He said that even a smile was charity. You never know how a smile could help someone's day, right? So there has to be sincerity in one's prayers, so that they dwell deep in the heart of the human being, and there has to be some sort of manifestation of that sincerity in works or deeds in the social world.

— 11 —

Intimacy and Compassion
AMINA WADUD

Amina Wadud is widely recognized as a mother of Islamic feminism. Her groundbreaking study *Qur'an and Woman* (2nd ed., 1999) is a classic work of contemporary Muslim thought, and her *Inside the Gender Jihad: Women's Reform in Islam* (2006) tells the story, much of it autobiographical, of the efforts toward gender equality among contemporary Muslims in many lands. Amina Wadud is emerita professor of Islamic studies at Virginia Commonwealth University.

— ⅃⅃ —

"And among His signs is that He created mates for you"—many say "of your own nature, from your own kind"—"and has made between you *muwaddatan warahma*," which these days I'm translating as "intimacy and compassion" (30:21).

Muslims still continue, I myself included, to encounter the Qur'an as a sacred text for the purpose of guidance. And one of the things that I have understood is that a person has to be guided from where they are to where they must next step. And there are, at least in the quantum physics way in which we look at the universe, infinitely many ways that they may step, and the end result of each step is that they then will be proceeding to the next location. In spiritual jargon we would say that they would be going to their next station, or their next location, their next *hal*.

One of the things about working with the Qur'an, with my own love of it and at the same time with this motivation of justice, is encountering the relationship between the Qur'an and law, and the relationship between that law and culture, and vice versa. I would also add the relationship of culture to law. I'm pretty emphatic about the desire to transform patriarchy into equality and justice. I'm also pretty inspired by the Qur'an to think that is part of the divine plan, part of the divine design. And yet, when you look at Muslim personal status law, and at Muslim patriarchal cultures (not that we are unique in having patriarchal cultures), there is a structure which I used to call the marriage of domination. There is a structure which is pretty repetitive: a man and a woman enter into a relationship which we know as marriage, or *nikah*, but they don't enter it on equal footing. In fact, the man is fully an agent. He tends to be the one who pursues the woman, and the woman therefore is a passive receptacle. In fact, the language of the marriage contract, as it was encoded in the law, is a contract of sale. That language is problematic because it makes her a subject, and in fact they even dealt with that in the law, because they were clear: she's not a subject; she's not a slave. So what exactly is being bought? And what exactly is for sale here? And if you look very closely at the legal literature, what is for sale is her genitalia. He purchases access to her body, and particularly her sexuality, by this contract of nikah. Well, in brief language, that just doesn't work for me. This is the structure of marriage that has been encoded in the law and reconfirmed in culture. I am Qur'an-centric: the Qur'an is at the center of my heart and my motivation. This is not a negation of *hadith*; it is not a negation of the *sunna* or the established practice of the Prophet, or the Prophet himself, upon him be peace. I say this because there are some people who, when the Qur'an is at the center, literally do *not* consider the Prophet to be important, nor his hadith, nor his sunna, and I'm not one of those people. So when the Qur'an is central, I grapple with the ways in which it has been used to reconfirm these notions. And in fact, in 4:34, it says that men have this *qiwama*, or guardianship, over women. Now, the qiwama model as it has been encoded in the law is hierarchical. Men are complete actors, women are passive receptacles, and a good woman therefore gets a man who will take care of her, protect her, and be responsible for her. He is the doer, and she is having these things done to her or for her. And that language in my mind cannot be made into language that I feel is inspired by the Qur'anic notion of *tawhid*, which is more reciprocal. And reciprocity is not going to ever come out of the discourse centered around a role of qiwama. What we have discovered (I say "we" because I'm not working on this alone) is that qiwama was encoded in almost every level of the legal literature about marriage, either inspired by culture or as an inspiration to culture. That qiwama is the language of patriarchy, and it is there in the Qur'an, there's no question about it. The fact that the Qur'an has that, and that the culture already had it, to me is a compensation for the context in which the Qur'an was revealed. But in no way is it the end of the story, because, and this is why I think it is important to look at these things in a relational way, the Qur'an also says, "And among His signs is that He created mates of like nature, from your own self, and has made between you intimacy and compassion." And muwaddatan warahma, "intimacy between you," in my mind cannot happen without fidelity, reciprocity, equality, mutual confirmation, along the lines of what I articulate as a relationship between equals. They don't have to be the same in order to be equally important, and that relationality is confirmed to be of a certain nature if you take into consideration muwaddatan warahma. "Loving mercy" or "compassion" to me is intimacy. So what we see is that the Qur'an actually has both of these in it, and the question then is how do we choose, and why do we choose. So in a patriarchal context, it's seemed quite natural to codify things along the lines of qiwama, which was the order and stayed the order and is still the order in some places of the world, but the Qur'an is eternal, and coincidentally, it also presents this other model. What we—that is, women activists working specifically on this—feel is that we need to construct the law to reform the patriarchy in that law toward more equality and reciprocity. We need to construct the law in such a way as to make the relationship of marriage a relationship of reciprocity and intimacy and compassion. So I'm very motivated by this passage as an inspiration for raising up the level of marital relations in Islam and among Muslims to such an extent that we take our partner as a meaningful reflection of our capacity to serve God. We don't take our partner for granted, nor do we take our partner as merely a utility that helps us to sustain licit sexual relations, although sexual relations are also a meaningful part of intimacy. So it's not an either/or thing; it is just that when you remove the reciprocity from sexuality, you have something else. When you sustain that intimacy, it is a transformative kind of spirituality, and the best sex is the sex that is holistic—that is, mind, body, and spirit. So I'm very much inspired both by this passage but also by the work that's being done in order to make this passage the rubric upon which we build marriages of equality, reciprocity for the future of Islam and Muslims.

Part of working on gender justice in Islam for me has always been motivated by my sense of, and my relationship to, the sacred. We have been in a discourse to articulate some idea of Islamic feminism. We have been in a discourse, myself included, where we were told emphatically that either you have Islam or you have feminism. Feminism was said to be secular, and many feminists, Muslim feminists included, demanded the removal of religion from the discourse about rights and human dignities. They felt that it got in the way, and certainly there was enough patriarchy encoded at various levels of religious practice and religious institution that one could make sense of that. But it was difficult for me to relinquish the spiritual motivations that I find in Islam, and I also noticed that the vast majority of Muslim women were inclined to identify as Muslim and did not want to leave Islam out of the discourse. The problem is that the representatives of Islam quickly, around the time of the end of the twentieth century, became components of the discourse of Islamists for political Islam, and therefore Islam became reified in its patriarchal form. The best we could do was simply surrender to the wisdom of that and accept our place as a complement to man's full reality. When I say "our place," I mean women. So both sides were in agreement: you cannot have Islam and human rights. I battled with this for quite some time, not wanting to give up one or the other, and I realized that was exactly the problem. The binary that was created meant that either you have Islam and its patriarchal manifestations or you have human rights in its secular, nonreligious manifestations. We had to rewrite the script, both the meaning and understanding through experience of Islam and the meaning and the understanding through experience of feminism. So Islamic feminism became the home for those of us who wanted emphatically to identify in terms of our justice movement specifically with Islam, and in my case with the spiritual worldview that is offered and practiced by believing Muslims. Feminism became the radical idea that women are human beings, and human beings from the Qur'anic perspective are agents of God. Part of our agency before God is to fulfill our destiny as his or her, God's, representative on the earth. So standing up for justice and standing up against patriarchy is in fact the fulfillment of our Islamic responsibility of moral agency. So for me, I spend a great deal of time negotiating between the places where people want to squeeze out either the spiritual motivations or the political motivations to say that you cannot have those two things at the same place, or to make spirituality the subject of politics, which is what I think the politics of piety is all about. I think that this is a kind of oxymoron where overt or external acts like longer scarves are taken as piety, as opposed to acts of conscientious resistance, acts of rejection of the limitations that are put upon the dignity of a person for whatever reasons that they would be exerted, and that this kind of defiance is something that is motivated not always from the most external manifestation of it, even when it must be manifest. So the inward must shine to the outward, and the outward must become the beautiful for the inward relationship with God, but it is not static. Because it's not static, you can't capture it by any symbol or any particular form and then expect that every time you return the grand epiphany will happen exactly that same way again. So it is in fact the essential element of dynamism in faith altogether; it's what we aspire to at least. When we do try to fulfill our rituals five times a day, we aspire every day to have that happen—and sometimes we're lucky. Most of the time we just perform the act and keep praying that it will be more successful as an opening to the face of God. So I have never experienced justice work without this element of confirmation, and it lights up for me the dark road that you must travel sometimes in order to resist patriarchy, hegemony, racism, sexism, homophobia, the class system. It is the light that shines for these liberation struggles, so I'm always delighted when I, in the Qur'an, can find those passages that reaffirm this in a way that will then also feed into reform and transformation of the law and the culture of Muslims toward more equality and reciprocity.

— ᠁ —

Ends and Means
MAHAN MIRZA

Mahan Mirza served as a college chaplain and a university professor prior to his current position as dean of faculty at Zaytuna College, the first Islamic liberal arts college in North America. His own interest in the liberal arts is reflected in the fact that he is an expert on the intellectual life of Abu Rayhan al-Biruni (973–1048), a polymath who wrote on natural science, including astronomy, mathematics, and geography, as well as philosophy and religion. His publications include serving on the editorial team of the *Princeton Encyclopedia of Islamic Political Thought* (2012).

— ᠁ —

Have you seen the one who denies the judgment? That is the one who casts aside the orphan, who neglects to urge the feeding of the needy. Woe to those who pray and are heedless of their prayers, who make a show but deny acts of kindness.

For a Muslim, the entire Qur'an is the word of God, but some verses rise as favorites in the heart of any believer. Sura 107 is one of those passages for me. The title in Arabic is al-Ma'un, which may be translated as "charity" or "neighborly kindness." *Al-ma'un* is the final word in the sura, and arguably the culmination toward which the entire passage inclines.

This sura begins with a question: "Have you seen the one who denies the judgment?" The last word, "judgment," is *din* in Arabic, and *din* can also mean "religion." Religion, and particularly Islam, with its emphasis on jurisprudence, has a prominent presence of law in it. Human beings are accountable; they are responsible for their actions, especially on the Day of Judgment. So the two concepts of religion and judgment meet on that day, just as they meet lexically in the word *din*.

The Day of Judgment is *yawm al-din*, and God is the owner and ruler of that day. Pious Muslims remind themselves of this fact many times each day in their prayers, when they recite the first sura, al-Fatiha, which acknowledges God as the owner and ruler (*malik*) of the yawm al-din. God is the ruler everywhere, but God has appointed human beings to be His vice-regents or deputies on earth (2:30). On the Day of Judgment, however, He will not give symbolic reign to anyone else. When reading the Qur'an, it is good to be aware of its subtle layers of intertextuality.

This sura begins with a question, which is a prophetic pedagogical method, analogous to Socratic dialogue. In *hadith* literature, it is common practice to pose a question that leads to further questions and eventually to an answer. The Qur'an poses questions similarly. "Have you seen the one who denies the judgment, or religion?" Sometimes, when speaking of this sura, I pause here if I have a primarily non-Muslim audience that is unfamiliar with the Qur'an. I then invite them to consider what it might mean to deny religion or to deny the judgment in the Islamic religious tradition. They tend to project their own ideas onto Islam and to answer that these are people who do not pray, or are not pious, or disobey God. The answer given in this sura, however, is very telling—and often surprises them.

The one who denies the judgment or religion is the one who repulses the orphan and does not urge the feeding of the needy. "Woe to the worshipers!" This is a strong indictment of people who have taken rituals, stripped them of their meaning, and then set them up as the ultimate purpose of their religion. This sura completely rejects that type of religiosity. These rituals are not ends in themselves but rather a means to a virtuous life. To confuse means and ends, while at the same time living a life devoid of virtue, is to deny the religion and the judgment. This is true even though, in many social contexts, a person whose life is in conformity to the exoteric aspects of religious teachings could be seen a great man or woman of God. Human beings tend to forget the inner aspect of religion, which is arguably its most important teaching. As the sura informs us, people can be heedless.

In just these few lines, the Qur'an has stated in very categorical terms that the one who denies religion and the judgment is the one who repulses the orphan and does not urge the feeding of the needy. Here a bit of context is helpful: in Arab society and culture, particularly in the seventh century, one's family and tribe provided a safety net. This social bond offered security and protection. Those who had lost their family, such as orphans, had to rely on the charity and goodwill of others. They lacked, institutionally, what was essential in order to flourish, or even to survive. A central part of the duty of a religious person, therefore, is to catch such people. The Qur'an teaches that this sort of concern is at the heart of a religious life.

The text continues: "Woe to those that pray and are heedless of their prayers." It is possible to observe the outward requirement to pray and yet do so with an inward hollowness. Pious Muslims seek to remember God at all times, and one path to such remembrance is to perform obligatory ritual prayer, or *salat*, five times a day. At one point during that formal, ritual prayer, one is required to recite verses of Qur'an, of one's own choosing. These short suras from the final portion of the Qur'an are often among those that are selected. As a result, it is possible that people recite these very verses from this sura in their prayer and then go out and shun the orphan and neglect to feed the needy. That is heedlessness. To heed one's prayer necessarily leads to a virtuous life. The ritual prayer is there to remind believers of what they should do and how they should live between times of prayer. Elsewhere in the Qur'an (20:14), Moses is addressed by God and told to establish the prayer "for my remembrance." Heedlessness is the opposite of remembrance, and remembrance of God is to care for the poor and the marginalized.

The Qur'an calls this heedless manner of prayer a show. Such prayer can be a social display, to entice others to think that one is good; this display can be a self-deception, in which one is convinced by empty acts of piety that one is virtuous. Here I am reminded of how the Qur'an speaks of those who are aware and of those who are not. When it comes to deceiving oneself or others, there can be a whole spectrum of self-knowledge and awareness. The Qur'an is nuanced in its recognition of the complexity of human psychology.

This powerful sura concludes with a contrast between making a mere show and practicing acts of common kindness. This charity or neighborly sympathy is at the heart of Muslim piety and ethics. It could be said that the entire sura leans toward this climactic note of kindness, al-maʿun. Like all but one of the 114 suras, this sura is prefaced by "In the name of God, the compassionate, the merciful," and it concludes with a call to compassion on the part of the believer.

— ١٢ —

Islam arose in a time of social change in Arabia. New technologies, such as a camel saddle that could carry much more weight than earlier designs, effected a revolution in trade.[5] Great influxes of wealth to successful merchants widened the gaps between the poor and the rich. In this context the Qur'an issued a moral demand to care for the socially disadvantaged, particularly orphans and widows, who had no adult male to advocate for their welfare in a patriarchal society. The later rise of powerful Muslim empires tempted the powerful to protect their wealth and privilege, but the text of the Qur'an and the example of the life of Muhammad remain as ideals for a just society. Muslim voices in this chapter have underscored the essential unity of the internal life of piety and the external commitment to justice. The next chapter focuses first of all on inward spiritual experience, but the emphasis on justice is by no means abandoned.

7

THE JOURNEY INWARD

Dealing as it does with the ineffable, mysticism is a difficult concept to define. Academic scholars of mysticism debate intensely just what the phenomenon is. For their part, mystics themselves tend to be sincerely humble and therefore refrain from identifying themselves as such. Furthermore, it is not a term of Islamic origin, and so some resist applying it to Muslims, fearing that it would impose a foreign concept from the outside. For all these reasons, caution is in order. Yet if mysticism may be taken, for the moment at least, as a powerful, intense experience of divine presence that tends to reorient one's life in profound ways, then perhaps the central theme of this chapter is mysticism, even if the Muslim speakers themselves would humbly shy away from that self-designation. They are not the only Muslims in this volume about whom that can be said.

In many religious communities, Muslim and beyond, the mystics and the advocates of social reform fall into separate camps and tend not to associate with the other side. Contemplatives and activists often mix like oil and water, whether that be in Islam, Judaism, or Christianity. Here, however, these two dimensions of the religious life remain integrated.

The name of the first Muslim teacher in this chapter has been withheld by request, and the reason for that will become evident. Survivors of abuse may need anonymity for their well-being. She speaks personally from experiences of great tribulation and triumphant joy. She issues a call for freedom from domination from those who insist that they alone can mediate between God and others. She reminds her audience that the Qur'an itself is a conversation, about which there is a further conversation. The Qur'an's call to recognize God alone as worthy of worship is also a call to liberation from oppressors' demands that they be idolized. That inward freedom blossoms into external freedom from abusive partners. This message of liberation is divine consolation.

— ‏‏ل ‏ —

Freedom from Pharaoh[1]

We then sent Moses to Pharaoh and his courtiers with Our signs, but they treated them wrongfully. See the consequences of those who spread corruption. Moses said, "Pharaoh, I am a messenger from the Lord of all the worlds, bound to report nothing about God but the truth, and I have brought you a clear sign from your Lord. Send the Children of Israel to go with me." He said, "If you have come with a sign, then bring it forth, if you are among the truthful." So Moses threw his staff and it became a serpent clearly, and then he drew out his hand and it was white for all to see. The courtiers among Pharaoh's people said, "This man is a learned sorcerer! He means to drive you out of your land. What do you command?" They said, "Put him and his brother off for a while, and send gatherers to all the cities to summon every learned sorcerer to you." The sorcerers came to Pharaoh and said, "Surely we will have a reward if we win," and he replied, "Yes, and you will be among those closest to me." They said, "Moses, either you throw first, or we will." He said, "You throw," and they did, casting a spell on people's eyes, terrifying them with great sorcery. Then We inspired Moses, "Throw your staff," and it swallowed their trickery. The truth was established, and their deeds were proven false. They were defeated and turned back in humiliation. The sorcerers were cast down prostrate and said, "We believe in the Lord of the worlds, the Lord of Moses and Aaron." Pharaoh said, "You have believed in Him before I have given you permission. This is a plot you have schemed to drive the people out of this city. You shall know: I will cut off your hands and feet on alternate sides, and then crucify you all." They said, "And so we have already returned to our Lord" (7:103–25).

The Consoling Qur'an[2]

To make a decision about which verse to discuss, I made *istikhara*. This means literally to seek out what would be good for one's situation. It is common practice for Muslims to make a prayer to God for understanding, open the Qur'an, and point a finger at a verse revealing God's message. I prayed, I opened the Qur'an, and I hit this verse: *Qalu inna ila rabbina munqaliboon* (7:125). They said, "We have already returned to our Lord."

My heart recognized this verse even though I had never spent time contemplating it and the story it is drawn from before. These verses depict Pharaoh and his sorcerers after Moses, *alayhi salam*, threw down his staff. By Moses' act, the sorcerers witnessed proof of the existence of God. They abandoned Pharaoh and fell down prostrate before the God of Moses. Pharaoh threatened to mutilate their bodies by cutting off their hands and feet before finally crucifying them. But the sorcerers replied to Pharaoh with full awareness of what is real and unreal, saying to him: "We have already returned to our Lord."

It is important that my finger settled on this verse and no other in that story, emphasizing that particular moment. This verse is the consoling moment. It is a moment when I read the Qur'an was with me through my suffering and my journey out of that suffering.

There has been a lot of discussion building over the last few decades in some Muslim scholarly circles about understanding the Qur'an as a conversation between God and the Prophet Muhammad, alayhi salam. Of course, there is wild difference of opinion on the nature of that conversation: Was it Muhammad's articulation—inasmuch as there was no veil between the Prophet and God and so the Prophet spoke from that reality—or is the Qur'an a living discourse between Muhammad and God and now between God and humanity?[3] But whatever one thinks about these supposedly radical perspectives, the Qur'an is traditionally understood to have been responsive to the Prophet and the early community's experience over the twenty-three years of its revelation. Verse after verse of the Qur'an speaks directly to the struggles faced by the Prophet, the community, and even individuals.⁴ *That is a conversation.*

Some examples: The verse "Certainly, with hardship there is ease" comes from a chapter of the Qur'an in which God reminds the Prophet, after a long period of desolation, that he was never left alone without divine care and attention (94). The stories of past prophets have been read as God's consolation to Muhammad and his community, reminding them that they are not alone in history; there have always been those who forcefully rejected God's message and mocked the prophets and their followers (11:49). The opening of the chapter of the Qur'an, entitled "She Who Disputes," directly addresses an old woman who came to the Prophet with a problem (58:1-4). It is said she was Khawla, a woman whose dotty old husband had irrevocably divorced her in a fit of pique. She and her husband needed their marriage reinstated. But the Prophet replied that, according to custom, nothing could be done. Khawla refused to accept this outcome and demanded that God solve her problem. Not long after, verses were revealed that honored her insistence, prohibited such divorces, and allowed for the reinstatement of her own. When the Prophet's wife, Aisha, heard about this, she said, "Glory to Him whose hearing encompasses all things!"⁵ The Qur'an is by its very responsiveness a conversation with God. The earliest Muslims called out to God, and so do we. Sometimes we even dispute with God, like Khawla. And God responded through the Qur'an then, and God responds now.

The outcome of that conversation, I believe, depends entirely on us. There is a verse in the Qur'an in which God says, "We have never sent a messenger except with the language of their people, so the messenger can make things clear to them" (14:4). God speaks to people not just in a linguistic form familiar to them but also in a cultural and psychological language they can understand. Another verse from the Qur'an states, "In this book, We have left out nothing" (6:38). Here the Qur'an explains that its message encompasses the entirety of the human experience. The Qur'an draws us into conversation with God by speaking directly to us. What people take from that conversation is in accordance with their intentions. Or said another way, people engage the language of the Qur'an in keeping with the capacity of their natures. For our intentions are bound to the limits of our distinct capacities in any one moment. There the burden of our freedom as the children of our primordial mother and father becomes utterly clear. The closing of the verse, "We have never sent a messenger except with the language of their people," says something about where those different intentions might take us. "God lets go astray whomever He wills and lets be guided whomever He wills. He is the Almighty, the All-Wise." Thus the same words in the Qur'an, read in keeping with individuals' distinct intentions, could be said to "produce" divine messages that misguide and guide alike.

My first lived experience with the distinct outcomes of humans' conversations with God was with verse 4:34, infamously called "the Beating Verse" because it prescribes beating as a last resort in trying to control rebellious women: "as for those women whom you fear will act rebelliously, first admonish them, then refuse to share their bed, then beat them." To the credit of their intentions, a great number of scholars in the past and present have interpreted the word that literally means "to beat" as "to maritally separate" instead. Other scholars have seen the revelation of this verse as severely limiting the unrestrained beating of women that every man considered his right at the time. Many scholars have followed the Prophet's example in placing restrictions on beating to such an extent that it becomes next to impossible to go through with it. The Prophet is reported to have experienced a crisis of conscience in the revelation of this verse and waited three days before reciting it. When the Prophet did recite it, the historian, Qur'an commentator, and legal scholar Abu Jafar al-Tabari (d. 923) reports that he prefaced it by saying, "God wanted one thing and I wanted another," and then he set about restricting its use.[6] Since all Muslims believe the Prophet is the finest expression of the Qur'an's guidance, then the issue should have been settled at once. But ill intent is powerful.

Other scholars ignored or argued away the Prophet's restrictions, allowing themselves and generations after to be led astray by a command of God. This verse was particularly hard for me, because a former partner chose misguidance out of a desire to control me emotionally and physically. And at the time, despite studying the sources myself, I was not aware of the Prophet's attitude or the other rulings. I was only aware that I was rebellious—our relationship had been volatile, to say the least—and that my partner had rights over my body. And he made use of his rights, trying to control my interactions with the outside world, throwing me around or throwing things at me when necessary, humiliating me, forcing sex on me, threatening to kill himself, and finally demonstrating that he could kill me if he wanted to.

But the core problem of this verse is not only with the permission to beat. If that were all, ill-intended interpretations could be more easily dismissed. The problem is that the verse begins by establishing male guardianship over women and ends with the guardian's responsibility to punish his wards. The verse opens, "Men are guardians over women because God has favored some over others and because they spend their wealth [on them]." As those who are familiar with family abuse are aware, violence is a function of the abuser's assumption that he or she has the right to control others. In these particular scholars' efforts to ignore the Prophet's intentions concerning this verse, they attributed statements to Muhammad that elaborated on this notion of control. In some of these reports, Muhammad does not just agree that beating women is necessary to keep them in line, he also expresses his frustration at women's recalcitrant behavior by declaring women's service to their husbands to be at the heart of their worship of God.

My partner's favorites were hadiths in which the Prophet is supposed to have positioned men as gods themselves or just one step lower as gatekeepers of their wives' salvation. In one, Muhammad declares, "If I could command someone to prostrate before anything other than God, I would command women to prostrate before their husbands" (Ibn Majah, Chapters on Marriage, #1853).[7] In others, Muhammad—otherwise famous for being a sensitive lover—is depicted commanding women to have sex with their husbands on demand, no matter the time or place (Tirmidhi, Chapters on Suckling, The Husband's Rights over the Wife, #1159). He is reported to have said that should a woman displease her husband by refusing sex with him, God and the angels will curse her until the morning (Muslim, Marriage, #3366, #3368). Other reports such as these create further causal links between a husband's satisfaction with his wife and God's judgment of her on the Last Day.[8] "Any woman who dies with a husband who is satisfied with her enters paradise" (Tirmidhi, Chapters on Suckling, The Husband's Rights over the Wife, #1161).

It doesn't matter that reports such as these can and should be ignored because their depictions are at odds with what else we know about the Prophet's character, and their content is theologically scandalous.[9] It is absurd to suggest that the Messenger of God, who sacrificed absolutely everything in order to guide people away from worshiping anything other than God, would then position men as nearly divine mediators and women as their worshipful servants.[10] Scholars who have been otherwise so attentive to theological niceties nevertheless have felt such idolatrous reports bear repeating for their "pedagogical value" in establishing proper male-female relations. In the case of marital rape, legal scholars codified it such that, with the payment of the dowry, a woman sells unrestricted use of her sex organs to her husband for the duration of the marriage.[11] Interpretations such as these draw a thread through the Qur'an's expression of male guardianship and hadith, unreliable or not, to create a complex of gendered power relations in which men are placed in the position of a god, or God's mediator, and women are placed in a position of *humiliation* before them. Their position is humiliating because as the Qur'an makes clear, over and over again, worshiping anything other than God is the gravest humiliation of the innate nobility of the human soul.

I lived in this state of humiliation by accepting abuse as intrinsic to worship. I studied the sources; I knew what was expected of me. The middle of the verse, after all, points to women's responsibility, stating that *righteous women are obedient*. Now, it hardly matters that this particular term for "obedient" refers to obedience to God alone in all but one case in the Qur'an, where it refers to God and His prophet alone. I had already come to accept that my partner was somehow in the position of God in the home and that obedience to him was obedience to God. The tradition, rooted in the language of the Qur'an, had turned me into an idolater. Don't get me wrong. I understand that I was a victim of gendered violence. But it was not until I began to experience my victimization as a form of idolatry that I was able to set myself free.

Muslim theologian Amina Wadud, who has been working through the Qur'an's sometimes heartbreaking complexity for decades, discusses how the Qur'an's call to worship God alone is explicitly at odds with patriarchy and other forms of oppression. These systems place some people in positions of power over others by obstructing the vertical reciprocity between God and the individual, and so too the possibility of horizontal reciprocity between the self and others. For Wadud, when the Qur'an is read by means of declaring God One, oppressive readings unravel and in fact become impossible to see, as it has been for those scholars who refuse to acknowledge that the Arabic in verse 4:34 can even sustain a meaning of "beat them."[12] And as it has been for those who read "guardianship" to demand only that men uphold their responsibilities as partners and fathers. The light of divine unity obliterates idolatrous readings.

And so I recognized the verse "We have already returned to our Lord" because it spoke so honestly of where I once had been and what it took for me to escape.

Before I left my partner, I had started to follow a Sufi teacher. In his lessons, he would always focus on the name "Allah." I learned that this practice of focusing on "Allah" is a beautiful path, but it presents temptations along the way. The teacher seemed to know what tempted me. Give me a simple statement that God is "One" and "obedience is due to God alone," and I will delve into elliptical conversations about the nature of reality, theological principles, and legal norms, thus forgetting about God in the process of trying to think about Him. I do not remember any lessons my teacher may have shared with his followers when we sat with him. I only remember "Allah, Allah,

Allah." And with that I fell into the practice of learning to worship God alone. *Moses had thrown down his staff.*

Little by little, my partner became more impatient and dis-
pleased with me, I became less willing to take it, and his language
became more derisive. His physical reminders of my position
in the household grew more frequent until finally he exploded
one day. Citing a prophetic report that he had used only metaphorically in the past, he demanded that I get on the floor and
actually prostrate before him. But I had already fallen down
prostrate worshiping "the Lord of the Worlds, the Lord of Moses
and Aaron." I was resolute and furious. I escaped into a nearby
room. But instead of recognizing what was growing within me,
my mind succumbed to the temptation to think it through and
make the worst of it.

I immediately thought of Sufi stories in which a scholar is
tested by a command to throw all his books in the river. The
books are his attachments, his learning, his autonomy. I thought
that my partner's demand that I prostrate before him was a
divine command to cast my ego into the river and submit to
him (which is exactly the opposite of the message of the story).
To my mind, I had failed the crucial test. Yet I could not make
myself return to him and prostrate before him. I sobbed and
begged God's forgiveness. I did not know that it was the beginning of my path out of the relationship.

But my partner knew it was the beginning of the end, and
things got dangerous. I had come to truly "believe in God before
he gave me permission," and this was the greatest betrayal. For
him, this was nothing but a scheme to destroy him, and everyone and everything in his world. As he put it, I was always "with
him or against him."

His threats to kill himself if I left him turned into threats
to kill himself and me. "He told me soon I would know what I
had done." He told me he could cut me open in my sleep. As the
sorcerers knew with Pharaoh, these were not empty threats. But
I had already returned to my Lord. Whether he killed me or not,
he had no more power over me. They said, "We have already
returned to our Lord."

It took years after that relationship ended to realize that I had passed the test. I had thrown my books—pharaonic readings of ill intentions—into the river. That first moment in which I truly began to worship only one God was a seed that unfolded over time in the action of living and growing. The Prophet, God love him, sat in a cave in Hira and received the whole of the Qur'an in one night. That was a divine seed that unfolded as verses of consolation and guidance for twenty-three years, in loving response to the needs of Muhammad's community as it grew and came to understand itself, and it continues to unfold in our hearts and minds as we grow and come to understand ourselves.

The consolation of the Qur'an is in that immediate, encompassing, enfolding, and unfolding conversation with humanity. The Qur'an recognizes the totality of our beauty and our ugliness. It recognizes our loss and our suffering, but also the loss and suffering of our oppressors. Most oppress because they have been oppressed themselves or suffer in some other way. It recognizes our moments of great joy, too, like when Mary's mother had just given birth to her and held her up for God to see, and called out to Him, "Look, it's a girl!" (3:35-36). And not just the great things—it recognizes the little things too, like watching birds overhead, their wings spreading and folding in again (67:19). It calls to us to see the map of our hearts in it, and through this, God's eternal presence and guidance. It draws us into the conversation with God about our simply being alive. And this is divine consolation.

— ١٢ —

Comfort and Signs
JONATHAN A. C. BROWN

Jonathan Brown describes the confluence of the personal and the eschatological. Human dignity persists despite limitations in a vast universe of death and life and coming cataclysm. In the midst of all this cosmic activity, human beings bear the responsibility to acknowledge and worship God and to exercise kindness toward others. The two passages that he chose elaborate on common themes of divine creativity and beneficence and of human caring. The first text does so from a cosmic perspective, and the second on an intensely personal, mystical scale.

Jonathan A. C. Brown is a professor of İslamic studies and Muslim-Christian understanding at Georgetown University and a recognized scholar of *hadith*. He has also written on Sufism, Islamic law, and Arabic lexical theory.

— ﻟﺍ —

Have you not considered that person who turned away,
who gave only a little bit, and was not beneficent?
Has he some knowledge of the unseen that he is able to see
*   and understand?*
Or was he not informed of what was in the book of Moses
*   and of Abraham,*
who was true in his covenant,
that no bearer of a burden bears the burden of another,
and that man only gets what he strives for,
and what he strives for will be appreciated?
Then he will be rewarded in a most complete way.
And does he not know that the ultimate destination of things
*   is to your Lord,*
that your Lord is the one who makes you laugh, who makes
*   you cry,*
that He is the one who brings death and brings life,
that He is the one who created the two genders, the male and
*   the female,*
from one drop, as it came forth.
And it is incumbent upon Him to bring about the second
*   creation,*
and that He is the one who makes you rich and content,
and that He is the Lord of the constellation Sirius,
and that He is the one who destroyed 'Ad, the community of
*   the past, and Thamud, for what remains of them?*
And the people of Noah indeed, they were even more unjust
*   and overweening,*
that the cities [usually understood to be Sodom and
*   Gomorrah], when they were covered up by what covered*
*   them.*

Of which signs of your Lord are you disputing?
This is a warner from the warners of old,
the eventual calamity is coming.
No one besides God can uncover it.
So are you surprised at this discourse,
and you laugh and you don't cry, enjoying your silly activities.
But rather prostrate to God and worship. (53:33-61)

I remember that when I was in college, I was driving home one day from school, thinking about these verses in my mind. I must have been about twenty-one years old or so. I felt that they had this incredible unity, presenting man with a very clear explanation of where you are in history and existence, in relation to meaning and truth. As I thought through these verses, they seemed to tell this story.

Have you ever considered this person who turned away from the messages of God, from truth? Such people don't want to be generous, to give to others in charity. They don't want to give of themselves. Do they have knowledge of the unseen? They seem so confident about what's right and what's wrong, that there is no God. They judge people who are religious in a snide and condescending way. What do they know? What truth do they have access to, that somehow they know that all the people in previous generations from the past who believed in God did not know? Weren't they told? Didn't they read what was in the books of Moses? Don't they remember the message of Abraham? And what are the important parts of this message? "No bearer of a burden bears the burden of another." You are only responsible for your own actions. You won't be blamed for anybody else and what they do. You are responsible for your one conduct and belief. Mankind is only judged by what he strives for. What he or she strives for will be seen; it won't be lost. So don't be afraid of death, of what happens after you die. Don't be afraid that you won't be remembered, that when your generation is past, you'll be a nothing, totally forgotten. You'll be judged by what you tried to do in this life, not by what you've accomplished. And what you sought to do will never be lost, even if no one ever knows about it, even if you die somewhere in a ditch, in a war, and no one ever knows who you are. What you tried to do will be remembered by God, and you will be rewarded for it most fully. "In the end we all go back to God." This whole creation will go back to its source. And that God is the one who makes you laugh and makes you cry, the one who brings happiness and sadness, not anything else, not anything you do. You can improve your understanding; you can take certain steps in your life to facilitate happiness, but ultimately this comes from God. God is the one who brings death and brings life. Many times in the Qur'an, when life and death are paired, death comes first. The classical Greek term for this rhetorical device is hysteron proteron, inverted word order, in which what comes first is mentioned last. It's like when you say you put on your shoes and socks. You don't put on your shoes and socks. You put on your socks and then your shoes. Yet, in Islamic cosmology, human beings lived before. We lived before creation in this moment in which God asked us, "Am I not your Lord?" All humans answered, "Verily you are our Lord" (7:172). And then you actually are dead. You are not alive. We all worry about what will happen at the end of this life when we die, but we don't worry about where we were before we were born, the centuries past, during the Hundred Years' War, during the Renaissance. You were dead; you did not exist. The Qur'an talks about God bringing the second life and the second death. You die twice, and then you're brought back to life twice, the final one being on Judgment Day. God made the two genders. God created you and can bring you back in whatever form He wants, in whatever way. He is the one who gives you wealth and makes you happy, makes you content. And it's not just this world. He is the Lord of all the worlds beyond this earth, in the heavens, in the things we see but just barely understand. He's the Lord of the people in the past, the one who brought them forth and destroyed them, for whatever reason, when they were overweening, and arrogant, and turned aside from his messengers. Such were the people of Noah, the people of Sodom and Gomorrah. So what do you dispute? What of this is something that you want to deny—and why? Do you have some knowledge that will tell you otherwise? This Prophet who is bringing this message is like the warners of the past. He's telling you that the end of the world will come someday, and there is no one besides God who knows when that will be. No one can prevent it. So why are you surprised by this message? Why is it so strange to you? Why do you think it's funny? Why don't you realize that it's serious? It's about your existence in this universe, this metaphysical space. And yet you just tarry in this world, doing silly things, and not worshiping God.

To me, this passage made sense as a unit. It's a very concise description of how things work. It both relates the power and dignity of human beings as agents of choice, to try to do good, and also sets this within the limits of a vast world in which God is in control. It is Stoic in that it holds that human beings are not in control of their environment, of what presents itself to them in their lives, but they are in control of their reactions and responses, in the way that they approach and deal with the challenges. For a Stoic, this approach has to do with happiness in this life, and aligning yourself with the natural order. For a Muslim, added to that, it's not just about this life. For millennia, the issue has been that you don't want just to not be when you die. You want to continue. One of the big answers to this over the centuries is that you have to do something to be remembered. The problem with that is that we remember certain people who may not have done anything, if the stories are false or changed, and yet we don't remember many people who may have done more. So if there is really to be some true and consistent way that human beings can have immortality, that goes beyond their life in this world, it has to be something that is not subject to the vagaries of history. It has to be something that will be assured it's fair. And that is in what you strive to do, either in the way you react or in the way you create or catalyze things, and that's what you'll be judged for. That for me is an important lesson. People always make fun of religion and say that it is a crutch. Yes, it's a crutch. And what does that tell you, that we are a species that needs a crutch. Humans need water, but that does not mean that it's not real. In fact, I would argue that the fact that everyone needs something means that it may really be. It's not something to be dismissed. It means something. There's a line in a Sherlock Holmes mystery, "The Adventure of the Cardboard

Box." Sherlock asks in effect, "What object is served by this circle of misery and violence and fear? It must tend to some end, or else our universe is ruled by chance, which is unthinkable." It is "unthinkable" to him why there's no reason why these things happen. It is conceivable to many people, today and in the past, but I would say that those people are not possessed of some insight. What reason do they have to think that meaning does not exist in this world, or beyond this life? They have no more idea about it than we do.

I have another small verse to talk about, a more personal, comforting one. This is from Sura 93, al-Duha, the Bright Morning Hours. *Duha* is the time right after the dawn, when the sun gets bright and in the desert the ground begins to heat up. The sand and the dirt start to get hot.

> *By the bright morning hour,*
> *and the night when it withdraws and becomes peaceful,*
> *your Lord has not forsaken you,*
> *nor has He become displeased,*
> *and surely what is to come is better than what has already*
>   *passed,*
> *and indeed soon God will grant you,*
> *and you will be well pleased.*
> *Did He not find you an orphan and give you shelter?*
> *Did He not find you lost and guide you?*
> *Did He not find you in need and bring you riches?*
> *So don't oppress the orphan,*
> *and don't turn away or scold the person who comes asking*
>   *you questions,*
> *but always speak about the bounty of your Lord.*

For me this is an interesting sura because it presents one of the big questions about the Qur'an. This sura is revealed to comfort the Prophet. It's in second-person singular, not plural. It's intimately part of the Prophet's life, yet when I read it, it speaks to me. It is real in my own emotional reaction. God does not despise you, has not left you. What comes is better than what's come before. God has given you so much. So don't refuse to give to others. You have to be caring, and polite, and kind to others, and always remember and speak about the bounties of your Lord and be grateful for what God has given you.

When I was about twenty years old, during the first summer after I'd become Muslim, I was traveling in Senegal and Mali. My friend Charles and I were taking a bus from the city of Bamako, the capital of Mali, to Mopti, which is a picturesque sort of mud-adobe city on the Niger River, then going up to Djenné and eventually to Timbuktu. At that time it was very difficult traveling. As we were waiting for the bus and a twelve-hour bus ride, it was hot, and my nose began to run. We got on the bus, and within an hour I had some full-blown illness that I had never had before. It was like going from zero to the worst flu that I'd ever had. I couldn't swallow, and my throat hurt so much it felt like it was bleeding. I was wondering if I had Ebola or some tropical disease, and it was terrible. I was miserable, and it was so hot, and the bus was so cramped and crowded. I remember that one man had a battery-powered boom box, playing the Police over and over again, songs like "Roxanne" and "Don't Stand So Close to Me." To this day I can't hear those songs. I wanted to strangle this man. I'd never been so miserable and scared in my life. I remember looking at the back of the seat in front of me and having this most profound moment, not of doubt, but of rejection of my religion and every religion. It was as if I had cleared away all the fear of doubting. It was a profoundly honest moment. And I said, "This is B.S.; God has never done anything for me." I reflected afterwards on what had happened. I didn't say that "There's no God"; I didn't say that there is nothing but this world, and that there's nothing beyond, no God. What I said was that God has never done anything for me. In Arabic the word for "unbelief" means "to cover something up," and in pre-Islamic Arabic, it means "ingratitude." So the concepts of unbelief and ingratitude are completely intertwined in the Islamic tradition. It's almost as if people can't really doubt. They can't really disbelieve because, from the Islamic perspective, you saw God once, before creation. You said, "Yes, you're my Lord." So I did not doubt God's existence; I said that God didn't do anything for me. Then, at the height of this moment, a voice came into my head. Not that I had genuine revelation, but like when the line of a song or movie comes into your mind uninvited. And the line was, "And did we not find you an orphan and give you shelter? Did we not find you lost and guide you? Did we not find you poor and enrich you?" And then a line from the next sura, which is often seen as closely linked to this one, "Did we not open your breast and expand your heart? Did we not set aside that burden that was breaking your back, and raise you up in dignity?" These came to my mind, and I realized all the good that God had done for me, not just in making me Muslim, but throughout my life, in giving me what I had and providing me with all this bounty. And in that moment, I felt like I was unified with some truth. I felt like all the coverings of the world had been removed, and I saw the actual structure of reality. I felt like we were all these dry leaves, twirling around the axis that was God. It was by dint of that axis, by being pulled into it, that we even exist. Life and death, as we know it, don't mean anything. There is no change between life and death. Being alive or being dead doesn't change what you really are. We are just this dead matter animated by God. I felt an incredible peace, unlike anything I've ever felt in my life, before or since. I remember looking out the windows of the bus, it was nighttime by then, and the whole sky was just a net of lightning. It wasn't loud, but the world around me, the trees and the dark, were illuminated. We arrived in Mopti, and I was still sick, but I have never felt more alive or healthier. In my life since then, I returned to normal life, where there are clouds of doubt that are created by our attachments to the world, by our laziness, by our ingratitude, by our own weaknesses, by the negative things in our surrounding—the things that encrust our hearts again. But I never really doubted what I believe. The details about Islamic law—if it says one thing or another, or whether or not I'm supposed to believe one thing or another—these matter, but they are not the core issues. I never doubted that core anymore. That moment was the truest moment of my life.

These two suras contain common themes of comfort and of the physical world as full of signs that point to the Creator. The two comment on one another. The first is intellectual, metaphysical. The other is more mystical, in the sense of direct contact. In

Arabic the word *dhawq*, "taste," would be used—an experiential understanding of the same truth.

— ٨٢ —

From Chaos to Union
HOMAYRA ZIAD

Homayra Ziad builds on the apocalyptic theme established by Jonathan Brown. She considers this from the Sufi dictum to "die before you die." The upside-down quality of apocalyptic cataclysm is internalized: the self is inverted. In the midst of all this overturning of normal reality, human accountability endures, as does the divine injunction to justice signaled by the reference to the unspeakable crime of burying an infant girl alive.

Homayra Ziad is assistant professor of religion at Trinity College in Hartford, Connecticut. Her particular interests include Sufism, women's studies, Qur'anic hermeneutics, and intellectual and cultural trends in Muslim India. She is passionate about interfaith engagement.

— ٨١ —

When the sun is overturned,
When the stars fall away,
When the mountains are moved,
When the ten-month pregnant camels are abandoned,
When the wild animals are gathered together,
When the seas are overflowed,
When the souls are paired,
When the infant girl who was buried alive is asked
For what sin was she killed,
When the pages are folded out,
When the sky is scraped open,
When hell is set ablaze,
When the garden is brought near,
A soul will know what it has prepared.
I swear by the moving stars, the planets that sweep along the
  sky,

By the night as it recedes, by the dawn as it gently breathes,
This is a saying of a noble messenger,
Endowed with power, his rank established, in the presence of
    the Lord of the Throne,
Obeyed and trustworthy there.
Your companion is not mad.
He saw him on the clear horizon,
And he is not withholding of the seen,
Nor is this a word of an accursed Satan.
Where are you going?
This is nothing but a reminder to all beings.
For those who will to walk straight,
You may not will except what God wills,
Lord of all beings. (Sura 81, al-Takwir)

I am attracted to apocalyptic scenarios. They appeal to the same part of me that is drawn to disaster films. This is not Schadenfreude. I'm not attracted to violence and pain. Instead, there is something in apocalyptic scenarios, the large-scale catastrophe, that confirms the fragility of our existence. I see how funny we are in our attempts to build civilizations, lay down codes of living, create structures and protocols. I do not mean to denounce these attempts. These are all ways in which we create lives that are accountable to God and to each other. Yet surely we know that everything can disappear in the blink of an eye! The Sufi tradition of "dying before you die" embodies the understanding that we only live fully when we know that we are always on the edge of extinction. I am drawn to the image of the candle burning brightest in the moment before it dies. I believe that we burn most fully when we are on the edge of being extinguished, knowing that at every moment we could be called to answer fully for what we've done.

   This apocalyptic passage, al-Takwir, looks at everything that is certain in our lives—the sun, the stars, the mountains, the seas, other living things. Strange things are happening. Objects that seemed enduring and practices that we imbued with certainty are upended, overturned, demolished. This passage is a beautiful example of how the Qur'an conveys meaning and does theology through stylistic devices. The poetic qualities of this passage serve the content of the message. Consider the repetitive use of the word "when":

When the sun is overturned,
When the stars fall away,
When the mountains are moved,
When the ten-month pregnant camels are abandoned.

Each use of the word "when" contributes to a buildup of tension. Each "when" presents to us a cataclysmic event that inverts our sense of reality. And then, when we come to the line "A soul will know what it has prepared," the tension suddenly breaks. The break at this line places an emphasis on human autonomy. On this day, we present to God what we have prepared. The preparation is in our hands. Before this line, every verb, in the original Arabic, was in the passive voice. The cataclysm is in the hands of God, and the human being is being acted upon, powerless before God's majesty. Then, at this line—"a soul will know what it has prepared"—the verb shifts to the active voice, granting us agency. Human beings have been handed a unique charge, by which we may choose whether we wish to seek self-perfection. By switching from the passive to the active voice, the Qur'an is doing theology, making a statement about human autonomy and accountability.

In Arabic, the predominant sounds in the first verses are heavy, evoking the cataclysm. Then, in the blink of an eye, the end rhyme changes, and there is a shift to breath-like sounds. In the verses that follow "A soul will know what it has prepared"— *I swear by the moving stars, the planets that sweep along the sky / By the night as it recedes, by the dawn as it gently breathes*—the sounds of the Arabic become breathy, as if the lines themselves are breathing a sigh of relief. Breath is the basis of life. In the Sufi tradition, spiritual practices are built around breath control. The root of these practices is the Qur'anic passage in which God gives life to Adam by breathing into him the divine spirit, or *ruh*. Much of what I have studied and practiced in the Sufi tradition is based around the breath. Part of the practice, or *tariqah*, of Naqshbandi Sufism, is *hush dar dam*, watching the breath.

This means placing awareness in every single breath, so that we may embody the Qur'anic verse that describes the relationship between God and Adam: "I breathed into him of My spirit." The consciousness of breath allows us to internalize the life-giving relationship of God to the archetypal human, to become aware of God's breath within us in the form of spirit.

Khwajah Mir Dard (1721–1785) was a beautiful Urdu poet, musician, and profound Naqshbandi Sufi theologian of Delhi. For him, the practice of hush dar dam is "perishing in the breath of the Merciful," or "becoming worthy of God's spirit." The Sufi master Muhyiuddin Ibn al-ʿArabi speaks of stages of self-perfection in which every human being connects spiritually to a particular prophet and dresses herself in their qualities. Dard connects hush dar dam to the stage of communion with Jesus, who the Qur'an lovingly calls *ruh Allah*, the Spirit of God. These breathing practices connect us to the ruh through friendship with Jesus, who was the perfect expression of the spirit. The Chishti Sufi tradition too offers us countless detailed analyses of the effects of breathing on human physiology, reflecting the connection between the Chishti path and yoga in South Asia. They describe how breath energizes the body and gives life to the heart. Scholar of Islam Scott Kugle tells us how Chishti masters focused on inversion of the breath, which leads to inversion of the self, turning us inside out.[13] The practice opens an entirely new channel in the body that energizes the heart, which in the Sufi tradition is the space in which the divine can most perfectly manifest. Inversion is a traumatic experience. And now I find myself linking the notion of inversion of self to the passage that we are studying together, the inversion of all that we hold certain in the world around us—in both cases, an inversion that manifests the Real.

In the midst of the cosmic upheaval of al-Takwir, the Qur'an inserts a denunciation of an act heinous to our contemporary moral sensibilities, but an acceptable cultural practice in seventh-century Meccan paganism: the burying alive of baby girls. "When the infant girl who was buried alive is asked for what sin she was killed . . ." The fragile newborn, deemed so worthless as to be disposable, is set among the sun, stars, mountains, sea, and skies—juxtaposed against all that is powerful and unchanging—and asked to point a finger at her murderers. It's hard to overemphasize the significance of this move. It is the Qur'an telling us, "Here is what you thought was so important. And here is what you thought was so unimportant." As the passage overturns the cosmos, it overturns social values that are not founded on ethical principles. This text is a warning to those who choose to follow in the footsteps of their ancestors rather than exercise their individual moral conscience. Social practices expressed in the language of tradition appear to be unchangeable. When our commitment to uphold tradition for its own sake takes on the greatest importance in our lives, we run the risk of losing our souls. It is not easy to go against the grain of social expectation. The Qur'an calls it the "steep pass"—our feet may slip, our breath turn ragged, but ultimately, what a view!

This passage calls upon the reader's capacity to imagine these cataclysms. Then it calls upon the reader's moral imagination to imagine a world—and to create communities—where the heinousness of this crime is so self-evident that it becomes unthinkable. People tend to read this as the denunciation of a single practice that thankfully no longer exists. Yet it still happens around the world. Girls are killed, sold, abused, for reasons of shame, honor, power, and cruelty. This text is not intended as a reason for us to be self-congratulatory but rather to consider the blind spots in our own society—child abuse, lack of access to health care, racial and gender injustice, military adventurism. We are living in a world in which apathy makes us culpable. This passage is a call to discover what we need to stand up for today—what is the equivalent of this crime in our time and in our own communities?—so that this question won't apply to us when we are called to judgment. And if we are unable to stand up for an issue on the public stage, we should at least be aware of what we ourselves are engaged in on a daily basis. This is a call to take account of ourselves and our own actions.

There is a tension in this passage that is found throughout the entire Qur'an, the tension between individual accountability and God's overpowering will. At the end of this sura, we find these words:

Where are you going?
This is nothing but a reminder to all beings.
For those who will to walk straight,
You may not will except what God wills,
Lord of all beings.

The passage begins with an intimate question, as though someone were to stop me on the road, shake me by the shoulders,
and speak right in my face. I love the directness of this question.
These are the words of a friend who cares deeply for me and
worries that I'm messing up my life and need to stop. These are
the words of a friend who enrolls me in a twelve-step program.
But then the passage goes on to say that I may not will anything
that God does not will. I'm told that I'm on the wrong path and
that I must will myself to walk straight—but that everything I
do is really the will of God. The passage appears to take away my
agency. In my mind, however, the very existence of the Qur'an
assumes moral agency. The Qur'an is an invitation, and that invitation assumes a choice to accept it or reject it. That choice cannot be wrested from us so crudely. So how do we hold these two
ideas in tandem? How do we walk that line? How we do reach
that point when the distinction between human and divine will
no longer matters?

I think the structure of this passage provides an answer. We
begin with chaos and cataclysm. "When the sun is overturned, /
When the stars fall away": This is the first great jolt. Waking up
to the vagaries of life. The realization, in some way or another,
that there is no such thing as solid ground. Everything that I hold
on to with pride—possessions, relationships, accomplishments
(in short, my ego)—is a fistful of dust.

And then comes the accounting of myself: "When the pages
are folded out." At first, it is harsh—I beat myself up every day.
I am the one at whom the infant child points her tiny finger. My
life has been a series of missteps. I wonder if there is any hope
for me.

But in time I calm down. "By the night as it recedes, by
the dawn as it gently breathes": I move into my breath. I gain
a semblance of control, the ability to slow down and become

meditative. I learn to forgive myself for what I could not have avoided and ask God to help me avoid the same mistakes in the future. Self-accounting becomes a practice, a way of life.

"This is a saying of a noble messenger": I appreciate anew the life story of our beloved Prophet. I turn to him, I grow in love for him, and seek to learn from him.

"You may not will except what God wills, / Lord of all beings": I pray that I keep breathing, that the process of inner clarity and growing self-awareness allows me to discern more clearly the path that God intends for me. Perhaps one day, when I breathe away the chaos, when the mists slowly clear, it will be harder to discern whose will is really at work. I hear anew the words of the poet Iqbal:

> *Raise the self to such exalted heights, that before every divine decree, God will turn to the servant and ask, Tell me, what do you wish your destiny to be?*[14]

— ١٢ —

Taken together, the voices in this chapter reflect on how the Qur'an connects overwhelming divine presence to human ethical behavior. The mystical meeting with God is also a summons to responsibility, justice, and kindness. These thinkers take us full circle, back to Ovamir Anjum's reflections on the opening sura of the Qur'an, where divine encounter requires a human response.

CONCLUDING REFLECTIONS

The Rich Diversity among North American Muslims

The breadth of teachings offered by these Muslim leaders and scholars offers some hint of the wide spectrum of Muslim thought in North America. While it is admittedly not an easy season to be a Muslim here in an age of such suspicion, distrust, and misrepresentation, at the same time it is intellectually and spiritually an extraordinary time and place to be a Muslim thinker and believer. Muslims from a great variety of ethnic and sectarian backgrounds, each with its own distinctive expressions of Islam, meet here and respond to the particular challenges and opportunities of North America in the early twenty-first century. Political and social realities that created tensions among these groups in their places of origin often have less meaning in this new context, allowing for a vibrant coming together of people and ideas. Just as Muslims found unique and pertinent manifestations in other lands and cultures, distinctly North American expressions are evolving in response to contemporary needs and conditions. The gathering of voices in this volume attests to the vitality and creativity of the Muslim community as they discover how to be faithful to their tradition in an era of much change.

Text and Interpretation

This book began with the suggestion that a religious community with a complex Scripture faces a twofold task of articulating what is the core message of its Scripture and of framing an interpretive method for dealing with apparent conflicts within its sacred text. In this intellectually fertile season in the North American Muslim community, the voices in this volume offer a wide range of reflections on these questions, though with much agreement on many matters.

Common themes included the oneness of God,[1] divine mercy,[2] divine and human kindness,[3] justice,[4] human dignity,[5] the possibilities and the limitations of human knowledge,[6] and the need to live in the awareness of divine presence.[7] Many spoke of religious diversity as a divine intention and therefore of the importance of respect and cooperation among different religions.[8] Others advocated for human creativity[9] and the importance of concrete deeds of goodness rather than rituals alone.[10] These and more were held forth as the core of the message of the Qur'an. Taken together, they describe a universe with a compassionate Creator and with human beings who are capable of creating a society characterized by goodness to one another and by devotion to God.

Implicitly and explicitly, the Muslims in this book addressed the question of interpretation of their Scripture. Mohammad Hassan Khalil, Sohaib Sultan, and Zeki Saritoprak offered what might be called a hermeneutic of generosity: the Qur'an must be read from its centeredness in mercy, a wide mercy that permits both Muslims and non-Muslims to flourish both in this life and the next. Similarly, for Zayn Kassam, the face of God is to be seen everywhere, and so it is imperative to treat all with compassion and respect for their dignity. For Hassan al-Qazwini, ethical directives in the Qur'an are to be understood in light of divine values that are shared among faiths, such as kindness and care for those in need.

Others spoke of, or showed through their example, particular ways of reading. Kecia Ali showed that the Qur'an does not conform to cultural expectations, and so reading it requires intense attentiveness and openness. Asma Barlas stressed that it is not a closed text, so one does not decide in advance what it means. Amina Wadud noted that believing Muslims should read the Qur'an with an eye to the transformation of Muslim culture toward more equality and reciprocity. One should not read it in such a way that it narrows the mercy of God. Jamal Badawi pointed out that Islam's sacred text must not be used to justify senseless and unnecessary violence. In the words of the anonymous speaker in the previous chapter, "the light of divine unity obliterates idolatrous readings." The Qur'an lends itself to deeply inward readings, as shown by Homayra Ziad, Jonathan Brown, and Maria Dakake.

Ovamir Anjum declared that if one does not feel a sense of awe, of the presence of the Merciful One who is eager to communicate that the world is good, then one is not really encountering the Qur'an. All these and still more principles of interpretation were offered.

Some reflected on the question of who has interpretive authority of interpreters and why. Zeki Saritoprak, Fareeha Khan, Jamal Badawi, and Sohaib Sultan found strength in Islam's long tradition of interpretation and commentary. Emran El-Badawi and Mohammad Hassan Khalil showed how some traditional commentators might surprise contemporary readers with readings that have been forgotten or largely laid aside. The anonymous scholar paid tribute to Ibn al-ʿArabi even as she moved into new directions. Dawud Walid and Rashad Abdul Rahmaan spoke of respect for the classical tradition but also of the need for interpretation that addresses the distinct situation of North American Muslims, particularly those of African descent. Asma Barlas held that the text itself gives authority to the reader, answerable to something higher within oneself. As in other religious communities, matters of authority are contested in this era of change. This can result in conflict, but it can also lead to creativity and growth as Muslims search for how to live out their faith in new cultural settings. In this regard it is also important to recognize that it is not only relatively recent newcomers to North America (or their descendants) who are changing Islam, but also longtime residents of North America who are newcomers to Islam.

Reading, Listening, Responding

Readers without much background knowledge of Islam may have been surprised by the richness and complexity of Qur'anic interpretation offered by the voices in this volume, who have proven worthy reading companions for those who come as guests to their holy book. Taken together, they have shown how Muslims struggle to be faithful to their religious community, how to be faithfully critical of the community's shortcomings (which all communities with high ideals have), and how to call their community to greater faithfulness.

If, as is hoped, readers have listened with openness to these Muslim teachers, some may be wondering how to respond. If, by their act of generous listening, they have allowed themselves to be moved by the power and beauty of what they have heard, have they somehow compromised their own religious convictions?

234 QUR'AN IN CONVERSATION

For Christian and Jewish readers, some of what they heard was rather familiar. The figures of Abraham, Joseph, Moses, and (for Christians) Mary are familiar from the Bible, even as the details of their stories are varied. There are parallels and analogies with Jewish and Christian ways of interpreting Scripture. Mystics in synagogue or in church have read the Bible allegorically, referring to inward spiritual experiences, as is evidenced in the fourteenth-century *Zohar*,[11] the great kabbalistic commentary on the Torah, or the twelfth-century Cistercian monk Bernard of Clairvaux's sermons on the Song of Songs.[12] Among Christians, during the Protestant Reformation, allegory came largely to be rejected, as was the felt need to read with the guidance of tradition, since the great medieval commentators of western Europe were Catholic and therefore held to teachings that Protestants cast aside. The modern tradition brought new ways of reading for both Jews and Christians, including the historical-critical method employed by Emran El-Badawi in his research into the Qur'an. Recent decades have witnessed the rise of liberationist readings, including feminist and womanist approaches, with which Kecia Ali, Zayn Kassam, Asma Barlas, and Amina Wadud are familiar.[13] These comparisons are offered simply to suggest possible entry points that may be familiar to non-Muslims, not to impose classifications from external religious communities upon these Muslim thinkers.

Elsewhere in this book, the ethical conclusions that these Muslim teachers have drawn from Scripture may have struck a recognizable note, even though the scriptural texts differed significantly from the Bible. At yet other times, the text and the interpretation were new concepts. These moments are also important and instructive. For example, for those who seek to understand their Muslim neighbors and their faith, it is essential to grasp how central the Prophet Muhammad is. Although it is implicit in every chapter in this book, Fareeha Khan, Hassan al-Qazwini, and Fazeel S. Khan, among others, particularly showed how Muslims regard Muhammad not simply with the respect due to a messenger of God but also with abundant warmth and affection. The depth of that love for Muhammad is instructive for outsiders who want to understand Islam, and it can be edifying even for non-Muslims to observe, even if it is not a part of their religious practice, because it is beautiful.

Many of these Muslim teachers have shown how it is possible to be influenced and enriched by the ideas of others outside one's community and yet remain fully committed to one's fundamental convictions and religious identity. Asma Barlas drew on philosopher Paul Ricoeur to think about hermeneutics. Emran El-Badawi stated that a deeper knowledge of ancient Jewish and Christian texts can lead to a fuller understanding of the Qur'an. Zayn Kassam expressed her admiration for theologian Sallie McFague and found harmony between her ideas and a Qur'anic ideal of pluralism and responsible care for the environment.

If these Muslims can maintain their rootedness in Islam and nonetheless fruitfully engage non-Muslim texts and ideas, then it seems feasible that non-Muslims can similarly be enriched by an encounter with the Qur'an. To witness faithful Muslims engage their Scripture with energy, self-honesty, intellectual vitality, and love can inspire others to do the same with their foundational texts. There will be occasions of convergence, just as there will be occasions of profound difference. Whether the conversation is face-to-face or within one's own mind, Muslim and non-Muslim conversation partners may come to agree on how to disagree, in a way that honors the integrity and beauty of each Scripture. Articulating that "how" can be wonderfully liberating, even exhilarating.

ARABIC TERMS

adab	proper behavior, courtesy, good character
alayhi salam	"Upon him be peace," a phrase used in piety after the name of a prophet
amshaj	mixed
ansar	the Helpers, the citizens of Medina who offered support to the Muslim immigrants from Mecca
aql	intellect
asbab al-nuzul	the occasion or circumstances accompanying a revelation of a passage from the Qur'an
asir	captives of war
as-salaamu ʿalaykum	"Peace be with you," a traditional Muslim greeting
awwal	first; origin
aya (pl. *ayat*)	verse of the Qur'an; also sign
baruz	manifestation
barzakh	meeting place of the ocean and the river in Sura 18, where the two waters meet but do not touch; barrier or separation between the physical and spiritual realms, where souls rest before the resurrection
dhawq	taste; used to describe spiritual experience
dhikr	a remembering or commemoration
din	religion, way of life; also judgment, requital
fard al-kifayah	community obligation that can be fulfilled by some members on behalf of all
al-Fatiha	the Opening, the first chapter of the Qur'an

fatrat	the people of *fatrat* are those who did not hear the revelation to Muhammad
fitra	nature, often human nature, and its natural knowledge of morality
hajj	the pilgrimage to Mecca
hanif	pre-Islamic monotheist who is not a Jew or a Christian
haqq	truth, right, pl. (*huquq*) rights
al-Haqq	the Real, the Truth; one of God's 99 names
hur	pure; attendants in paradise
ijaza	formal qualification granting authority to teach
ijmaaʿ	consensus of the scholars
ijtihaad	scholarly opinions
ikhbat	humility
'ilm laduni	knowledge from My (God's) presence
injil	Gospel
istikhara	to seek the good; to open the Qur'an and point a finger at a verse for guidance
jihad	struggle, exertion, effort
jinn	a class of spiritual beings, neither angel nor human
kafur	a drink of paradise
kalimah	Word; used to refer to Jesus as the Word of God
khalifa	successor, representative, vice-regent
kuffar	unbelievers, those who are disobedient or ungrateful
kufr	disbelief, ingratitude
maʿrifa	(spiritual) knowledge
maʿruf	that which is known
maʿun	kindness
majma al-bahrayn	the meeting of the two seas
al-mal	property, wealth
Malik	Master, king owner—name for God
maqasid	objective
milla	religion
miskin	poor
mu'minun	believers
mubashshirat	good news
mufʾlihun	successful ones
muhajirun	the Migrants, the Muslims of Medina who took up residence in Medina

mujaddid	one who renews or revives, reformer
muqatta'at	unconnected letters that are found at the start of some suras
mushrikun	those who associate the worship of God with another deity; polytheists
nabi	prophet
nafs	self, being, soul; sometimes the lower self
naskh	abrogation or supercession of an earlier revealed verse
nikah	marriage
qiwama	guardianship
qiyaas	analogical deduction
Rabb	another title for God, the caregiver (also sovereign)
rahma	loving mercy
Rahman, Rahim	merciful, compassionate—names for God
rasul	messenger, a prophet who brings a Scripture
ruh	breath, spirit
sabr	patience
sadaqa	charity
sakeena	tranquility
salat	ritual prayer
shirk	associating others with God
sunna	example from the life or teachings of Muhammad
sura	chapter of the Qur'an
ta'wil	deeper interpretation of the Qur'an
tafsir	commentary on the Qur'an
takhsees	specifying and limiting the ruling of a verse
talab	a desire to seek or learn
taqwa	consciousness of God, regardfulness, awareness
tarbiyah	education, caring for a child
tariqah	Sufi order
tawhid	the oneness of God
wali	patron, protector, religious guide
yawm al-din	Day of Judgment
zakat	purification, alms, giving of charity
zamharir	a section of hell that burns with its coldness
zill	shadow

NOTES

Introduction

1   In general, since the time of the apostle Paul, Christians have not felt bound to observe all the laws of Deuteronomy. For Paul, Christ brought freedom from the Jewish law. In extant ancient Christian commentary on the Bible, this passage is simply ignored. The multivolume *Ancient Christian Commentary on Scripture* thoroughly researched early Christian literature in multiple languages but located no explanations of this passage (Joseph T. Lienhard, *Exodus, Leviticus, Numbers, Deuteronomy*, Ancient Christian Commentary on Scripture, Old Testament 3 [Downers Grove, Ill.: InterVarsity, 2001]), which at least supports the point that this passage was not central to their understanding of Christianity. As an example of a much later voice, in his *Lectures on Deuteronomy* (English translation in vol. 9 of his *Works* [St. Louis, Mo.: Concordia, 1960], 215), Protestant reformer Martin Luther allegorizes this passage: the son is a son of the church, and the death is not physical. In general, Luther's understanding of biblical law is that its purpose is to drive people to the grace of Christ because the law is impossible to fulfill.

    Jewish tradition offers a different approach. This law is part of the Written Torah, which is interpreted by the Oral Torah, preserved in the vast corpus of rabbinic wisdom gathered in the Talmud, which treats this law in tractate *Sanhedrin*. There the rabbis "attenuated the force of this law by making the son's violation much more stringent than the text suggests, essentially eliminating cases in which the penalty would apply." Bernard M. Levinson, in Adele Berlin, Marc Zvi Brettler, and Michael Fishbane, *The Jewish Study Bible: Jewish Publication Society Tanakh Translation* (Oxford: Oxford University Press, 2004), 415. One Talmudic sage stated that the conditions that would result in the death penalty for this offense "never occurred and never will occur." W. Gunther Plaut, *The Torah: A Modern Commentary* (New York: Union of American Hebrew congregations, 1981), 1484.

2   Different branches of Christianity would make different choices. For many Prot-
     estants, for example, the biblical center of gravity would be Paul's statement
     that justification comes by faith (Rom 3:28). For many Orthodox, who espouse a
     theology based on God sanctifying the cosmos through the incarnation, the cen-
     tral truth of the Bible is that in Christ the Word became flesh and dwelt among
     humankind (John 1:14).

3   The literature on biblical interpretation and hermeneutics is immense. A
     glimpse of possibilities can be seen in John Barton, *The Cambridge Companion to
     Biblical Interpretation* (Cambridge: Cambridge University Press, 1998); and in John
     F. A. Sawyer, *The Blackwell Companion to the Bible and Culture* (Oxford: Blackwell,
     2006).

4   See the accounts, for example, in Carl Ernst, *Islamophobia in America* (New York:
     Palgrave Macmillan, 2013); John Esposito and Ibrahim Kalin, *Islamophobia: The
     Challenge of Pluralism in the 21st Century* (Oxford: Oxford University Press, 2011);
     and Nathan Lean, *The Islamophobia Industry: How the Right Manufactures Fear of
     Muslims* (London: Pluto Press, 2012).

5   Ingrid Mattson, whose words appear in the next chapter, has authored *The Story
     of the Qur'an: Its History and Place in Muslim Life*, 2nd ed. (Oxford: Wiley-Blackwell,
     2013).

6   The author met, in person or virtually, with these Muslim teachers and then
     transcribed and edited the recordings of these encounters. Many preferred to
     maintain the spoken quality of the conversations, while others opted for a less
     informal tone, adding to the variety of presentations in the chapters that follow.
     Unless noted otherwise, all explanatory notes are added by the author.

7   This diversity is suggested in the title of Vartan Gregorian's *Islam: A Mosaic, Not a
     Monolith* (Washington, D.C.: Brookings Institution, 2003). For a sense of the range
     of interpretations of the Qur'an throughout its history, see the two volumes of
     Mahmoud Ayoub, *The Qur'an and Its Interpreters* (Albany: State University of New
     York Press, 1984–1992).

Chapter 1

1   A *hadith qudsi* ("holy narration") is a saying of Muhammad that is of divine origin
     but not of the same status of revelation as the Qur'an. Traditionally understood,
     the text of the Qur'an is direct divine speech. A hadith qudsi is words of divine
     inspiration but expressed in human speech. This hadith is cited often in Islamic
     spirituality. See, for example, the mystic-poet Rumi's use of it in William C. Chit-
     tick, *The Sufi Path of Love: The Spiritual Teachings of Rumi* (Albany: State University of
     New York Press, 1983), 47, 56, 71; and the highly influential mystic Ibn al-ʿArabi's
     references to it as noted in William C. Chittick, *The Sufi Path of Knowledge: Ibn
     al-ʿArabi's Metaphysics of Imagination* (Albany: State University of New York Press,
     1989), 66, 126, 131, 204.

2   John Calvin, *Institutes of the Christian Religion* (Philadelphia: Westminster, 1960).
     Book 1 is "The Knowledge of God the Creator," while book 2 is "The Knowledge
     of God the Redeemer in Christ." In this authoritative translation by the great
     scholar Ford Lewis Battles, these two books are five hundred pages long, which
     may indicate the importance of the topic to Calvin.

3   A translation may be found in John of Damascus, *Saint John of Damascus: Writings* (New York: Fathers of the Church, 1958).

4   See Thomas Aquinas, *Summa theologiae: Latin text and English Translation, Introductions, Notes, Appendices, and Glossaries* (Cambridge: Blackfriars, 1964).

5   See Moses Maimonides, *The Guide of the Perplexed*, trans. Shlomo Pines (Chicago: University of Chicago Press, 1963).

6   A pivotal study of the role of knowledge in Islam is Franz Rosenthal, *Knowledge Triumphant: The Concept of Knowledge in Medieval Islam* (Leiden: Brill, 1970). On p. 2 he writes:

> For *'ilm* [knowledge] is one of those concepts that have dominated Islam and given Muslim civilization its distinctive shape and complexion. In fact, there is no other concept that has been operative as a determinative of Muslim civilization in all its aspects to the same extent as *'ilm.* . . . There is not a branch of Muslim intellectual life, of Muslim religious and political life, and of the daily life of the average Muslim that remained untouched by the all-pervasive attitude toward "knowledge" as something of supreme value for Muslim being.

> In his chapter on worship in T. J. Winter, ed., *The Cambridge Companion to Classical Islamic Theology* (Cambridge: Cambridge University Press, 2008), William C. Chittick wrote that in Islamic theology, "The importance of knowledge cannot be overstressed. . . . Ali put it his way, 'There is no good in a worship without knowledge, and there is no good in a knowledge in which there is no understanding'" (221).

> For important studies of the role of knowledge in the theology of Islamic spirituality, see Chittick, *Sufi Path of Knowledge;* and John Renard, *Knowledge of God in Classical Sufism: Foundations of Islamic Mystical Theology* (New York: Paulist Press, 2004).

7   Abu Hamid Muhammad Ibn Muhammad al-Ghazali (c. 1058–1111) has exerted an enormous influence on Muslim thought. A distinguished polymath, he wrote on theology, philosophy, religious law, and spirituality or mysticism. Note: because most readers of this book will not be Muslim, the dates are given in the calendar of the Common Era familiar in the West.

Taqi ad-Din Ahmad Ibn Taymiyya (1263–1328) was another scholar fluent in multiple religious and secular disciplines. Because he wrote at the time of the Mongol invasions, there is a distinct edge to his writings. Eager to preserve both Islamic religion and the intellectual achievements of Muslim culture in a time of threat, his language against non-Muslims, or even fellow Muslims who threatened Arabic civilization (the Mongols had converted to Islam), could be harshly critical. As a result, Ibn Taymiyya has become a favorite of ultraconservative Muslims. Thoughtful scholars such as Ovamir Anjum who appreciate the subtlety of Ibn Taymiyya's thought offer a more nuanced view of this important thinker.

Shams al-Din Abu Bakr Ibn Qayyim al-Jawziyyah (1292–1350) was the most prominent disciple of Ibn Taymiyya. His vast output includes works on theology, ethics, religious law, and commentary on the Qur'an.

8   Passages set off in italics are words of the Qur'an.

9   Clive Staples Lewis (1898–1963) was a scholar of medieval English literature, a

novelist best known for his children's books *The Chronicles of Narnia*, as well as *The Great Divorce* and *The Screwtape Letters*, and a lay Christian apologist who authored such works as *Mere Christianity*, a favorite of many conservative Christians.

10 Hans Küng (b. 1928) is an important progressive Catholic theologian. Perhaps his most influential work is *On Being a Christian*. He is a significant promoter of ecumenical and interfaith understanding and has written about Judaism and Buddhism, as well as a large volume entitled *Islam: Past, Present, and Future*. While still recognized as a priest by the Catholic Church, his controversial stance on papal infallibility resulted in the Vatican revoking his permission to teach Catholic theology.

11 The Muʿtazilites were a philosophical school that flourished in the eighth and ninth centuries in the cities of Basra and Baghdad. They emphasized the role of human rationality. Their particular traits included an insistence on human freedom over predestination and a rejection of the notion (accepted by many) of the Qurʾan as participating in God's eternal nature, as in their eyes this undermined the fundamental Islamic teaching on the absolute unity of God.

12 In his *Conferences* 9.31, Cassian quotes the early monastic Antony as saying, "It is not perfect prayer when the monks are aware of themselves or even that they are praying." (Non est perfecta oratio in qua se monachus, vel hoc ipsum quod orat, intellegit [Joannes Cassianus, *Joannis Cassiani opera Omnia*, Patrologia Latina 49 (Paris: Migne, 1865), col. 808]).

Chapter 2

1 This is a wide-ranging group. Rashid Rida was an important voice for Muslim reform in the first part of the twentieth century. Sayyid Qutb resisted both indigenous political tyranny and Western imperialism in the Muslim world. He was an Egyptian journalist rather than a trained Muslim scholar, but his enormous, multivolume commentary *In the Shade of the Qurʾan* is a call to return to Islamic purity and is a favorite of Muslim extremists. Farid Esack is a contemporary South African Muslim who is a tireless advocate for justice. Abdulaziz Sachedina grew up in Africa of Indian descent, teaches in a university in Virginia, and is a significant Muslim ethicist. Mahmoud Ayoub is a Lebanese Muslim scholar, also a long-time professor in the United States, and a major Muslim thinker in the realm of interfaith relations. T. J. Winter, a convert to Islam and a professor in the United Kingdom, is an important theologian.

2 Mahmud Ibn ʿUmar al-Zamakhshari (1075–1144) was a Qurʾan commentator, grammarian, lexicographer, and theologian. His commentary on the Qurʾan achieved canonical status in the Muslim world: hundreds of manuscript copies survive, many printed editions were undertaken in the last two centuries, and his commentary was itself commented upon by later scholars from the thirteenth century to the present. Ibn Taymiyya, whom we met in the previous chapter, accused al-Zamakhshari of Muʿtazilite tendencies, but these did not tarnish the authority of his commentary on the Qurʾan, which has remained a standard component of Muslim learning for centuries.

3 Rashid Rida (1865–1935) was a major leader of an Islamic movement of

reinvigoration and reform. Along with other Muslim thinkers such as Jamal al-Din al-Afghani (1839–1897) and Muhammad ʿAbduh (1849–1905), he proposed a modernist vision of Islam that intellectually embraced the findings of science and that politically resisted corrupt governments and imperialist domination by European forces.

4   See Michel Cuypers, *The Banquet: A Reading of the Fifth Sura*, trans. Patricia Kelly (Miami: Convivium Press, 2009); and Carl W. Ernst, *How to Read the Qurʾan: A New Guide, with Select Translations* (Chapel Hill: University of North Carolina Press, 2011).

5   Theodor Nöldeke (1836–1930) was a pioneer of modern Western scholarship of Islam. He published his influential *Geschichte des Koran* (*History of the Qurʾan*) in 1860.

6   These are deities of pre-Islamic Arabia.

7   The references here are to early Syriac Christian thinkers and controversialists. Most writings of the theologically elusive Bardaisan (ca. 155–222) have not survived, and his questionable reputation is derived chiefly from those who wrote against him, sometimes centuries after his time. Aphrahat wrote some polemics against Jewish doctrines and practices in the early fourth century, apparently at a time when some Christians of his day were promoting the adoption of Jewish elements into Christianity in that region. Isaac of Nineveh wrote in the seventh century. He is best remembered as a writer on ascetic and monastic spirituality. Nestorians and Jacobites (or Monophysites) arose during the fierce theological debates about the relationship between divine and human natures essences in Christ, and the implication of this relationship for salvation, that raged from the fifth century onward.

8   Fred Donner's views may be found in his *Muhammad and the Believers: At the Origins of Islam* (Cambridge, Mass.: Harvard University Press, 2010).

9   These early Christian texts share some similar material with the Qurʾan, such as the story of Jesus fashioning clay birds and then miraculously bringing them to life (Thomas 1:3; Qurʾan 3:49 and 5:110) and the account of Mary in the temple before the birth of Jesus (James throughout; Qurʾan 3:35ff.) The Qurʾanic passage on Mary is the focus of Kecia Ali's conversation later in this chapter.

10   These are three outstanding classical scholars and historically influential commentators on the Qurʾan: Abd Allah Abu Muhammad Abd Allah Ibn Muslim al-Dinwari Ibn Qutaybah (d. 889), Abu Jafar Muhammad Ibn Jarir al-Tabari (d. 923), and Abu al-Fadl ʿAbd al-Rahman Ibn Abi Bakr Ibn Muhammad Jalal al-Din al-Khudayri al-Suyuti (1445–1505).

11   Ibrahim Ibn ʿUmar al al-Biqaʿi (1407–1480) composed a lengthy commentary on the Qurʾan in which he discussed both the canonical texts of the Hebrew Bible and the New Testament.

12   Paul Ricoeur (1913–2005) was a major philosopher of the last century who wrote about memory, history, freedom, evil, symbolism, ethics, narrative, the nature of language, and more. Asma Barlas' interest here is in Ricoeur's reflections on the interrelatedness between the act of interpretation and the experience of an enhanced understanding of selfhood.

13   Mahmud Muhammad Taha (1936–1985) was a Muslim reformer who called for

modernization of shariah law. He gave primacy to the earlier or Meccan portions of the Qur'an, which were revealed before the Medinan verses, which contain most of the legal pronouncements of the Qur'an. In other words, the spirit of the early revelations of the Qur'an, with their emphasis on justice and care for the marginalized, is given priority over the specific legal material. This in turn allows for change in law that fits modern times but adheres in principle to the Qur'an's overarching message. His proposal was perceived as a critique of the shariah law imposed by the then government of Sudan, resulting in a show trial and his execution.

14   We have already met the great philosopher and mystic Ibn al-'Arabi in the first chapter, and his name will come up again later in this book. Often regarded as the first existentialist philosopher, prolific Danish writer Søren Kierkegaard (1813–1855) was an ethicist, social critic, and religious thinker, as well as a literary critic and composer of fiction.

15   Because our conversation at various points assumed familiarity with her argument in the above-mentioned article, Asma Barlas kindly gave me permission to incorporate some of its insights into this report of our conversation.

16   Although the Bible does not contain this story, pre-Islamic Jewish commentary on the Genesis story of Abraham tells a similar tale. See James L. Kugel, *The Bible as It Was* (Cambridge, Mass.: Harvard University Press, 1997), 133–38.

Chapter 3

1   These are prominent Muslim experts of religious jurisprudence from the fifteenth, eighteenth, and twentieth century, respectively.

2   'Umar Ibn Abdul-Aziz (682–720) was a Daiesascus caliph in the Ummayad Dynasty. His short reign, from 717 until his death by poisoning in 720, is remembered for his piety and charity.

Chapter 4

1   The English philosopher John Locke (1632–1704) was a major figure of the European Enlightenment and is remembered best for his contributions to political philosophy, religious toleration, and theory of knowledge.

2   The war in Vietnam was a lengthy conflict, extending from the mid-1950s through the mid-1970s, which reflected the worldwide tensions in the Cold War between the United States and the Soviet Union and their respected allies. This protracted conflict became increasingly unpopular in the United States by the mid-1960s, when the presence of U.S. military advisors was supplemented by ever larger numbers of combat troops, dependent upon conscription in a time when young people who were influenced by the civil rights movement and its emphasis on social justice and nonviolence questioned the moral legitimacy of the war.

3   Stokely Carmichael (1941–1998) was a prominent advocate for social justice, associated successively with the civil rights movement, the Black Power Movement, and the Black Panther Party.

4   Whitney Young (1921–1971) was an important civil rights leader, best known for his leadership in the National Urban League, an organization dedicated to overcoming racial discrimination. With Whitney Young as executive director, the league moved from cautious advocacy to full participation in the civil rights movement.

5   Ingrid Mattson is a Muslim scholar and leader whose words appear earlier in this volume, where she is more fully introduced.

6   Sayyid M. Syeed was for a long time the Secretary General of the Islamic Society of North America. In recent years he has focused his work in the interfaith sphere as the national director for the Office for Interfaith and Community Alliances for the Islamic Society of North America.

7   Often cited as one of the most influential Muslims internationally, Hamza Yusuf is a convert to Islam who spent many years in study in traditional Muslim settings. He is cofounder and president of Zaytuna College, a recently established Muslim liberal arts college and the first of its kind in North America. The bold experiment of Zaytuna College is represented in this volume by the voice of its dean of faculty, Mahan Mirza, whose words are in a later chapter.

8   Fazlur Rahman (1919–1988) taught Islamic studies at the University of Chicago for many years. The author of numerous influential works, he has been described as a reforming, modernizing voice within Islam.

9   In Hindu traditions, *bhakti* is the religious path of intense devotion. *Ginans* are devotional poems and hymns often associated with the Nizari branch of Ismaili Shi'ites in South Asia. Both bhakti and ginans are frequently associated with ecstatic worship and with recognition of the spirit of devotion across religious boundaries.

10   The term "Parsis" refers to Zoroastrians of Persian origin who settled in South Asia.

11   Sikhism began in the north Indian region of Punjab, founded by Guru Nanak in the fifteenth century. The Sikh religious community describes its ideals as constant remembrance of the one formless God, human equality, service and generosity, and rejection of empty rituals.

12   Goan Christians trace their roots to the Portuguese colonization and evangelization efforts in the Indian state of Goa, along that country's west coast.

13   Sallie McFague, who taught for many years at Vanderbilt University, is a prominent feminist theologian who has written about the role of metaphor in theology, applying that concept in her description of the earth as God's body. In her 1993 book *The Body of God: An Ecological Theology*, she makes a case for panentheism.

14   Both Asma Barlas and Amina Wadud appear in chapters 2 and 6 of this book, respectively.

Chapter 5

1   http://www.muslim.org/who.htm.

2   His translation and commentary on the Qur'an are available at http://www.muslim.org/english-quran/index.htm. It is this translation from which Fazeel S. Khan quotes below. Many of his progressive ideas are also found in his important

book *The Religion of Islam*, which is available at http://www.aaiil.org/text/books/
mali/religionislam/religionofislam.pdf.

3   The Qur'an identifies the Sabians as a monotheistic religious group. They are
mentioned positively along with Jews and Christians in the Qur'an (2:62, 5:59, and
22:17).

4   Muhammad Asad, *The Message of the Qur'an* (Bristol: Book Foundation, 2003),
969n15. Muhammad Asad (1900–1992) was one of the most influential European
Muslims of the twentieth century. A linguist, journalist, diplomat, and modernist thinker, he is best known for his translation of the Qur'an, *The Message of
the Qur'an*, a work that includes extensive footnotes that draw on a wide range
of Islamic learning. Among the many classical authorities cited by Asad is the
philosopher and theologian Fakhr al-Din al-Razi (1149–1210), whose formidable
commentary on the Qur'an has been greatly influential in Muslim history.

Chapter 6

1   The four dominant schools of religious jurisprudence in Sunni Islam are known
as Hanafi, Shafi'i, Maliki, and Hanbali. The jurist Muhammad Ibn Idris al-Shafi'i
lived from 767 to 820. Kecia Ali, who appears in an earlier chapter, wrote a book
on him, *Imam Shafi'i: Scholar and Saint* (Oxford: Oneworld, 2011).

2   Qur'an 5:32.

3   Qur'an 5:8.

4   James 2:17.

5   See Michael A. Sells, *Approaching the Qur'an: The Early Revelations* (Ashland, Ore.:
White Cloud Press, 1999), 7.

Chapter 7

1   Unlike elsewhere in this volume, the notes in this section are the work of the
Muslim scholar rather than the author.

2   My theological outlook is heavily indebted to the work of Muhyiddin Ibn al-'Arabi,
Amina Wadud, and Ann Holmes Redding. I have taken from each, I hope accurately and in keeping with spirit of their work, but ultimately this reflection
should be read as a personal interpretation of the Qur'an through their work.
Thanks to all those who helped with this piece; I know you understand why I
cannot mention your names.

3   On these and related readings, see the work of Amina Wadud, Nasr Abou Zaid,
Mohammad Arkoun, Fazlur Rahman, and Abdul Karim Soroush.

4   The locus classicus of the responsive nature of the Qur'an is the *asbab al-nuzul*
literature, which documents the traditional accounts of the occasions of descent
of individual passages. On asbab al-nuzul literature, see Andrew Rippin, "Occasions of Revelation," in *Encylopaedia of the Qur'an*, ed. Jane Dammen McAuliffe, 6
vols. (Leiden: Brill, 2001–2006), 3:569–73.

5   On Khawla, see Mohja Kahf, "Braiding the Stories: Women's Eloquence in the
Early Islamic Era," in *Windows of Faith: Muslim Women's Scholarship and Activism*, ed.
Gisela Webb, 147–71 (Syracuse, N.Y.: Syracuse University Press, 2000).

6   On the interpretation of this verse, past and present, see Ayesha Chaudhry,

Domestic Violence and the Islamic Tradition: Ethics, Law and the Muslim Discourse on Gender (Oxford: Oxford University Press, 2014).

7   These numbers refer to location of the hadith in the classical collections of Ibn Majah, Tirmidhi, Muslim, and Abu Dawud (ed.).

8   Chaudhry, *Domestic Violence*, 41–44.

9   It is reported the Prophet said, "If you hear a hadith that your heart accepts, that your mind and body are at ease with, and you feel that it is acceptable to you, then it is even more acceptable to me. If you hear a hadith that makes your skin cringe, and your hearts or minds turn against it, and you feel that it is inconceivable (*baʿid*) to you, then it is even more inconceivable to me." On this hadith and its use by hadith scholars, see Jonathan A. C. Brown, "The Rules of Matn Criticism: There Are No Rules," *Islamic Law and Society* 19 (2012): 356–96.

10   While the hadith of prostration ostensibly forbids one to prostrate before another, it is sometimes cited in sections on marriage in the hadith collections to express the extent of a husband's rights over his wife: Abu Dawud, Book of Marriage, #2140; Tirmidhi, Chapters on Suckling, The Husband's Rights over the Wife, #1159; Ibn Majah, Chapters on Marriage, #1853.

11   See Kecia Ali, *Marriage and Slavery in Early Islam* (Cambridge, Mass.: Harvard University Press, 2010).

12   On the "Tawhidic Paradigm," see Amina Wadud, *Inside the Gender Jihad: Women's Reform in Islam* (Oxford: Oneworld, 2006), and her many online essays on the subject.

13   Scott Kugle, *Sufis and Saints' Bodies: Mysticism, Corporeality, and Sacred Power in Islam* (Chapel Hill: University of North Carolina Press, 2007), 238–40.

14   This is Homayra Ziad's own translation from Urdu of a much-loved passage from *ghazal* number 33 in part 2 of Muhammad Iqbal, *Bal-e-Jibril* [Gabriel's wing] (Lahore: Sheikh Mubarak Ali, 1935). The title of the poem may be translated "Why should I ask wise men about my origin?" and the original may be viewed at http://www.allamaiqbal.com/works/poetry/urdu/bal/text/index.htm.

Concluding Reflections

1   See Zeki Saritoprak, Fareeha Khan, Jamal Badawi, James E. Jones, Zayn Kassam, and the anonymous contributor.

2   See Ovamir Anjum, Mohammad Hassan Khalil, Jamal Badawi, Zeki Saritoprak, Sohaib Sultan, Fareeha Khan, Eboo Pate, and Fazeel S. Khan.

3   See Hassan al-Qazwini, Fazeel S. Khan, Ovamir Anjum, Suʿad Abdul Khabeer, Mahan Mirza, Mohammad Hassan Khalil, and Jonathan Brown.

4   See Dawud Walid, James E. Jones, Amina Wadud, Homayra Ziad, Eboo Patel, Zayn Kassam, Jamal Badawi, Suʿad Abdul Khabeer, Asma Barlas, and the anonymous scholar.

5   See Zayn Kassam, Eboo Patel, Ayesha Chaudhry, and Homayra Ziad.

6   See Ingrid Mattson, Maria Dakake, and Ovamir Anjum.

7   See Rashad Abdul Rahmaan, James E. Jones, Sohaib Sultan, Eboo Patel, and Homayra Ziad.

8   See Fazeel S. Khan, Zayn Kassam, Eboo Patel, Jamal Badawi, and Emran El-Badawi.

9   See Su'ad Abdul Khabeer, Eboo Patel, and Rashad Abdul Rahmaan.

10   See Rashad Abdul Rahmaan, Fazeel S. Khan, Dawud Walid, and Sohaib Sultan.

11   A new English translation of the *Zohar* is underway: Daniel Chanan Matt, *The Zohar* [Sefer ha-Zohar] (Stanford, Calif.: Stanford University Press, 2004). For a useful introduction, see Arthur Green, *A Guide to the Zohar* (Stanford, Calif.: Stanford University Press, 2004); and Daniel Chanan Matt, *Zohar: The Book of Enlightenment* (New York: Paulist Press, 1983).

12   A complete English translation is available: Bernard of Clairvaux, *On the Song of Songs*, 4 vols. (Spencer, Mass: Cistercian, 1971–1980).

13   For a survey of the history of biblical interpretation, see "Interpretation, History of," in *The Oxford Companion to the Bible*, ed. Bruce M. Metzger, Michael D. Coogan, Philip S. Alexander, Karlfried Froehlich, and Jerry H. Bentley, Oxford Biblical Studies Online, http://www.oxfordbiblicalstudies.com/article/opr/t120/e0350 (accessed September 10, 2013). See also the essay "Jewish Interpretation of the Bible," in Adele Berlin, Marc Zvi Brettler, and Michael Fishbane, *The Jewish Study Bible: Jewish Publication Society Tanakh Translation* (Oxford: Oxford University Press, 2004), 1829–1919. For examples of feminist and womanist readings, see Carol A. Newsom, Sharon H. Ringe, and Jacqueline E. Lapsley, *Women's Bible Commentary* (Louisville, Ky.: Westminster John Knox, 2012).

FURTHER READING ON
INTERPRETATION OF THE QUR'AN

Published commentary on the Qur'an by North American Muslims is recent and only beginning. The following books are suggested for readers who want to know more about the interpretation of the Qur'an over history, particularly among the classical sources.

Gätje, Helmut. *The Qur'an and Its Exegesis.* Translated and edited by Alford T. Welch. Oxford: Oneworld, 1996. This book is a useful place to begin for a sampling of classical Muslim commentary on the Qur'an, arranged topically.

Ayoub, Mahmoud. *The Qur'an and Its Interpreters.* Vol. 1. Albany: State University of New York Press, 1984. Vol. 2, *The House of 'Imran.* Albany: State University of New York Press, 1992. These two volumes draw on the lengthy history of interpretation of the Qur'an and together treat the first three suras of Islam's sacred text.

Ali, Maulana Muhammad. *The Holy Qur'an.* Columbus, Ohio: Ahmadiyya Anjum Isha'at Islam, Lahore U.S.A., 1995. Available at http://www .muslim.org/english-quran/index.htm.

Asad, Muhammad. *The Message of the Qur'an.* Bristol: Book Foundation, 2003.

Each of these translations contains extensive notes, many of them based in the classical commentators yet also offering insights by the translators themselves.

For readers seeking more detailed commentary, again drawn chiefly from classical sources, the following series are valuable.

The Institute of Ismaili Studies in London is producing a series entitled *An Anthology of Qur'anic Commentaries*. The first volume has appeared:

> Hamza, Feras, and Sajjad Rizvi, and Farhana Mayer, eds. *On the Nature of the Divine*. London: Institute of Ismaili Studies; Oxford: Oxford University Press, 2008.

Fons Vitae Publishing and the Royal Aal al-Bayt Institute for Islamic Thought are publishing a series entitled *Great Commentaries on the Holy Qur'an*. To this date these volumes have appeared: vol. 1, *Tafsir al-Jalalayn* (2007); vol. 2, *Tafsir Ibn Abbas* (2008); vol. 3, *Al-Wahidi's Asbab al-Nuzul* (2008); vol. 4, *Tafsir al-Tustari* (2011).

Fons Vitae has also published *Spiritual Gems: The Mystical Qur'an Commentary Ascribed to Imam Ja'far al-Sadiq*. Translated and annotated by Farhana Mayer. Louisville, Ky.: Fons Vitae, 2011.

PARTICIPANTS

Su'ad Abdul Khabeer is assistant professor of anthropology and African American studies at Purdue University. She researches the intersection of race, religion, and popular culture, including young Muslims and hip-hop. She has written for the *Washington Post*, *The Root*, and the *Huffington Post*.

Rashad Abdul Rahmaan is an imam of Masjid Sultan Mohammed and assistant director of education at Clara Mohammed School in Milwaukee, Wisconsin, where he is also very active in interfaith dialogue in numerous settings.

Kecia Ali is associate professor of religion at Boston University. Her books include *Sexual Ethics and Islam: Feminist Reflections on Qur'an, Hadith, and Jurisprudence* (2006), *Marriage and Slavery in Early Islam* (2010), and *Imam Shafi'i: Scholar and Saint* (2011).

Hassan al-Qazwini is the imam of the largest mosque in North America, the Islamic Center of America in Dearborn, Michigan. He has written *American Crescent: A Muslim Cleric on the Power of His Faith, the Struggle against Prejudice, and the Future of Islam and America* (2007).

Ovamir Anjum is the Imam Khattab Chair of Islamic Studies and associate professor in the department of philosophy and religious studies at the University of Toledo. He has written *Politics, Law, and Community in Islamic Thought: The Taymiyyan Moment* (2012) and is at work on a translation and analysis of Ibn Qayyim's *Madarij al-Salikin* (Ranks of divine seekers).

Jamal Badawi is professor emeritus of commerce and religion at St. Mary's University in Halifax, Nova Scotia. His books include *Gender Equity in Islam: Basic Principles* (1995) and *Leadership: An Islamic Perspective* (1999).

Asma Barlas is professor of politics and director of the Center for the Study of Culture, Race, and Ethnicity at Ithaca College. Her books include *"Believing Women" in Islam: Unreading Patriarchal Interpretations of the Qur'an* (2002), *Re-understanding Islam: A Double Critique* (2008), *Islam, Muslims, and the U.S.: Essays on Religion and Politics* (2004), and *Democracy, Nationalism, and Communalism: The Colonial Legacy in South Asia* (1995).

Jonathan A. C. Brown is associate professor of Islamic studies and Muslim-Christian understanding at Georgetown University. His books include *Misquoting Muhammad: The Challenges and Choices of Interpreting the Prophet's Legacy* (2014), *Muhammad: A Very Short Introduction* (2011), *Hadith: Muhammad's Legacy in the Medieval and Modern World* (2009), and *The Canonization of al-Bukhari and Muslim: The Formation and Function of the Sunni Hadith Canon* (2007).

Ayesha S. Chaudhry is assistant professor of Islamic studies and gender studies in the department of classical, Near Eastern and religious studies and the Institute for Gender, Race, Sexuality and Social Justice at the University of British Columbia. She has written *Domestic Violence and the Islamic Tradition: Ethics, Law and the Muslim Discourse on Gender* (2014).

Maria Dakake is associate professor of Islamic studies at George Mason University. She is one of the editors of the *HarperCollins Study Qur'an* and is the author of *The Charismatic Community: Shiʿite Identity in Early Islam* (2007).

Emran El-Badawi is assistant professor of Arabic language and literature and director of the Arabic program at the University of Houston. He is also codirector of the International Qur'anic Studies Association and has written *The Qur'an and the Aramaic Gospel Traditions* (2013).

James E. (Jimmy) Jones is associate professor of world religions at Manhattanville College, where he holds a concurrent appointment in African studies. He also serves as visiting professor at the Graduate School of Islamic and Social Sciences and has been director of the Al-Azhar University Arabic Summer Immersion Program. He contributed a chapter to *Peace-Building by, between, and beyond Muslims and Evangelical Christians* (2010).

Zayn Kassam is the John Knox McLean Professor of Religious Studies at Pomona College in Claremont, California. Her books include *Introduction to the World's Major Religions: Islam* (2005) and an edited volume, *Women and Islam* (2010).

Mohammad Hassan Khalil is associate professor of religious studies at Michigan State University. He is the author of *Islam and the Fate of Others: The Salvation Question* (2012) and the editor of *Between Heaven and Hell: Islam, Salvation, and the Fate of Others* (2013).

Fareeha Khan is an affiliated scholar at Willamette University. She is advisory editor of the *Oxford Encyclopedia of Islamic Law* and is completing her first book, *The Ethical Contours of a Fatwa: Women, Sufism and Islamic Law in Late Colonial India.*

Fazeel S. Khan is by profession a civil rights attorney who also serves as secretary of the Lahore Ahmadiyya Islamic Society and editor of *The Light and Islamic Review.*

Ingrid Mattson holds the London and Windsor Community Chair in Islamic Studies at Huron University College at the University of Western Ontario in London, Canada. Formerly she was professor of Islamic studies, founder of the Islamic Chaplaincy Program, and director of the Macdonald Center for the Study of Islam and Christian-Muslim Relations at Hartford Seminary, as well as the president of the Islamic Society of North America. She has written *The Story of the Qur'an: Its History and Place in Muslim Life* (2nd ed., 2013).

Mahan Mirza served as a college chaplain and a university professor prior to his current position as dean of faculty at Zaytuna College, the first Islamic liberal arts college in North America. He is an editor of the *Princeton Encyclopedia of Islamic Political Thought* (2012).

Eboo Patel is founder and president of Interfaith Youth Core, an organization that partners with colleges and universities to advance interfaith leadership. He has served on President Obama's Inaugural Faith Council and is the author of *Acts of Faith: The Story of an American Muslim, the Struggle for the Soul of a Generation* (2007) and *Sacred Ground: Pluralism, Prejudice, and the Promise of America* (2012).

Zeki Saritoprak holds the Nursî Chair in Islamic Studies at John Carroll University. He is editor and cotranslator of *Fundamentals of Rumi's Thought: A Mevlevi Sufi Perspective* (2004); editor of a critical edition of al-Sarakhsi's *Sifat Ashrat al-Sa'a* (1993, in Arabic); and author of *Al-Dajjal in Islamic Theology* (1992, in Turkish).

Sohaib Sultan is Muslim life coordinator and chaplain at Princeton University. He has written *The Koran for Dummies* (2004) and *The Qur'an and Sayings of Prophet Muhammad: Selections Annotated and Explained* (2007).

Amina Wadud is professor emerita of Islamic studies at Virginia Commonwealth University. Her books include *Qur'an and Woman* (1992) and *Inside the Gender Jihad: Women's Reform in Islam* (2006).

Dawud Walid is executive director of the Michigan chapter of the Council on American-Islamic Relations. He also serves as an imam. He is a former writer for the *Muslim Observer* and *Illume* magazine and currently serves as a political blogger for the *Detroit News.* He is regularly consulted and interviewed by news media from Al-Jazeera to the *Wall Street Journal.*

Homayra Ziad is assistant professor of religion at Trinity College in Hartford, Connecticut. She is cochair of the American Academy of Religion's Interreligious and Interfaith Studies Group and coeditor for the Palgrave series Interreligious Studies in Theory and Practice. She is working on two books, the first on the interplay of religious and literary aesthetics in the work of the renowned eighteenth-century theologian and poet of Delhi Khwajah Mir Dard, and the second on Islam and humor.

INDEX OF ANCIENT SOURCES

JEWISH AND CHRISTIAN SCRIPTURES

SUBJECT AND CONTRIBUTORS INDEX

*Location of contributor conversations are noted with bold page number
(e.g., Abdul Khabeer, Su'ad, 147, **173–81**, 181, 249n3)*

N.b.: The Arabic definite article is *al-*. When using Arabic terms in English it is acceptable to reference terms with or without this article. In this index, words will generally be found listed under the first letter of the noun itself. Some cross-references are provided for the reader's ease (*e.g.*, al-Fatiha; *see* Fatiha).